Who Bears the Lifetime Tax Burden?

Who Bears the Lifetime Tax Burden?

DON FULLERTON
DIANE LIM ROGERS

THE BROOKINGS INSTITUTION
WASHINGTON, D.C.

Copyright © 1993
THE BROOKINGS INSTITUTION
1775 Massachusetts Avenue, N.W., Washington, D.C. 20036

Library of Congress Cataloging-in-Publication data:

Fullerton, Don.
    Who bears the lifetime tax burden? / Don Fullerton, Diane Lim Rogers.
      p. cm.
    Includes bibliographical references and index.
    ISBN 0-8157-2992-8 (cl: alk. paper)—ISBN
  0-8157-2993-6 (pa: alk. paper)
    1. Tax incidence—United States.   2. Taxation—United States.
I. Rogers, Diane Lim. II. Title.
HJ2322.A3F85 1993
336.2'94'0973—dc20   92-44669
                                        CIP

9 8 7 6 5 4 3 2 1

THE BROOKINGS INSTITUTION

The Brookings Institution is an independent organization devoted to nonpartisan research, education, and publication in economics, government, foreign policy, and the social sciences generally. Its principal purposes are to aid in the development of sound public policies and to promote public understanding of issues of national importance.

The Institution was founded on December 8, 1927, to merge the activities of the Institute for Government Research, founded in 1916, the Institute of Economics, founded in 1922, and the Robert Brookings Graduate School of Economics and Government, founded in 1924.

The Board of Trustees is responsible for the general administration of the Institution, while the immediate direction of the policies, program, and staff is vested in the President, assisted by an advisory committee of the officers and staff. The by-laws of the Institution state: "It is the function of the Trustees to make possible the conduct of scientific research, and publication, under the most favorable conditions, and to safeguard the independence of the research staff in the pursuit of their studies and in the publication of the results of such studies. It is not a part of their function to determine, control, or influence the conduct of particular investigations or the conclusions reached."

The President bears final responsibility for the decision to publish a manuscript as a Brookings book. In reaching his judgment on the competence, accuracy, and objectivity of each study, the President is advised by the director of the appropriate research program and weighs the views of a panel of expert outside readers who report to him in confidence on the quality of the work. Publication of a work signifies that it is deemed a competent treatment worthy of public consideration but does not imply endorsement of conclusions or recommendations.

The Institution maintains its position of neutrality on issues of public policy in order to safeguard the intellectual freedom of the staff. Hence interpretations or conclusions in Brookings publications should be understood to be solely those of the authors and should not be attributed to the Institution, to its trustees, officers, or other staff members, or to the organizations that support its research.

Foreword

THE QUESTION of who pays the taxes in the United States is of great concern not only to policymakers and economists but to all segments of American society. For many years the Brookings Institution sponsored a statistical research program to aid in understanding the distribution of tax burdens by income class. The program resulted in two seminal studies by Joseph A. Pechman: *Who Bears the Tax Burden?* coauthored with Benjamin A. Okner, in 1974; and in 1985, *Who Paid the Taxes, 1966–85?*

Those two books have set the standard for virtually all studies of the distributional effects of alternative tax rules, including those undertaken by the U.S. Treasury Department, the Congressional Budget Office, and the Joint Tax Committee. Households are ranked from rich to poor on the basis of a comprehensive measure of annual economic income, and effective tax burdens are computed at each level.

The current volume, by Don Fullerton and Diane Lim Rogers, continues this Brookings tradition. As in Pechman's earlier work, the primary concern is the relative taxation of rich and poor. If only annual income is measured, however, the lowest income group may include some people who are just getting started on a high-income career, some who have retired from a high-income career, as well as others who are persistently poor. To better identify and separate the rich and poor, this book employs a lifetime definition of income and tax. It estimates lifetime wage profiles for individuals, classifies them into groups defined by the level of lifetime income, and calculates the long-run burden on each group. In addition, the authors build a general equilibrium model able to compute the effects of each tax on wage rates, interest rates, and the prices of goods purchased by consumers. The model also sheds light on the efficiency of resource allocations under alternative tax regimes.

Don Fullerton is professor of economics at the University of Virginia and visiting professor of economics and public policy at Carnegie Mellon; Diane Lim Rogers is assistant professor of economics at Pennsylvania State University. They acknowledge their great intellectual debt to Joseph Pechman, who not only laid the analytical foundation for all such research in tax incidence but encouraged them to work on this topic and made several key suggestions. They are also grateful for the assistance they received from many other people. Hilary Sigman undertook most of the work on chapter 5, performing all the calculations with the Consumer Expenditure Survey and estimating the consumption preference parameters. Cheryl Colner made additional calculations for distributional results; and John Karl Scholz and Charles Ballard supplied useful data.

Henry Aaron, Charles Ballard, Jane Gravelle, Ed Olsen, James Poterba, Joel Slemrod, and Jon Skinner made extensive comments on earlier versions of the book. They encouraged the authors to reformulate parts of the model, recalculate results, and revise the text.

Other suggestions were provided by seminar participants at the Brookings Institution, Carnegie Mellon University, the University of Kentucky, the National Bureau of Economic Research, the Pennsylvania State University, and the University of Virginia. Along the way, the authors benefited from expert typing and other help from Sheryl Huweart, Bev Lecuyer, Peggy Pasternak, Rhonda Richardson, Betty Smith, and Donna Mae Weber.

The authors are grateful for financial support from the University of Virginia's Bankard Fund and the National Science Foundation.

The views expressed here are the authors' alone and should not be ascribed to the persons or organizations whose assistance is acknowledged or to the trustees, officers, or staff members of the Brookings Institution.

BRUCE K. MAC LAURY
President

March 1993
Washington, D.C.

Contents

Tables

Figures

CHAPTER ONE

Introduction and Summary

DEBATES about tax policy arise every year, and legislative changes occur almost as often. But who bears the ultimate burden of these taxes? Both households and producers can adjust their behavior, buy less of a taxed good, or invest in a different industry. The burden is shifted, like a hot potato, as each person tries to pass it on to someone else. Where does it land?

The legal liability to pay taxes we call "statutory incidence," but the ultimate burden of the tax is its "economic incidence." Consider the corporate income tax as a clear example of the difference. The law says that the corporation and hence its shareholders are responsible for paying this tax. Economic models and common sense agree, however, that the burden may be shifted by changes in behavior. Corporate managers may shift the burden forward to consumers by raising prices. They may shift it backward onto labor by cutting wages. Conceivably, they might hold down interest payments, royalties, or rents, thereby shifting the burden sideways onto noncorporate owners of capital.

When burdens are shifted, policymakers need estimates of the ultimate economic effects of each tax. With many groups trying to pass the same potato simultaneously, such estimates require an economic model that captures as many household and producer actions as possible and reflects both short- and long-term consequences. While much research has explored this issue using annual data on household incomes and expenditures, this book considers the multiple effects of taxes on individuals over their entire lifetimes.

Two Approaches to Tax Incidence

Economists have long grappled with the distributional effects of taxes, and their efforts have produced some useful results. Theoretical models show, for

1

example, how mobile capital-owners can avoid a tax in one sector by moving into another sector, thus bidding down the rate of return in the untaxed sector and creating further effects on other individuals.

Economists use these models to identify the specific parameters of an effect, such as the ability of taxed firms to substitute labor for capital, untaxed firms to absorb more capital, and consumers to substitute away from the taxed output. Economists can then build empirical models to estimate these parameters. Finally, they build computational models to incorporate those estimated behaviors and to calculate the movement of capital and labor, the change in the rate of return and wage rate, the burdens on investors and workers, the change in the price of each output, and the burden on consumers.

These existing studies of tax incidence fall into two general categories. One approach begins by dividing all households into groups based on some measure of their annual income. Data are collected on wages and salaries of households in each group, capital income (such as interest and dividends), and expenditures by commodity. Shifting tax burdens from one group to another can then be measured from estimated changes in wages, interest rates, and commodity prices. This is the approach taken by many scholars and all government agencies that measure the distributional effects of taxes.

A problem with this approach, however, is that the group with the lowest annual income is a mixed bag. It includes some young workers just starting their careers who will likely earn more later, some retirees who had earned more earlier, some people with volatile incomes who just had a bad year, and, finally, the perennially poor. Policy concerns must differ for these four types of individuals: some are really poor, some are comfortable, and some are actually very rich. Even if careful study shows that a particular tax change redistributes from a high-income group to a low-income group, little is known about what happens to the welfare of individuals who move among the annual income classes during their lives. Indeed, most people move up the income scale during working years and then back to low income upon retirement.

The second approach divides all households into groups by age, then uses a "life-cycle" model to specify individual lifetime plans for saving and consuming during working years and dissaving and consuming during retirement years. Such a model is used to calculate equilibrium prices over time and to report present value changes in lifetime tax incidence. These studies focus on how taxes affect savings incentives, capital formation, and future productivity. They can also simulate a tax change, estimate effects on wage rates and interest rates, and measure redistributions between young and old.

A problem with this second approach is that it considers only one kind of

Figure 1-1. *Two Lifetime Profiles*[a]

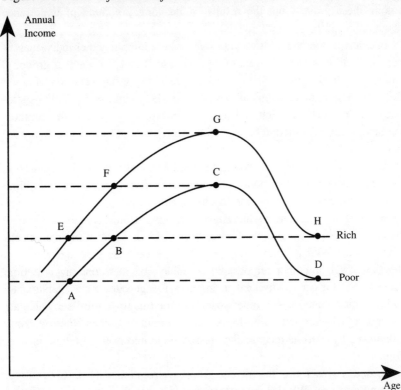

a. Typical studies that use annual income measure would link points horizontally; those that use an age measure would link them vertically.

individual in each age group. Different generations are alive at one time, and the model can calculate effects on these different age groups, but not on individuals within the group. This kind of model misses the fundamental distinction between rich and poor, a distinction that plays prominently in any policy debate about the distributional effects of taxes.

To illustrate the distinction between the two approaches, suppose that the economy included only the two types of individuals depicted in figure 1-1. One type has relatively poor lifetime prospects, advancing with age through points A, B, C, and D. The other type has relatively rich prospects, and advances with age through points E, F, G, and H. The typical annual incidence study would take individuals at point G as the highest-income group, lump together individuals at points F and C for the second group, lump together those at points E, B, and H for a third group, and assign those at points

A and D as the poorest group. They might then find how taxes redistribute among these groups, but the results would convey nothing of importance about either of the two individuals.

In contrast, the typical life-cycle study would lump together individuals at points A and E as the youngest group, those at B and F as another group, C and G as a third group, and D with H as the oldest group. The model could then calculate redistributions among the old, the young, and middle generations, but not between rich and poor. Neither of these approaches captures the fundamental distinction between the two types of individuals in this economy.

This book combines the two approaches to capture the fundamental distinction between rich and poor individuals classified on the basis of lifetime income. Our combined approach has five major steps.

We start with data from the Panel Study of Income Dynamics (PSID), which incorporates thousands of observations of individuals over an eighteen-year period.[1] With all individuals together, we estimate the wage rate as a function of age and other demographic variables. We then construct a lifetime wage profile for each individual, using actual wage rates for available years and predicted wage rates in other years. We use this wage profile to calculate the individual's present value of potential lifetime earnings, then we rank individuals by lifetime income and classify them into twelve lifetime income groups.

Second, for each lifetime income group, we reestimate the wage profile as a function of age. We also estimate age profiles for the personal income tax and for government transfers such as social security. The estimated wage profile rises and then falls over time for all groups, but the steepness and the timing of the peaks differ. Groups that earn relatively more of their income earlier in life must save more for retirement and are likely to bear more burden from taxes on capital income. Also, we add to each group's lifetime income an estimate of inheritances. These are highly concentrated at the top of the income distribution, and they also affect taxes on capital income.

Third, we use data from the Consumer Expenditure Survey (CES) to estimate how people allocate consumption among specific commodities. These choices depend on age and income. If a tax is found to affect relative product prices, it may burden some groups more than others.

Fourth, we build a general equilibrium simulation model that encompasses

---

1. The PSID is a data base compiled by the Institute for Social Research at the University of Michigan.

all major U.S. taxes, many industries, both corporate and noncorporate sectors within each industry, and consumers identified by both age and lifetime income. It is not a model of annual decisionmaking, but a life-cycle model in which each individual receives a particular inheritance, a set of tax rules, a wage profile, and a transfer profile. Each then plans an entire lifetime of labor supply, savings, goods demands, and bequests. We also look at each industry's use of labor, capital, and intermediate inputs. We can then simulate the effects of a tax change on each economic decision through time. We calculate new labor supplies, savings, capital stocks, outputs, and prices. With effects on ages in all years, we can also calculate the change in economic welfare for groups ranging from lowest lifetime income to highest.

Fifth, we evaluate the effects of each U.S. tax by comparing its estimated burdens with those of a proportional tax (where the burden is the same fraction of income for all groups). In our lifetime framework, a progressive tax is one in which the lifetime tax burden as a fraction of lifetime income rises as lifetime income rises, and a regressive tax is one in which the lifetime tax burden as a fraction of lifetime income falls as lifetime income falls. We simulate the effects of each tax before 1986, of the Tax Reform Act of 1986, and of other proposed changes.

We find that the personal income tax, the largest single source of revenue, is progressive. The lowest income group bears a burden of about 5 percent of lifetime income, whereas the highest income group's burden is about 19 percent of income.[2] In contrast, sales and excise taxes are found to be regressive, because heavily taxed goods like alcohol and tobacco constitute a higher fraction of low-income groups' spending. The payroll tax is also rather regressive, for reasons described later.

So far, these results are much like those of existing studies that measure annual burden as a fraction of annual income. But important differences arise for a tax on capital (such as, in this model, the state and local property tax). In a snapshot picture of the economy at one point in time, the share of capital owned by high-income groups is even larger than their share of income. Therefore the burden of a tax on capital is progressive. In the more dynamic context of our lifetime calculations, however, capital holdings are changing

2. When we simulate the removal of the personal tax, revenue is recovered through a proportional tax at a 9.6 percent rate. Tables and figures will show the gains to each group from this replacement. The highest income group gains 9.0 percent of income, so their personal income tax burden must be 18.6 percent of lifetime income. The lowest income group gains −4.3 percent with this 9.6 percent replacement tax, so their personal income tax burden must be only 5.3 percent of income.

over time. High-income groups still have high capital shares, because they receive larger inheritances (and leave larger bequests), and because they have very steeply peaked earnings profiles that peak relatively early in life. We find that groups in the middle of the lifetime-income classification are those whose earnings peak relatively late in life. Low- and high-income groups that earn relatively more early in life must save relatively more to smooth out the entire lifetime path of consumption. Thus taxes on capital affect both high- and low-income groups more than those in the middle.

Since the property tax reduces the net rate of return to capital in our model, it affects both high- and low-income groups. This tax on capital is not progressive but creates a U-shaped burden. This tax also raises the cost of housing, however, so it has an extra burden on low-income households that spend a high fraction of income on housing.

Our results for the corporate income tax are even more surprising. In the standard analysis, the corporate income tax reduces the net rate of return to all owners of capital. Since these capital owners are in high-annual-income brackets, the tax is said to be progressive. If the corporate income tax reduced the net rate of return in our model, it would burden both low- and high-income groups more than those in the middle. Here, however, the corporate income tax does *not* reduce the net rate of return because it collects very little revenue in our base year.[3] Any tax that might have been collected on the return to equity is largely offset by interest deductions, investment tax credits, and accelerated depreciation allowances. When we simulate the removal of the corporate tax system of credits and deductions, the overall rate of tax in this sector falls only from 46.6 percent to 42.1 percent. The remaining rate reflects personal taxes and property taxes on corporate-source income.

The corporate tax does not affect the overall rate of return, but it does affect the cost of production in particular industries. It reduces costs for industries receiving more than the average amount of investment tax credits and accelerated depreciation allowances, and it raises the relative cost of other outputs such as tobacco and gasoline. Because these goods constitute a high fraction of low-income budgets, the tax has a *regressive* effect.

Finally, we simulate the effects of specific reforms and proposals. Typically, to estimate distributional effects of a change such as the Tax Reform Act of 1986, academic researchers and government agencies have used the framework of annual tax incidence. Indeed, part of the motivation for the

---

3. This revenue is calculated from observed capital stocks, an assumed 4 percent net rate of return, and effective tax rates that reflect the statutory tax rules for different assets under 1984 law. It thus reflects a long-run equilibrium, not short-run profit fluctuations.

1986 Tax Reform Act was to reduce tax on the lowest-annual-income group. But is this reform still distributionally appealing in the lifetime perspective? Using our lifetime incidence model, we find that all groups gain from this reform. It is not clearly progressive or regressive, but it improves the efficiency of resource allocation. We look at other possible reforms, such as the integration of corporate and personal income tax systems, and we perform considerable sensitivity analysis.

We develop these themes in considerable detail. We provide specific functional forms for production and for lifetime decisionmaking, and we display all estimates of earnings profiles, preference parameters, and other sources of data. We specify every step so that other researchers can replicate our model. To be accessible to a wider audience, however, we devote the rest of this chapter to a complete but nontechnical description of the model and results.

The Theory of Tax Incidence

Researchers have long recognized that tax burdens are shifted through changes in supply and demand behavior and thus through changes in prices. In such analyses, they have found it convenient to distinguish between prices of consumption goods and prices of the factors of production such as labor and capital. When a tax increases the price of a good, we say purchasers are burdened on the "uses side." When a tax decreases returns on a factor of production that provides a source of income, we say affected persons are burdened on the "sources side." The overall effect on each household depends on the fraction of the budget spent on each commodity, and on the fraction of income received from each factor of production such as labor and capital.

The simplest possible example is an excise tax on a single commodity, where the industry employs only a small share of the total labor and capital of the economy. In this case, changes in its use of these factors would not affect the economy-wide wage or rate of return to capital. Assuming constant returns to scale, the industry can produce at any level with the same costs per unit output. Under these assumptions, a "partial equilibrium" model, with supply and demand for just that one commodity, would be appropriate. The cost of production is raised by exactly the amount of the tax, so the equilibrium price rises by just the amount of the tax. The entire burden is on the uses side. Although buyers curtail purchases at the increased price, no effect is felt on the sources side. Accordingly, most excise taxes are assumed to burden households in proportion to expenditures on the taxed commodities.

For many purposes, however, that model is too simple. If the industry is large, the tax may reduce the demand for labor or capital enough to affect wages or the return to capital. In the short run these factors may go unemployed, but in the long run they are expected to be employed by other industries. If the taxed industry is labor intensive relative to the rest of the economy, the excess supply of labor may only be re-employed at a lower wage rate. If the industry is capital intensive, investors driven elsewhere may find a reduced net rate of return. Burdens are felt on the sources side of income. The partial equilibrium model then needs to be discarded in favor of a "general equilibrium" analysis that can encompass simultaneous changes in factor markets as well as product markets.

Conversely, a partial equilibrium model might be appropriate to analyze a tax on just one factor of production. Consider a wage tax, on either employers or employees, but remember that the burden can be avoided by changes in behavior. If workers cannot adjust their labor supply behavior because they need to work forty hours a week regardless, they get stuck with the entire burden of the wage tax. The employer's share of the tax cannot raise the gross-of-tax cost of labor to the firm, or employers would want fewer workers. Regardless of the statutory incidence, producers are only willing to use the same amount of labor if they pay the same gross-of-tax wage. Therefore the net wage falls by the full amount of the tax, and the entire burden lies on the sources side of income. Because production costs are unaffected, none of the burden shifts to the uses side. For reasons such as these, the payroll tax is often assumed to burden households in proportion to their income from labor.

Again the analysis is too simple, however, if workers can change their behavior. If labor supply is reduced, firms may need to attract back those workers by paying a higher gross wage. Most of the tax may still be borne by workers, but some may be passed on to producers in the form of higher costs and ultimately on to consumers in the form of higher prices. The increase in costs would be greater for labor-intensive industries than for others, so the increase in prices would be greater for those outputs than for others. Burdens are felt on the uses side of income. The partial equilibrium model again needs to be discarded in favor of a general equilibrium analysis that can encompass simultaneous changes in different product markets as well as factor markets.

The need for a general equilibrium analysis becomes even more immediately apparent when we consider a tax on one factor of production in only one sector or industry. A tax such as the corporate income tax might be expected to affect both the rate of return to corporate investment and the price of corporate output. In order to deal with factor markets and product markets simultaneously and make explicit calculations about these several prices and quantities, some simplifying assumptions are essential. Many of these assumptions are relaxed by the more complicated general equilibrium model used later in this book, but important insights can be gained from the simplest general equilibrium model with just two inputs and two outputs. All skill categories are lumped together into one factor of production called "labor," and all asset categories are lumped together into one factor of production called "capital." Both the corporate output and the noncorporate output are produced using labor and capital with constant returns to scale, and all markets are perfectly competitive. Each factor is in fixed total supply, perfectly mobile between sectors, and fully employed. Labor and capital would then move from one sector with a lower net wage or net rate of return, to the other, with a higher net wage or rate of return, until an equilibrium is reached and these net factor returns are the same for both sectors. Finally, these initial analyses typically assume a closed economy, with no international trade in factors or products.

The first such general equilibrium model of taxation was developed by Arnold C. Harberger in 1962. Since the corporate income tax applies to the normal return to equity investors in the corporate sector only, Harberger characterized it as a tax on all capital in that one sector. Assuming no other taxes or other distortions in the economy, he solves for the change in the net rate of return as a function of specific parameters such as the ability of corporate producers to substitute out of capital and into labor, the ability of noncorporate producers to absorb the factors that leave the corporate sector, and the ability of consumers to substitute between the two outputs. As capital leaves the corporate sector and bids down the rate of return in the other sector, some of the burden is shifted to those other owners of capital on the sources side. As the gross-of-tax cost of capital increases in the corporate sector, competitive producers raise the equilibrium price of corporate output, and some burden is shifted to consumers on the uses side. Those consumers buy less of the taxed output, so corporations cut back production. If corporate firms cannot readily substitute labor for capital, they may reduce their use of both labor and capital. If those firms are capital intensive, the fall in the demand for capital may reinforce the fall in the rate of return to capital. If those corporate firms are labor intensive, however, the demand for labor may fall by more than the demand for capital. In this case the equilibrium wage may fall, and some of the burden may be shifted onto workers. Finally, as investors and

workers move into the noncorporate sector and pull down its cost of production, the price of noncorporate output may fall. Anyone with large purchases
of this noncorporate output may actually gain on the uses side.

Using "plausible" values for the important substitution parameters, Harberger thinks it likely that the full burden falls on all owners of capital. Still,
those who spend more than the average fraction of income on corporate products may lose while those who spend more than the average on other outputs
may gain. The general equilibrium model is designed to capture both the
sources side and the uses side simultaneously. Even this simple model allows
for multiple outcomes, however, so the incidence of the corporate income tax
has been the subject of considerable controversy.

Since Harberger's pathbreaking analysis, other researchers have considered additional complications such as immobile factors of production, imperfect competition, land as a separate factor, short-run adjustment costs,
multiple industry outputs, and increasing returns to scale.[4] These additional
possibilities do not reduce the degree of controversy. In particular, much attention has focused on the assumptions of fixed factor supplies. These assumptions might be justified by the claim that capital accumulation is not
responsive to the net rate of return and labor supply is not responsive to the
net-of-tax wage.[5] Of course, empirical studies have measured the factor supply responses, and these estimates can be incorporated, but then the analysis
must be expanded to an intertemporal framework that allows one period's
savings response to affect the next period's capital stock. Additional avenues
are then open for the shifting of burdens: if savers "avoid" the tax by reducing
their savings, then less future capital implies a lower marginal product of
labor and a lower future wage.[6]

Finally, we note the distinction between the distributional effects and the
efficiency effects of a tax. When individuals try to avoid the tax by changing
their economic behavior, they may be able to shift part of the burden onto
others and thereby change the distributional effects of the tax. Estimates of
this economic incidence are essential for informed policymaking. These

4. Useful reviews of this voluminous literature are provided by McLure (1975), Shoven and
Whalley (1984), and Kotlikoff and Summers (1987).

5. Alternatively, the fixed factor supply assumption might be justified not on empirical
grounds but simply to avoid the complications of savings behavior and capital growth. Static
models can further investigate the effects of taxes on the allocation of labor and capital, all else
equal.

6. Empirical estimates of labor supply responses are reviewed in Burtless (1987). The effects
of taxes on savings and capital formation are discussed in Bovenberg (1989). Dynamic studies
of tax incidence are summarized in Kotlikoff and Summers (1987).

changes in economic behavior may also affect efficiency, however, both in production and in consumption. Under the presumption that private firms try to maximize profits by selecting the most efficient mix of labor and capital in their production process, any tax that alters that mix results in less efficient production. This efficiency cost can be captured in the ultimate measures of consumer welfare. Similarly, we presume that individuals with no taxes would make the "right" choices about how much to work, how much to save, and how much of each commodity to consume. Taxes that affect these choices have efficiency costs that also affect consumer welfare. These efficiency costs give rise to "excess burden," to the extent that the total cost to consumers is larger than the revenue from the tax.[7] General equilibrium models that quantify these behavioral changes can calculate both the distributional effects and the efficiency effects of a tax.

Clearly all such information is relevant to policymakers who must choose among alternative tax rules. These policymakers need the best possible information in order to balance competing objectives. An attempt to raise the proportion of taxes collected from the rich may further distort their factor supply and consumption decisions and thereby decrease economic efficiency. It may even increase burdens on the poor more than on the rich. This book describes a model that can make these trade-offs explicit. We use the model to find the effects of each tax on all prices and quantities, the allocation of resources, the efficiency of economic decisionmaking, and the distribution of after-tax incomes.

Empirical Work on Tax Incidence

Joseph Pechman and Benjamin Okner's *Who Bears the Tax Burden?* (1974) is still the most widely cited empirical study of tax incidence across households. The authors use the theoretical developments just described to specify several possible outcomes for the burdens of each tax, and apply these scenarios to actual data on the annual incomes and expenditures of a large sample of households. Merging data files from a sample of 72,000 households, they capture information on demographic characteristics such as age and family size, and tax return items such as income from dividends, interest, rent, capital gains, and wages and salaries for each household. To classify

---

7. A thorough discussion of excess burden is in Auerbach (1985), for example. Taxes also create administrative and compliance costs that are not captured in our model.

households into income groups, they use a measure of "economic income" that includes transfers, the household's share of corporate retained earnings, and the imputed net rental income from owner-occupied homes.

They then consider alternative assumptions about the shifting of each tax, and add up the burdens for each group in each case. Pechman and Okner assume for all cases that the burden of the personal income tax remains with the household, the employee part of the payroll tax remains with the worker, and the burden of sales and excise taxes falls on consumption. The employer share of the payroll tax is sometimes allocated to workers, and it is sometimes split half to workers and half to consumers. The property tax is assumed to affect either the return to landowners specifically or all capital owners generally. Finally, for the corporate income tax, they consider several cases with different proportions of the burden on shareholders, capital owners, wage-earners, and consumers.[8]

For each combination of assumptions, Pechman and Okner calculate the effective tax rate on each household, defined as the total tax burden as a fraction of economic income. The tax system is defined as "progressive" if this effective tax rate rises with income. Their results, shown in figure 1-2, indicate that the most progressive set of assumptions ("variant 1c") is not very different from the least progressive ("variant 3b"). In either case, the overall U.S. tax system is roughly proportional over the middle eight deciles. The effective tax rate is a bit higher, however, at the very tails of the income distribution.[9]

This finding has shaped the tax policy debate for the past two decades. The general perception is that the progressive effects of the personal income tax and the corporate income tax are more or less completely offset by the regressive impacts of payroll taxes, sales taxes, and excise taxes. Richard A. Musgrave and others (1974) conduct a similar analysis and arrive at a similar conclusion. In contrast, Edgar K. Browning and William R. Johnson (1979) find that the U.S. tax system as a whole is highly progressive. They assume that sales and excise taxes raise product prices, but government transfers are

---

8. The burden of the corporate income tax is assumed to fall fully on shareholders (in proportion to dividend receipts); or on all capital (in proportion to income from all investments); or half on shareholders and half on all capital income; or half on all capital income and half in proportion to consumption; or one-fourth to consumption and one-fourth in proportion to wages.

9. At low-income levels, the effective tax ratio is high because the denominator is small. For these reasons, when we designed the model described later in this book, we followed a suggestion by Joseph Pechman to subdivide the top and bottom groups. Instead of having just ten deciles, we separate the poorest 2 percent from the rest of the low-income decile and the richest 2 percent from the rest of the top-income decile.

Figure 1-2. *Effective Rates of Federal, State, and Local Taxes under the Most and Least Progressive Incidence Variants, by Population Percentile, 1966*

Effective tax rate (percent)

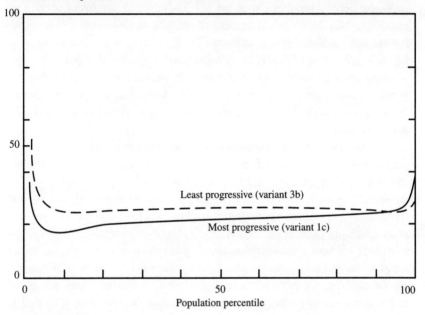

Source: Pechman and Okner (1974).

indexed to provide the same real benefits, thus protecting low-income transfer recipients. These taxes do not fall on consumption generally but only on consumption out of factor income.[10]

These studies have three problems in common. First, they classify households by annual income alone and do not use longer time periods. Second, they consider alternative assumptions about the distributional burdens of a given amount of tax. They trace the dollar flows, but they do not calculate

---

10. Pechman (1985) is a revised version of the Pechman and Okner study. In comparing 1985 to 1966, Pechman finds that while the distribution of income before taxes is virtually unchanged, the 1985 tax system is less progressive. Thus the after-tax distribution of income is more unequal. The decreased progressivity is the result of an upward trend in payroll tax rates, a downward trend in corporate and property taxes, and the individual and corporate income tax cuts of 1981. Browning (1986), however, indicates that the data used by Pechman are biased (understating transfers and overstating labor income for the poorest groups) and that appropriate adjustments to the data would cause the 1985 system to appear no less progressive than the 1966 system. Pechman (1987) corrects the peculiarities in his data, and finds that his revised estimates indeed indicate virtually no change in progressivity.

changes in consumer welfare. Thus they cannot address issues of efficiency. Third, these studies use incidence results from different kinds of models. The approach is not necessarily "partial equilibrium," because they may assume particular general equilibrium effects of taxes on factor returns or on product prices, but they do not calculate these effects in a single model. It is not clear, for example, whether partial shifting of the corporation tax to consumers is logically consistent with partial shifting of the payroll tax to consumers.

In addressing these last two problems, other researchers have built explicit general equilibrium models that specify all demand and supply behaviors. They then calculate the effect of each tax on each price, quantity, and consumer welfare.

A comprehensive general equilibrium model for annual tax incidence analysis is fully described in Charles L. Ballard and others (1985). The study shows how taxes raise the cost of production and affect the demand for labor and capital in each of nineteen industries that use both primary factors and intermediate inputs. By examining expenditures in twelve income groups that receive income from labor, capital, and indexed government transfers, their model shows how consumer demand depends on product prices and factor supplies depend on net factor return. Thus taxes may affect both behaviors. By establishing a benchmark equilibrium with current tax rules and initial prices and quantities, they were able to simulate the effects of a change in any particular tax: a decrease in the demand for labor leads to a fall in the wage, just as a decrease in the demand for capital leads to a fall in the rate of return. The set of prices is adjusted until supply equals demand simultaneously for every good and factor.

It is useful to compare these two kinds of annual incidence studies. The main advantage of the first kind is that it can employ detailed microdata on thousands of households. The computer program makes one pass through each household, calculates income, allocates it to an income group, and adds its taxes to that group's burden. In contrast, a general equilibrium model might take many iterations until it finds a set of prices at which quantities supplied equal quantities demanded in all markets. For these repeated calculations, the sample must be reduced or aggregated.

The main advantage of this second kind of study is that it uses a structural model that derives its demand and supply behaviors from explicit production functions and utility functions. The advantage is not that tax incidence is "calculated rather than assumed," because the structural model itself requires many assumptions about functional forms and elasticity parameter values. Varying the ease with which labor can be substituted for capital in production (the elasticity of substitution) will generate different amounts of burden shifting, the same way that the first kind of study may assume different amounts of burden shifting.

Rather, the advantages are more subtle. First, the analyst can see explicitly how results are tied to a particular elasticity parameter that we might be able to estimate. Second, incidence results are consistent because all tax burdens interact simultaneously rather than acting independently. Third, the effect at each income level can be measured explicitly by an index such as the "equivalent variation," the amount of income the individual would accept to forgo the tax change.[11] Fourth, this explicit welfare measure can include excess burdens. Whereas the first kind of annual incidence study allocates burdens across households that sum to total taxes paid, the second kind calculates losses in welfare that account for tax-induced distortions. These losses may sum to a figure larger than total taxes paid.[12] For these reasons, we use an applied general equilibrium framework in our calculations below.

All of the studies discussed so far use the annual incidence approach. Since Lawrence H. Summers' 1981 article, a number of authors have incorporated a lifetime perspective into tax incidence analysis. Alan J. Auerbach, Laurence J. Kotlikoff, and Jonathan Skinner (1983) specify lifetime utility in a general equilibrium model that distinguishes among fifty-five overlapping "generations."[13] Each year a new generation of adults is "born," plans a lifetime of earnings and consumption, and decides how much to save. The model has only one sector and produces one consumption good, as it is intended only to examine the incidence of a general consumption tax, wage tax, or income tax.

Under this model, a tax change affects labor supply, savings, capital accumulation over time, and all future prices. The model is theoretically elegant and generates some interesting results. Since the elderly have already planned for their retirement, for example, their consumption may be higher than in-

11. This index is an "exact" utility-based welfare measure, as defined explicitly at the end of chapter 2. It uses status-quo prices to value the change in utility.

12. This last effect may be small, especially in one-period models that do not account for changes in savings and capital formation. The original work of Harberger (1966) found excess burden at about 0.5 percent of income. Excess burdens may differ by income, however, if higher-income individuals have different factor supply elasticities or face different marginal tax rates. Moreover, efficiency effects may be much larger in dynamic models with intertemporal effects on savings, capital formation, and growth (Judd, 1987). Our lifetime model does calculate changes in savings, so the explicit welfare measures may become important.

13. The initial model by Auerbach, Kotlikoff, and Skinner (1983) is fully described in the book by Auerbach and Kotlikoff (1987). A review of other lifetime models appears in Kotlikoff and Summers (1987).

come (and their wages may be zero). Therefore the switch from an income tax to a consumption tax would increase burdens on the elderly and allow higher welfare for future generations. Conversely, the switch to a wage tax would provide a windfall gain to the elderly, at the expense of future generations.[14]

These life-cycle models do not incorporate detailed data on actual economies with disaggregate goods and heterogeneous consumers. The models are designed to evaluate redistributions between generations, not within a generation. In other words, the "young" group includes both lifetime-rich and lifetime-poor (points A and E in figure 1-1) as does the old group (points D and H). As a consequence, these models cannot address the very basic incidence question about the distribution of tax burdens between rich and poor.

Just a few studies have considered the incidence of taxes across different lifetime income categories. Using Canadian data, James B. Davies and others (1984) construct lifetime histories of earnings, transfers, inheritances, savings, consumption, and bequests. Measuring lifetime income, classifying households, and adding up the burdens under alternative incidence assumptions, the authors use the same basic approach as Pechman and Okner but extend it to a lifetime context. They arrive at two major conclusions. First, personal income taxes are less progressive in the lifetime context, while sales and excise taxes are less regressive. Thus the Canadian tax system is just as mildly progressive in the lifetime framework as it is in the annual framework. Second, lifetime results are less sensitive to variations than are annual results. Both conclusions proceed from the fact that the distribution of lifetime incomes is less unequal than the distribution of annual incomes.

James M. Poterba (1989) focuses on sales and excise tax burdens in the United States. Appealing to the permanent income hypothesis of Milton Friedman (1957), he uses current consumption as a proxy for lifetime income in order to classify households. Sales and excise taxes may be regressive for annual income, but they are closer to proportional for consumption. Therefore they must be more proportional to lifetime income than to annual income. He thus agrees with Davies and others that sales and excise taxes are less regressive in the lifetime context. Andrew B. Lyon and Robert Schwab (1990) use data from the Panel Survey of Income Dynamics in a model of life-cycle behavior to find that cigarette taxes are just as regressive, and al-

---

14. Ballard (1983) and Seidman (1983) also employ overlapping generations models with lifetime utility maximization in general equilibrium. Ballard includes more disaggregation of production, and Seidman includes bequests and inheritances.

cohol taxes are slightly less regressive, when measured with respect to lifetime income rather than annual income.

Comparing Annual and Lifetime Perspectives

Current consumption decisions certainly depend on horizons longer than one year. In the "permanent income" theory of Friedman (1957), individuals average their income over long horizons. They take that average to be the permanent component of income, and deviations from that average to be the transitory component. They borrow or save in order to achieve a smooth consumption path based on permanent income.

The "life-cycle" model extends the horizon to an entire lifetime.[15] In its simplest version, individuals receive no inheritances, face no uncertainty, and can borrow or lend at a single interest rate. People are assumed to know all future earnings, so they can calculate lifetime wealth as the present value of those earnings (discounted at the single interest rate). On the basis of lifetime wealth and assumed preferences, they can plan the timing and composition of consumption. That is, they maximize a lifetime utility function subject to a lifetime budget constraint. The individual can borrow or lend but must pay off all debts before the date of death. Thus, the lifetime budget constraint requires that the present-discounted-value of consumption must be equal to the present-discounted-value of income. An interpretation is that current well-being is better measured by lifetime income than by current income.

Many researchers who study income distributions have recognized that the distribution of lifetime income is a better index of differences in welfare than the distribution of annual income. Some studies have computed both such distributions and compared the results.[16] All of these studies find that the distribution of lifetime incomes displays less inequality. For example, N. S. Blomquist (1981) finds 32–42 percent less inequality in the value of lifetime labor endowments than in annual labor endowments. Thus, to the extent that individuals are life-cycle utility-maximizers, the annual measure can be a poor proxy for the lifetime measure.

15. Originally presented by Modigliani and Brumberg (1954), and Ando and Modigliani (1963).

16. These studies include Lillard (1977a, 1977b), Moss (1978), Irvine (1980), Blomquist (1981), and Slesnick (1986). Moss provides an excellent discussion of the important issues concerning the measurement and distribution of lifetime incomes, and the implications for evaluating the incidence of government programs such as social security. Other citations are provided in Poterba (1989).

Why do these measures differ? Let us examine a case in which the two measures are identical. If each person's income never changed over time, annual income would mirror permanent income. Each path in figure 1-1 would be flat, and individuals would not change annual income categories. The poorest annual income category would include the same individuals as the poorest lifetime category.

But this is generally not the case. Lifetime income profiles are generally not flat, but humped: incomes generally rise during early years, level off during middle years, and fall during retirement. This pattern puts young and old lifetime-rich individuals into low annual-income groups and creates different annual and lifetime groupings.

A second difference can arise simply with income volatility. Self-employed individuals with a mid-range permanent income might be placed into a high-annual-income category, or a low-annual-income category, depending on the year taken for study. Employed workers subject to temporary lay-offs may experience similar fluctuations in annual incomes.

A third distinction is that, while the annual incidence of capital taxation depends on fixed capital endowments, the lifetime incidence of capital taxation depends on inheritances and on the shape of the *earnings* profiles. Milton Moss (1978), for example, finds that the rich have profiles that are more hump-shaped. In order for them to achieve a smooth path for consumption, then, they must save early in life and bear more burden of capital taxation. In contrast, the poor typically have profiles that are flatter, lower, and more irregular. In our results, we find that incidence depends not only on the height of the peak but on the timing of the peak. For example, we find that the earnings of middle income groups tend to peak later in life, so those groups do not accumulate as much savings relative to richer and poorer groups. The burden of capital taxation falls on those whose earnings peak early and who therefore save more for later.

A fourth difference is that the composition of lifetime income varies less than the composition of annual income. Differences in capital share of annual incomes that arise from the average amount of life-cycle savings are not relevant in the lifetime perspective. The only relevant differences in the composition of lifetime income come from bequests and inheritances, or from variations in the timing of earnings relative to consumption. Therefore taxes that change relative factor prices have less effect on the sources side. Similarly, all individuals progress from one set of consumption goods when young to another set of consumption goods when old. The composition of spending may still depend on income, in the lifetime perspective, but it does not depend on age. Therefore taxes that change relative goods prices have less effect on the uses side.

These considerations suggest that *all* distributional effects of taxes are likely to be muted in the lifetime context. The progressivity of the personal income tax places low tax rates not just on the lifetime poor, but also on the lifetime rich who are young. In addition, high personal taxes may be paid by lifetime-poor individuals who happen to be at the top of their earnings hump. However, a progressive annual tax structure generates heavier burdens on individuals with more humped lifetime income profiles, all else equal.

A fifth distinction is that, though the annual perspective takes annual income as "ability to pay taxes," the lifetime perspective takes lifetime income as a measure of total ability to pay over one's lifetime. A misconception here is that the lifetime perspective mandates lifetime accounting to calculate current tax liability. Not so. Tax collections can still be based on annual accounts. But the lifetime perspective provides a useful yardstick to help evaluate any such tax system. For "horizontal equity," two individuals with similar lifetime income should pay similar total lifetime taxes. In addition, for "vertical equity," higher lifetime incomes could be associated with higher lifetime tax burdens. Whether or not actual taxes are based on an annual accounting system, policymakers should be concerned with both "short-run equity" and "long-run equity." With borrowing constraints, for example, the timing of tax payments can be important. Still, the fairness of a tax should be evaluated both on how current taxes reflect current ability to pay and on how lifetime taxes reflect lifetime ability to pay.[17]

Other differences are more subtle, such as what to include in the measure of income. In the annual perspective, income includes wages and salaries, entrepreneurial income, and all forms of capital income such as interest, dividends, and capital gains. One might impute all corporate-source income through to shareholders. Annual income may be realized or accrued, and it may be before or after taxes and transfers. Similarly, annual taxes may be realized or accrued. In contrast, a lifetime measure of income requires no capital income at all. Lifetime income would include only gifts received, inheritances, and labor income, although these would be discounted by the

---

17. Even if economists believe lifetime income more accurately reflects the economic status of individuals, and even if equity in taxation is desired, it may not be possible to design a tax system that directly taxes individuals according to lifetime income. Some economists therefore advocate the adoption of consumption-based taxes. Since consumption more accurately reflects lifetime income and economic well-being, it is thought that a consumption tax system would be more equitable than the present annual income tax system. See Bradford (1986, chap. 8) for a thorough discussion of equity issues in taxation.

net rate of return to capital. Any capital income received at any point during
the lifetime would then reflect not different levels of well-being but simply
different choices about when to consume: two individuals with identical paths
for labor incomes and inheritances will have the same lifetime income, even
if one prefers later consumption and thus has higher initial savings and capital
income.

We note, however, that while lifetime income is independent of capital
income, lifetime tax burdens are not. The lifetime burden of our tax system
will be affected by consumption and savings behavior, since capital income
is included in the income tax base. For two individuals with the same lifetime
income, the current system places a larger burden on the one with more savings and delayed consumption. Therefore the lifetime perspective still requires information on savings behavior and capital income.

This brings us to a final important difference between the annual and lifetime perspectives. Data on capital income by annual income category are
readily available, given that households must report interest and dividend
income on their annual tax returns. With the lifetime perspective we are not
so fortunate. Data covering the entire lifetime profiles for labor income do
not exist, let alone data on the composition of income (capital relative to
labor) by lifetime income category. The panel data that are available, such as
the Panel Study of Income Dynamics, can be used to predict lifetime labor
income profiles with some degree of confidence, but the survey lacks ade-
quate information on returns to capital.

Thus, in the lifetime perspective, we are forced to rely on a model to
construct lifetime patterns of savings and wealth. The model of lifetime decisionmaking can be chosen on the basis of some demonstrated empirical
acceptability, but then the model determines each group's consumption, savings behavior, and capital income through time. The obvious starting point
for a model of lifetime tax incidence would be a version of the life-cycle
model that could be modified by the consideration of bequests, liquidity constraints, the degree of foresight, and even differences between interest rates
for lending and borrowing. This approach has the advantage of a rigorous
framework for subsequent economic analyses using the model.[18]

---

18. Because the model determines the path for savings and capital income through life, we
cannot use available data on any one year's savings and wealth at different ages. The problem is
that panel data on capital are not available. One year's data are enough to support an annual
model, but not a lifetime model. Observations of uneven consumption patterns across different
ages, and of saving during retirement, would be difficult to explain in a model of lifetime
decisionmaking.

In particular, note that the choice of model will surely affect the savings path and therefore the lifetime incidence of capital income taxation. For this reason we need to clarify that our model employs the basic life-cycle framework, with perfect capital markets, one interest rate, and no liquidity constraints. We incorporate bequests, however, as is necessary to explain the observed U.S. capital stock.[19] Nevertheless, the lack of panel savings data and the complexity involved in simulating such data may limit the use of lifetime incidence as an operational policy tool.

Finally, we note a frequent objection to the assumption of perfect capital markets with unlimited borrowing and lending at a single rate of interest. This assumption is important both because it greatly simplifies the computations of the model and because it ensures that lifetime income is unambiguously better than annual income for measuring the distribution of welfare. Borrowing and lending are not unlimited, of course, and they are not subject to a single interest rate. Thus, one says that consumers are "liquidity constrained."[20] In the extreme case where no borrowing *or* saving is possible, current period income or utility *is* a proper measure of well-being. Pechman's 1990 study suggests that lifetime measures are impractical or impossible to determine, and that even if they could be determined, lifetime incomes cannot be regarded as a satisfactory measure of current well-being.

On the other hand, *any* borrowing or lending can reduce the validity of annual income as a measure of welfare. Even if borrowing is prohibited, one's own saving and dissaving can break the relationship between current consumption and income. In addition, even if individuals are not able to borrow against all future income, they may be able to borrow against some future years for some purposes such as a mortgage on a house. Thus, even if lifetime income is not a perfect measure of economic well-being, we feel it is a better measure than a simple snapshot of annual income.

The Measure of Lifetime Income

In order to classify consumers, we must first specify who is being classified. That is, we must choose the unit of analysis. In annual studies such as Pechman and Okner (1974), consumers are categorized according to total

19. Kotlikoff and Summers (1981).
20. See the empirical study done by Zeldes (1989). His results are somewhat mixed, but he does find that an inability to borrow against future income affects the consumption of a sizable subset of the population.

household income. This makes good sense, since the well-being of an individual depends not simply on his or her own income or wealth, but on the income or wealth of the entire household. Our income tax system uses the household as the unit of analysis for similar reasons. In the lifetime perspective, however, it becomes extremely difficult to think about the "lifetime" of a household. Household composition varies tremendously over an individual's lifetime due to marriage, births, divorce, deaths, and the moving out of adult children. The concept of "lifetime household income" is complicated even in theory, but especially in practice. For this reason, the lifetime perspective may typically examine burdens across individuals rather than households. Still, one can assign shares of total household labor income or inheritances to the different individuals in the household.[21]

Whether the unit of analysis is the individual or the household, classification may also depend upon whether labor supply is taken as fixed or variable. Individuals with fixed labor have no opportunity to make distorted labor supply decisions, so labor taxes have no excess burden. A model with fixed labor can still be used for distributional analysis, however, to measure annual or lifetime burdens from labor taxes, capital taxes, or any consumption taxes. The income classifier would include this fixed labor income.

With variable labor, however, the definition of income is not so obvious. Suppose, for example, that two individuals with the same "true" level of welfare make different choices about how much to work. One earns more labor income to spend on market goods, but has less leisure time. The other person takes more leisure, but has less to spend on market goods. They are equally well-off, one would suppose, but their labor incomes differ. In order to classify them into the same level of well-being, we need a broader definition of income. We define "endowment income" as the value of total time available: the wage rate times the maximum number of hours that could be worked (for example, eighty hours a week). The individual then decides how much of this endowment income to spend on market goods (by working), and how much to spend on leisure. Choosing to take another hour of leisure means giving up the hourly wage, so the "price" of leisure is the forgone wage. The individual still makes choices subject to a budget constraint, but now the budget constraint requires that spending on market goods (prices times quantities) plus spending on leisure (the wage rate times hours of leisure) cannot exceed the value of endowment income (the wage rate times total

---

21. In calculations for each household, the husband and wife are each assigned half of their combined incomes or inheritances in each year.

hours available). With this definition of income, two persons with the same wage rate and time availability will be classified into the same income group, even if they choose different amounts of work.[22]

In a model of annual incidence analysis, fixed labor supply means that the income classifier includes annual income from labor and capital. The assumption of variable labor supply dictates the use of annual endowment income (from total time plus capital). But the issues are strictly analogous in a model of lifetime tax incidence. With a fixed labor supply each year, lifetime income is the present-discounted-value of labor income plus gifts and inheritances received. In a lifetime model with variable labor supply, the discounting includes each year's total endowment of time. When the individual is free to choose the number of hours to work, "ability to pay" is best reflected by the total value of the individual's labor endowment.[23]

In our model, with variable labor supply, we adopt the endowment definition of lifetime resources. All individuals are assumed to have 4,000 hours available each year. Then, using the different wage profiles for each individual, we calculate the present value of each year's wage rate times total hours. We use this measure to classify individuals into groups. This choice will affect classification if, for example, two individuals with the same earned income differ in the value of leisure taken. Then, for each group, we add a separate estimate for inheritances received.

This labor endowment definition of income is also used as a measure of well-being for the denominator of the effective rate of tax on each group. This choice will affect relative tax burdens if, for example, income groups vary systematically by the fraction of hours actually worked. In our model, high-income groups work fewer hours than low-income groups. They "spend" more of their endowment on leisure, but taxes do not apply to leisure. Taxes do apply to work effort, and to consumption of earned labor income. As a consequence, all U.S. taxes look more regressive than if all groups worked

22. This type of model is well suited to analyze labor supply choices, and thus tax distortions, but all leisure hours are voluntary. We concentrate on consumer and producer choices and assume that markets clear in order to solve for equilibrium price effects that indicate long-run tax incidence. Thus the model does not encompass other market imperfections, involuntary unemployment, or other macroeconomic problems. An accurate determination of individual welfare levels would clearly depend on problems like unemployment, but long-run tax incidence depends primarily on behavioral changes that affect market prices of goods and factors.

23. To the extent that hours of labor supply are not subject to individual choice, the full endowment might not be an appropriate measure of ability to pay. One may say that when unemployment is involuntary, for example, leisure hours contribute positively to lifetime utility but not to ability to pay.

the same amount. An immediate implication is the importance of measuring differences in hours worked by each lifetime income group, despite the obvious difficulties.

This discussion has listed a number of ways in which our lifetime income and classification differ from previous studies such as Pechman and Okner (1974). The differences include recognition of hump-shaped earnings profiles, the volatility in annual income, the timing of the peak in earnings, the exclusion of capital income, the use of a life-cycle model, the individual as the unit of account, and the decision to include leisure in the total value of endowment. But do these issues really matter? How is lifetime classification and incidence different from the standard classification and incidence?

To estimate lifetime incomes, we require longitudinal data for many individuals over many years. This analysis has only recently become possible, because the University of Michigan's Panel Study of Income Dynamics has been asking the same questions of the same individuals for more than eighteen years. We wish to estimate the wage rate as a nonlinear function of age, so that for each individual in the sample we can predict the wage rate for years that come after as well as before the sample period; multiply the actual or estimated gross-of-tax wage rate by a total number of hours per year (for example, 4,000) to get the value of the endowment; and calculate the present value of this endowment for each person. These levels are used to classify individuals into twelve groups according to lifetime ability to pay. We are also interested in the timing of income, because the shape of an individual's lifetime income profile determines the composition of annual income. Groups with earlier and more pronounced peaks must save for later consumption, so they will have higher observed ratios of capital to labor income. Therefore we reestimate the nonlinear wage profile separately for each of the twelve groups. In addition, we require information on the time path of personal income taxes paid and transfers received, in order to set up a consistent benchmark data set with a path of consumer spending out of total available net-of-tax income. The remainder of this subsection summarizes these econometric procedures; chapter 4 presents the detail.

From the PSID, we draw a sample of 500 households that includes 858 adult individuals and draw information on wages, taxes, transfers, and various demographic variables for the years 1970–87. We include heads and spouses in our sample and consider the individual as the unit of analysis. At this point, if we were to use each individual's own wages in the classification, most of the poorer individuals would be spouses and most of the richer ones would be heads. But of course the individual's well-being depends on the combined resources of the household. Therefore we assign to each individual the average resources of the household before we classify them into lifetime income groups. Thus two married individuals will always be assigned to the same lifetime income category.[24]

We assume that each economic lifetime spans sixty years, from chronological age 20 through 79. Because our PSID data cover only eighteen years of each individual's lifetime, we require predictions about the rest of the years that are not observed. We generate these predictions from an initial set of econometric regressions on our full sample of 858 individuals. Separate regressions are used to predict wage rates, taxes, and government transfers, each as a nonlinear function of age and of demographic variables such as education, race, and sex. To improve the fit, these initial regressions are run separately for heads and spouses. We use fixed, individual-specific effects, to allow individuals with similar demographic characteristics to have systematic differences in their levels of lifetime income.[25]

These initial estimations are used to forecast and backcast wages, taxes, and transfers for the out-of-sample periods in each individual's economic lifetime. In addition, the initial wage regressions are used to assign the potential wage for any period in which the individual did not choose to work.[26] After incorporating estimates of the wage, tax, and transfer amounts for years without data, we compute the individual's present value of labor endowments ("lifetime income"), before and after taxes and transfers. We determine the lifetime labor income of each individual, as well as an average for the household.[27] Heads and spouses are then treated as individual entities, and each is categorized according to his or her average household lifetime income.

Part of chapter 4 compares the annual and lifetime income distributions

24. Also, our sample of households is not purely random, because we use only households that remain in the sample and that retain the same marital status for the entire 1970–87 period. Given the stability of family composition in our sample, it would seem inappropriate to assign a husband and wife to two separate lifetime income categories.

25. The fixed-effects generate differences in the constant terms across individuals in the regressions. This can be viewed as a way of accounting for unobserved differences in ability or motivation. We find these differences very important. In the wage estimation for heads, for example, the adjusted R-squared increases from 0.274 to 0.681 when we go from a model without individual-specific effects to one with these effects.

26. The wage regressions are performed on a sample that excludes years with zero wages. The selection bias in such a procedure is found to be very small, given that we account for individual-specific effects. This issue is discussed further in chapter 4.

27. The average household lifetime income is simply the average of the lifetime income of the head and the lifetime income of the spouse, if any. For those who are unmarried, the individual and average measures of lifetime income are the same.

and classifications. We confirm the results of previous studies that find lifetime income distributions are much more equal than the annual counterparts.
A measure of income dispersion is the coefficient of variation, the ratio of the
standard deviation to the mean. Here we find this coefficient is 1.298 for
annual incomes and only 0.456 for lifetime incomes. For consistency with
Pechman and Okner (1974), the annual measure is transfer-inclusive household income.

Perhaps more important for our analysis, we find that the annual income
categories do not match up with the lifetime income categories for the same
individuals. For each of our 858 individuals, we calculate annual income in
1984 for classification into annual income deciles. As it turns out, only 21.1
percent of the individuals in our sample are in the same annual and lifetime
income deciles, and only 46.1 percent are within plus-or-minus one of the
same decile. Most of the differences in these classifications occur when someone who is lifetime-rich is very young or very old and earns low annual
income. If we label the bottom 30 percent of the population the "poor" and
the top 30 percent the "rich," we find that 13.8 percent of the annually poor
are lifetime rich, and 2.6 percent of the annually rich are lifetime poor. We
conclude that the annual and lifetime classifications are too different to assume that lifetime incidence will be similar to annual incidence.

For the purposes of our analysis of lifetime tax incidence, we sort the
individuals in our sample into twelve categories based on lifetime income
before taxes and transfers. For these categories, we use the eight middle deciles, plus a split of the highest decile and lowest decile. The highest decile
is split into the top 2 percent and the next highest 8 percent; the lowest decile
is divided into a bottom 2 percent and the next lowest 8 percent. We choose
this division because of a belief that the very richest and very poorest of the
population may be very different from the not-so-rich and the not-so-poor,
both in terms of their lifetime income profiles and their economic decisions.

After all the individuals in our sample are assigned to one of the twelve
lifetime income categories, we reestimate the econometric relationships that
predict the wage rate, taxes paid, and transfers received in each category. In
this final set of regressions, however, the only independent variables are age,
age squared, and age cubed. The coefficients on these age variables define
life-cycle profiles that differ across lifetime income categories. Each lifetime
income category has its own age profile for wages, taxes, and transfers, and
we interpret these profiles as a description of a representative individual in
each group.

We thus concentrate on differences between groups and ignore differences within each group. We want to measure effects of taxes on "vertical equity," the distribution of burdens between high and low income groups, defined on a lifetime basis. But in doing so, we miss the effects of taxes on "horizontal equity," the relative burdens for different individuals at the same income level. We limit the number of consumer types to these twelve income groups, because, for the simulation of every tax policy change, the general equilibrium model must evaluate supply and demand of every consumer type at every trial set of prices in the search for an equilibrium.[28]

Although the tax and transfer profiles are used only to generate the initial benchmark equilibrium, the wage profiles are taken as constant and exogenous to our model. Individuals face no uncertainty about their future path of wages. We capture differences between these predetermined paths, and we capture the movements of individuals among annual income levels, but we ignore any movement between lifetime income groups.

The wage profiles represent the paths of lifetime endowments and are therefore extremely important to our analysis. Differences across the lifetime income categories in the shapes of these profiles are critical in the determination of the lifetime incidence of taxes. The final wage profiles for several of the lifetime income categories are illustrated in figure 1-3. Each is the profile for a representative individual in the category. Groups 1 and 2 represent the lowest 2 percent and next lowest 8 percent of the lifetime income distribution, respectively. Group 4 represents individuals between the 20th and 30th percentiles, and Group 9 consists of those between the 70th and 80th percentiles. Group 12 is the top 2 percent of the population, and group 11 is the next highest 8 percent.

From figure 1-3 it is apparent that individuals in the higher lifetime income categories are characterized by wage profiles that are more peaked. The richest lifetime income category (group 12) appears to be significantly more peaked than the second richest (group 11), which suggests that our split of the top decile is important. Because we use life-cycle consumption behavior in our model, the increasing peakedness implies that higher lifetime income categories will save more for retirement and will have higher ratios of capital to labor income. This ratio is key to the determination of the lifetime incidence of capital taxes relative to labor taxes.

In figure 1-3 we can also see that these wage profiles peak at different

28. Heterogeneity within each income group is interesting not only because it affects horizontal equity but because it could affect results on vertical equity. Since relationships between taxes and capital formation are not linear, within a group, the tax on the average person is not the same as the average of taxes on different persons.

Figure 1-3. *Wage Profiles for Selected Groups*

1984 dollars per hour

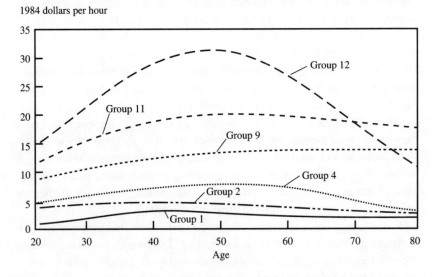

points in the life cycle. For the first few income groups, the peak age has a slight upward trend, as group 2 peaks at age 39, group 4 peaks at age 47, and group 9 peaks at age 64. Then, at higher levels of income, the peak wage years come earlier, at age 50 for group 11 and at age 47 for group 12. Thus the middle-income groups, with the later earnings peaks, do not need to save as much for retirement. The lowest income groups and the highest income groups have earlier peaks, save more during life, and bear more burden of capital taxation. Thus the timing of the peak is important in determining tax incidence.

A Description of the Model

This section provides an overview of the entire general equilibrium simulation model. We try here to describe its features in general terms and to justify some of the assumptions. Later chapters provide specific equations, data, and other detail.

In our research, we address several primary concerns. First, we want to capture important influences of taxes on diverse household choices in labor supply, savings, and the consumption of commodities. We therefore specify utility functions and budget constraints that incorporate these choices, and we assume utility-maximizing behavior in order to solve for each factor supply and consumption demand as a function of income and prices. Second, we want to capture effects of taxes on each producer's use of labor and capital. We specify production functions and assume profit-maximizing behavior in competitive markets to solve for each factor demand as a function of factor prices. Third, we want to find the net impact of taxes when these behaviors are considered simultaneously. These concerns dictate the use of a general equilibrium model. Consumers must make intertemporal decisions about present and future consumption in order to capture the effects of taxes on savings, capital formation, and growth. The utility function must include leisure as an alternative to consumption, and it must include a variety of consumer goods that may be taxed at different rates. Taxes in the model must be flexible enough to reflect the diverse effects of all federal, state, and local tax instruments.

Consumer Behavior

To structure these diverse concerns, we assume that consumer decisions are made in stages. To begin, the individual calculates the present value of potential lifetime earnings. This endowment is supplemented by government transfers, reduced by taxes, discounted at the after-tax interest rate, and augmented by a fixed initial inheritance. For simplicity, we assume that the consumer expects the current interest rate to prevail in all future periods.

One part of this lifetime endowment must be saved for a bequest upon death.[29] We model such behavior because we are concerned that life-cycle saving by itself may only explain about half of the observed capital stock.[30] In our model, part of the capital stock is attributable to the fact that individuals receive exogenous inheritances and are required to leave comparable bequests at the end of life. Incidence results depend on the differences in these inheritances among groups. To achieve balanced growth in this model, each group must add some additional savings to their inheritance before they make their bequest.

The rest of the present value of income is available for spending. The consumer maximizes a lifetime utility function, in stages, and this maximization provides all demands as functions of incomes and prices. In the first

29. For a discussion of motivations for individual bequests and the ways taxes affect the size of bequests, see Bernheim (1991).

30. Kotlikoff and Summers (1981).

decision stage, the consumer chooses how much to spend each period. This choice depends on our assumption for the individual's rate of time preference (0.005 in the central case) and the elasticity of substitution among time periods (0.5 in the central case). The consumer's choice about how much to spend each period is also affected by changes in the net rate of return (which starts at 0.04 in the central case). We later test the sensitivity of results to all of these specific numerical assumptions.

At the second stage, the consumer allocates one period's "spending" between leisure and other consumption goods. This choice depends on our assumption regarding another elasticity of substitution (0.5 in the central case). We allow individuals to "buy" more leisure at a price equal to the forgone net-of-tax wage, instead of buying other goods. This choice is affected by taxes, and it also depends on age. Individuals in this model never fully retire, but the weight on leisure increases with age after they reach age 60, in a way that reflects actual choices.

In the third stage, individuals decide how to allocate current consumption spending among seventeen particular goods (such as food, alcohol, tobacco, utilities, housing). This decision function is specified such that a consumer at a given age buys a set of seventeen "minimum required purchase" amounts and then allocates remaining spending according to a set of seventeen "marginal expenditure shares." These thirty-four parameters are estimated for each of twelve age categories using data from the Consumer Expenditure Survey, as described in chapter 5. This functional form has several important implications. By making a portion of spending nondiscretionary, it reduces the sensitivity of total consumption and saving to the net rate of return. In addition, because discretionary income may be spent in proportions different from minimum requirements, actual purchase proportions depend on total income. Required spending is relatively high for housing and gasoline, while discretionary spending is relatively high for clothing, services, and recreation. Thus the rich and the poor buy different bundles and bear different burdens on the uses side.

This framework also allows us to use the same utility function for everyone in the model. In previous efforts, rich and poor individuals spend in different proportions because they have different preferences and differ in fundamental characteristics. We feel it is very arbitrary to assume that even if the poor were to receive additional income, they would still spend it as if they were poor. It seems more natural that a poor person with more money would begin to behave like a rich person. That is, the primary distinction between rich and poor is the amount of income they receive. Therefore, in our model, everyone has the same preference parameters. The poor spend more on goods with high minimum required expenditures because they are poor, and the rich spend more on goods with relatively high marginal expenditure shares.[31]

In the fourth stage of our consumer's allocation process, expenditure on each consumer good is divided by fixed coefficients among components drawn from a list of producer industries. No real "decision" is made here, but this step allows us to match consumption data using one definition of commodities with production data using a different definition of commodities. For example, expenditure on the consumer good "appliances" is composed of portions from metals and machinery, from transportation, and from the trade industry.

Then, in the fifth and final stage of the decision tree, the consumer takes the spending on each industry output and allocates it between the corporate sector and the noncorporate sector. We assume that the corporate output is not identical to the noncorporate output in the same industry. Hand-carved furniture, for example, is not the same as manufactured furniture. The consumer chooses the amount of each, using a weighting parameter based on initial observed corporate and noncorporate shares of production within each industry, and using another elasticity of substitution (5.0 in the central case). This allows us to capture the observed coexistence of both sectors within an industry, despite different tax treatments. If the outputs were identical, a higher tax rate would drive one sector out of production. The degree of similarity is reflected in the elasticity of substitution. The other purpose of this specification is to capture ways in which changes in corporate taxes affect relative product prices and quantities demanded of the outputs of each sector.

Producer Behavior

We use a similar decision tree to model producer behavior in each sector of each industry. Each output is produced by many competitive firms using production functions in stages, with constant returns to scale. These assump-

31. Thus we do not investigate the possibility that the rich and the poor have different rates of time preference. This possibility may be important, especially in annual income models, because it may help explain differences in capital accumulation. Here we do not try to explain why some are rich and some are poor. Instead, the differences in potential earnings profiles are exogenous. We want to investigate the effects of these endowment differences without mixing in effects of other differences, such as in preferences.

tions are typical in this literature, because they guarantee that sales revenue is exhausted by payments for inputs, with no excess profits for the firms. Thus each output price can be calculated directly from the use and price of each factor of production. Also, for computational simplicity, we assume no externalities, no adjustment costs, and no uncertainty.[32]

In the first stage of production, output is composed of a fixed coefficient combination of value-added and intermediate inputs. Each of the nineteen industries uses the outputs of all other industries, in fixed proportions. Thus we capture the effect of one product price on another. In the second stage, value-added is a function of labor and "composite" capital. The weighting parameters are based on observed labor and capital in each industry, and the elasticity of substitution varies by industry (between 0.68 and 0.96, in the central case). Thus a tax on labor can induce the firm to use more capital instead, and vice versa. It also raises the cost of production, and thus output price, in any industry that uses a high proportion of the taxed factor.

In the third and final stage of the production tree, composite capital is a function of five asset types—equipment, structures, land, inventories, and intangible assets. These types are defined by important tax differences such as the investment tax credit for equipment and the expensing of new intangible assets created through advertising or research and development. The weighting shares are again based on the observed use of these assets in each industry, and the response to tax differentials is again specified by an elasticity of substitution (1.5 in the central case).

Government Functions

Government in this model conducts several functions. It pays transfers to individuals according to the estimated lifetime transfer profiles discussed in the previous subsection. It produces an output for sale through an industry called "government enterprises," and it produces a free public good through a composite combination of its use of labor, capital, and purchases of each private industry output. The weights in this combination are based on observed government purchases, and the elasticity of substitution is one. The

32. Other studies consider the effects of monopoly power and returns to scale—for example, Harris (1984). Effects of externalities are investigated in Ballard and Medema (1991), and adjustment costs in Goulder and Summers (1989). We ignore these complications to concentrate on features that are required to calculate lifetime tax incidence for groups with different lifetime incomes.

level of this public good is held fixed in all simulations, because any tax change is accompanied by an adjustment that ensures equal-revenue yield. A final government function, of course, is to collect taxes.

Taxes

Each tax instrument enters the model as a wedge between the producer's price and the consumer's price. The payroll tax, for example, applies an ad valorem rate to each producer's use of labor, so the gross-of-tax wage paid by the producer is higher than the net-of-tax wage received by the worker. Similarly, sales and excise taxes appear as ad valorem rates on each consumer good, so the gross-of-tax price paid by the consumer exceeds the net-of-tax price received by the seller.

The personal income tax is a little more complicated, to enable us to capture its progressive effect on tax burdens. The actual U.S. personal tax system imposes higher effective tax rates on higher incomes through a graduated rate structure with a changing marginal tax rate. For some purposes, we must calculate the effects of individual choices at each possible marginal tax rate in order to determine utility-maximizing behavior. Our primary goal, however, is to measure the distributional effects of the tax. For this purpose, it is sufficient to use a set of linear tax functions that approximates the U.S. system, with a negative intercept for each group and a single marginal tax rate (0.3 in the central case). Although all individuals face the same marginal tax rate, average tax rates still increase with income due to the negative intercepts. We do not model the many exemptions and deductions. The important point is that these simpler, linear tax functions can replicate the observed data on personal taxes actually paid by each group.

The state and local property tax and the U.S. federal corporate income tax raise the producer's gross-of-tax cost of capital, for each asset type, relative to the investor's net-of-tax rate of return. This cost of capital is the gross rate of return that must be earned on the asset to be able to pay all necessary taxes and still yield the required net rate of return. The cost of capital for each asset depends on the statutory corporate tax rate, depreciation allowances at historical cost, the rate at which inflation erodes those allowances, the rate of investment tax credit, and the required rate of return for the firm. This required rate of return depends, in turn, on the going market rate and the personal taxation of interest, dividends, and capital gains. A similar cost of capital formula applies to the noncorporate sector. This treatment allows the producer's choice among assets to depend on relative tax rules, and the price of output in each industry to depend on the relative use of assets with different effective tax rates.

Other Specifications of the Model

Other assumptions help to close the model in a way that accounts for all flows and that helps facilitate computation. We ignore international mobility of labor or capital, but allow for trade of industry outputs. Also, the value of imports must match the value of exports; the government's expenditures and transfer payments must match tax revenue; and, the value of personal savings must match the value of investment expenditures. Producer investment is not the result of firms' intertemporal optimization, but instead follows personal savings from consumers' optimization. The amount of personal savings is growing over time, because consumers' labor earnings are growing through population and technical change. On the steady state growth path, the capital stock grows at exactly the same rate as the effective labor stock.

Data for this model derive from many different sources, adjusted to represent 1984 as the base year. In addition to the survey data used to estimate wage profiles and preference parameters, we use the National Income and Product Accounts for an input-output matrix, labor compensation by industry, government purchases, and international trade. These data are combined with other published and unpublished data such as on capital allocations and inheritances. Detail is provided in chapter 3; consistency adjustments are described in chapter 6.

For some parameters, such as the elasticities of substitution, we assume particular values. For other parameters, such as those describing preferences across goods, we use econometric estimates. Finally, for remaining parameters, we "calibrate" from data on actual allocations. We use the demand functions, and all initial prices and observed quantities, to solve backward for the value of the parameter that would make that quantity the desired one. This procedure establishes a "benchmark" equilibrium, with existing tax rules and prices, so that all consumers are buying the desired quantities and supplying the desired amounts of each factor, while producers are using their desired amounts of factors to produce the desired output.

Thus, using all these parameters together, we can solve for an equilibrium with unchanged tax rules that replicates the benchmark-consistent data. This provides an important check on the solution procedure. From this benchmark, we can alter any particular tax rule and see how much more or less the consumers want to buy of each good. The solution algorithm then raises the price of any good in excess demand, and lowers the price of any good in excess supply, until it finds a set of prices where the quantity supplied equals the quantity demanded for every good and factor. It "simulates" the effect of the tax change, to calculate all new prices, quantities, and levels of consumer utility. Our measure of the tax burden is the "equivalent variation," the dollar value of the change in utility measured in terms of benchmark prices.

A Summary of Results

The effects of each separate tax instrument can be measured by comparing the benchmark equilibrium, with the tax, to a simulated equilibrium without it. If we were just to remove the tax, in a balanced budget incidence analysis, the effects of the tax removal would be mixed up with the effects of the necessary reductions in government spending and transfers. We therefore recover the revenue with a proportional tax on all endowments of labor. In this "differential" incidence analysis, the effects of each tax are compared with those of a proportional tax that raises the same revenue. Each tax can then be judged progressive or regressive, relative to that proportional alternative. The endowment tax base is a hypothetical alternative, because it includes the value of leisure, but it provides a nondistorting alternative against which to measure the efficiency of each tax. More important, this "proportional" alternative takes the same fraction of all consumers' true economic income or well-being.

Using this kind of calculation, we summarize the results for each tax in figure 1-4. These results correspond to our central case parameterization. Ignore the additive nature of this stacked-bar graph for the moment, and consider only one tax at a time. For the personal income tax, shown at the bottom of each bar, results appear moderately progressive. In this model, the entire personal income tax can be replaced by a 9.6 percent tax on all endowments. The lowest lifetime income group loses 4.3 percent of lifetime income when the personal income tax is replaced with this flat 9.6 percent endowment tax (so their personal tax burden must have been about 5.3 percent of endowment). The highest income group gains 9.0 percent with the 9.6 percent replacement (so their personal tax was about 18.6 percent of endowment). These two groups each contain only 2 percent of the population, however. Most of the action is in the middle ten groups, accounting for 96 percent of the population, where the personal income tax is not quite so progressive.

Figure 1-4.   *Welfare Effects of Removing Each Tax, Standard Case*

Equivalent variation as percent of lifetime income

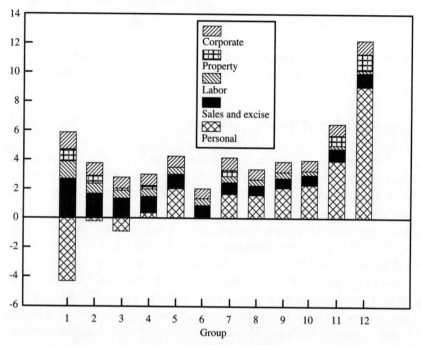

The rate roughly parallels the flat replacement tax for most of these groups, though perhaps 2 percent more for the top few deciles.

We also note that the total gain is positive, about 0.7 percent of the present value of lifetime income for all groups of all ages. This measure of efficiency reflects the personal income tax distortions in labor supply and savings behavior. Since the average present value of lifetime income is almost a million dollars in 1984, this 0.7 percent figure amounts to about $7,000 per lifetime.

The next largest tax category includes state and local sales taxes plus federal excise taxes. The blackened part of the bar graph in figure 1-4 shows that replacement of these taxes (with an 8.5 percent endowment tax) provides 2 percent gains to low-income groups and smaller percentage gains to high-income groups. Thus sales and excise taxes have regressive effects compared to the proportional replacement. They also have an efficiency effect equal to 0.3 percent of income, or $3,000 per lifetime.

Chapter 7 provides other detailed results from these simulations, including new prices, incomes, labor allocations, and capital accumulations. It shows how U.S. sales and excise taxes raise the prices of particular goods such as alcohol, tobacco, and gasoline. In addition, chapter 5 shows these same goods have estimated minimum required purchases that are large relative to their marginal expenditure shares. These goods constitute relatively large fractions of low-income budgets, and thus the selective nature of these taxes makes them regressive. In this model, a tax at the same rate on all consumption commodities would be nearly proportional on a lifetime basis.[33]

Next, in figure 1-4, the payroll tax on labor is also somewhat regressive. Compared with the proportional replacement (at a 4.9 percent rate on endowments), it takes 1.2 percent more from the lowest income group and only 0.2 percent more from the highest income group. The model is not sufficiently refined, however, to capture the regressive effect of the cap on social security tax paid by high-income workers. Low-income groups take a somewhat lower fraction of their endowments as leisure, in our model, and therefore pay relatively less endowment tax than payroll tax. The efficiency effect is 0.1 percent of income, or 1.3 percent of revenue, figures that are smaller than for any other tax category.

The property tax has two effects in our model, as it does in the U.S. economy. First, it raises the cost of capital, primarily in housing. It thus reduces total demand for capital, reduces the equilibrium net rate of return to *all* types of capital, and places burdens on the sources side for those who own capital. A distinguishing feature of our lifetime model is that owners of capital are not just "the rich" but are people whose earnings peak relatively early in life and who must therefore save more to achieve the desired consumption path. A look at the wage profiles in figure 1-3 suggests that middle-income groups peak late, so the sources-side burden of this tax falls on other low- as well as high-income groups. Second, the property tax raises overall costs for housing providers and thus raises the equilibrium break-even price of housing services. Since this expenditure makes up a relatively high fraction of the budgets of low-income families, this tax has regressive effects on the uses side. In combination, figure 1-4 shows that this tax has a U-shaped distribution of burdens. Its replacement (with a 2.7 percent rate on endowments) provides gains at the top and at the bottom of the income distribution while leaving the middle-income groups unaffected. The efficiency effect is 0.2 percent of income, or 4.5 percent of revenue.

Finally, the corporate income tax is shown at the top of each bar in figure

33. If the present value of expenditures were exactly equal to the present value of the labor endowment, a flat-rate consumption tax would take exactly the same fraction of all lifetime incomes. In our model, however, the consumption tax base differs from labor endowment because of gifts and inheritances and because of leisure. Even a flat-rate consumption tax can be regressive if higher-income groups take more untaxed leisure.

1-4. In the traditional analysis, this tax reduces the net rate of return to capital and places sources-side burdens on owners of capital. It may also raise the price of corporate outputs relative to noncorporate outputs. In our model, with 1984 tax rules, the removal of the corporate tax has no effect whatsoever on the net rate of return to capital and thus no sources-side burden at all. The reason is that in 1984 this tax collected very little revenue: for the marginal investment, the positive corporate tax on the return to equity is virtually offset by the investment tax credit, accelerated depreciation allowances, and the deductions for payments of interest. The replacement tax on endowments only requires a 0.2 percent rate to acquire the same revenue.

The corporation tax does have effects on the uses side, however, because it raises some output prices and lowers others. It reduces the prices of outputs produced by industries with intensive use of tax-favored assets such as equipment and intangibles. An investment tax credit applies for equipment, in 1984, and expensing is allowed for advertising and research and development. The tax also raises the prices of outputs produced by industries with intensive use of other less-favored assets such as structures, land, and inventories. This effect on the uses side is somewhat regressive at the low end of the income distribution, because the corporate tax raises prices of goods with large minimum required purchases.

The corporate tax does not raise much revenue, but it still distorts producer choices in the use of tax-favored assets relative to other assets. The overall efficiency cost of the tax is 0.26 percent, relative to income, but 65 percent relative to the small amount of revenue. In other words, the corporate tax in 1984 was a particularly inefficient source of funds for government. Changes since 1984 are discussed in chapter 9.

Figure 1-4 provides a valuable visual image of the overall effects of all U.S. taxes together, with three caveats. First, although the heights of these bars display a distinct U-shaped pattern, the negative bars for the first three groups must be subtracted from the positive bars to get the net effect of all taxes. The net effects look a bit more progressive. Second, this progressive appearance stems primarily from a low overall burden in the bottom 2 percent group and a high overall burden in the top 2 percent group. If one concentrates on just the middle ten groups, covering 96 percent of the population, the overall effect of the U.S. tax system is roughly proportional or only slightly progressive.

Third, the effects of these separate tax replacements are not exactly additive. These tax instruments interact with each other in interesting ways, and the combination is not equal to the sum of the parts. We therefore also perform a simulation that removes all taxes simultaneously, requiring a 25 percent rate of tax on all labor endowments to achieve the same real value of revenue. This replacement has virtually no effect on the lowest income group, and it provides an 11 percent gain for the highest income group. Thus results appear progressive. Again, those small groups are unusual. For the middle ten groups, with 96 percent of the population, the current tax system imposes burdens (relative to the proportional tax alternative) that increase only from 3 percent to 5 percent of lifetime income.

The endowment tax replacement is proportional to a broad measure of consumer welfare, and it thus serves as a valuable basis for judging the distributional effects of each U.S. tax. It is also a nondistorting lump-sum alternative, and thus allows us to calculate net efficiency effects. It is only a hypothetical alternative, however, because the Internal Revenue Service would find it particularly difficult to enforce a tax on leisure, or on the amount that could potentially be earned. We therefore perform some additional experiments with the more realistic alternative of a uniform consumption tax on all commodities. This revenue could be collected as a national sales tax at the same rate on all final demands, or as a consumption-type value-added tax (VAT).[34] The two are equivalent for present purposes, because our model does not capture potential differences in administration, enforcement, and collection costs.

Figure 1-5 shows the effects of replacing each tax with this uniform consumption tax, using the same type of stacked-bar graph. The vertical scale is slightly different, but this figure conveys the same impression about overall progressivity as figure 1-4. The personal income tax still takes less from the first three income groups than would this proportional alternative, and takes more from the remaining nine groups. Actual U.S. sales and excise taxes are still regressive compared with this uniform sales tax, because they apply higher rates to the goods that are big expenditures for low-income families. The patterns of these burdens are also similar to those in the previous figure for the separate effects of payroll taxes on labor, property taxes, and corporate income taxes.

The same caveats also apply. The negative bar for the first group must be subtracted from the positive bar, so that the net effect is near zero. Also this group is only 2 percent of the population. The overall pattern for the middle

---

34. Value added for each firm is equal to sales revenue minus costs for material inputs and capital investments. The value of a finished consumption good is equal to the sum of the value added at each stage of production, so a tax on the finished good has the same economic effects as a VAT.

Figure 1-5. *Welfare Effects of Removing Each Tax, Standard Case —*
VAT Replacement

Equivalent variation as percent of lifetime income

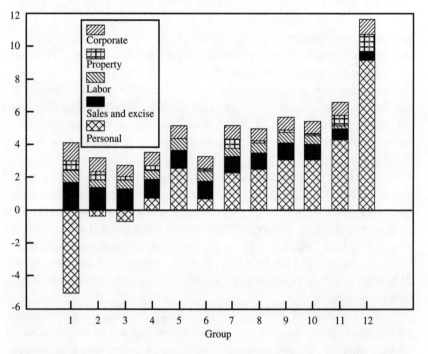

ten groups, with 96 percent of the population, is not very progressive. We
also remove all U.S. taxes simultaneously, but the replacement tax rate must
be 37 percent because the consumption tax base is smaller than the endowment tax base. Relative to this 37 percent consumption tax, actual U.S. taxes
take 2 percent less from the lowest lifetime income group, and 11 percent
more from the highest lifetime income group. For the middle ten groups,
these percentages vary only from 3 percent to 6 percent more than the proportional tax.

All of these simulations are based on a single set of assumptions about
values for certain parameters such as the various elasticities of substitution.
To determine the importance of these assumptions, and to see how the results
might be different, we set up the model with alternative sets of assumptions.
Chapter 8 includes a full description of variant A through variant H, with the
overall conclusion that our results are not very sensitive to these assumptions.

Here we summarize results just from variant A. Some of the most impor-

Figure 1-6. *Welfare Effects of Removing Each Tax, Case A*

Equivalent variation as percent of lifetime income

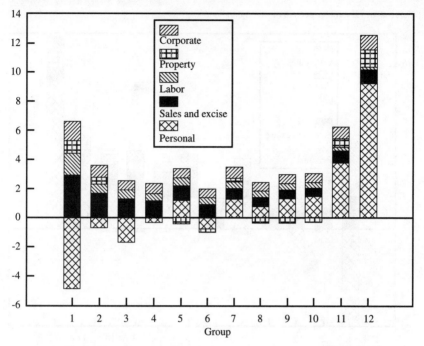

tant aspects of our model involve the savings behavior of consumers, the accumulation of capital relative to labor, and the resulting effects on factor prices. The parameters that most affect these outcomes are the rate of time preference, which determines the weight or importance placed on present consumption relative to future consumption, and the intertemporal elasticity of substitution, which reflects the consumer's flexibility. We use various empirical estimates of these parameters, and consistency conditions in our model, to choose 0.005 for the former and 0.5 for the latter. Many studies have found that the intertemporal elasticity of substitution is less than 0.5, however, so we use an alternative value of 0.25 in variant A. At the same time, to ensure that life-cycle behavior still generates the observed capital stock in our base year, we must use -0.005 for the rate of time preference.

Results for variant A are shown in figure 1-6 for the endowment tax replacement, and figure 1-7 for the VAT replacement. Tables of numerical results are thoroughly discussed in chapter 8, but these stacked-bar graphs seem to indicate that not much has changed. The personal income tax is still a bit

Figure 1-7. *Welfare Effects of Removing Each Tax, Case A—*
VAT Replacement

Equivalent variation as percent of lifetime income

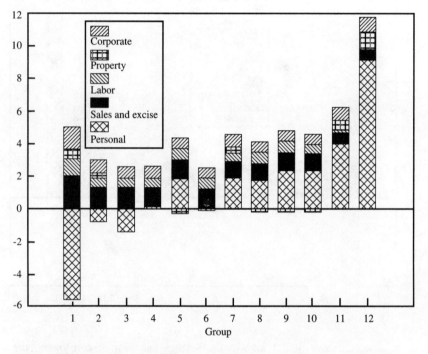

progressive, but the combined effect of U.S. taxes is still fairly flat across the
middle ten groups. One subtle difference, however, is that the property tax
burden is negative on some of the middle-income groups. The explanation is
that because savers are less flexible about when they consume, they are less
able to shift part of the burden of this tax on capital. The net rate of return to
capital falls more than in the central case, and the burdens on capital are more
pronounced. Capital owners who bear this tax in our model are the low- and
high-income groups that experience early peaks in their earnings and that thus
accumulate more capital for later consumption. In contrast, the middle-
income groups experience late earnings peaks and *gain* from having this tax
on capital instead of the flat-rate alternative.

Finally, chapter 9 provides details and discussion of calculations for the
Tax Reform Act of 1986 and other possible reforms. We capture all of the
major features of the 1986 act in our model, but not all the myriad details.
Most important, the 1986 act repealed the investment tax credit, altered de-

preciation allowances, and reduced the statutory corporate tax rate from 46 to 34 percent. These changes are expected to improve the allocation of resources between tax-favored assets such as equipment and other assets such as structures, but they might also raise the cost of capital and discourage investment. The act used the extra corporate tax collections to reduce personal taxes, in a revenue-neutral fashion. We do the same in our model, where the personal marginal tax rate can be reduced from 0.30 to about 0.28 with no change in government spending. As a consequence, all the lifetime income groups gain. These gains fall from about 0.5 for the lowest group to near zero for the highest group, but the overall gain is about 0.3 percent of total lifetime income. On average, this gain amounts to $2,610 per person, per lifetime, forever.

CHAPTER TWO

Theoretical Basis of the Lifetime Incidence Model

FOR OUR STUDY of lifetime tax incidence, we developed a general equilibrium model with multiple consumers and producers. Consumers are divided by lifetime income category and age. They maximize lifetime utility according to a life-cycle theory with bequests, by allocating consumption and leisure across periods. The production side of the model includes annual decision-making by profit-maximizing, competitive firms, and ignores distortions other than those generated by the tax system. By design, the model accounts for distortions caused by differing tax rates across time, among goods, between the corporate and noncorporate sectors, and among assets within each sector.[1]

Most U.S. taxes apply to many sectors of the economy, and a tax on one industry can affect factor returns and thus output prices in other industries. An effective analysis of the distributional and efficiency aspects of the tax system thus requires a general equilibrium study. Changes in prices of other goods and factors shift the burden of a tax, and these indirect, general equilibrium effects become more significant with larger taxes. Moreover, these effects contribute to the pattern of tax incidence among consumers. The lifetime incidence model shows how and to what extent individuals bear the ultimate burden of taxes.

Equally important, the model allows us to determine utility-based measures of welfare. These utility measures capture the effects of general equilib-

---

1. This combination of simplifying assumptions makes the complete model manageable, but other papers may address particular aspects in more detail. For example, Harris (1984) incorporates imperfect competition in a general equilibrium model of taxes, tariffs, and trade. Goulder and Summers (1989) incorporate forward-looking investment behavior by firms, Goulder and Eichengreen (1989) consider international flows of capital, and Ballard and Medema (1991) add pollution externalities.

rium price changes as well as the distortions that cause the burden of taxation to exceed the tax revenue paid. If distortions and price changes affect some lifetime income categories more than others, the distribution of the tax burden may be quite different from accounting measures of taxes paid. All price changes and distortions are captured in our calculation of the "equivalent variation" for each lifetime income category. The equivalent variation is the amount of income that would be "equivalent" in terms of utility to the policy change. It is the amount necessary to attain the new level of utility at the old set of prices.

In this chapter we first describe the features and equations of the dynamic consumption side of the model, and follow with a presentation of the production side. Next, we discuss the government and foreign sectors and describe the U.S. tax system model. We then explain the mechanics of the model through discussion of the computational procedure. Finally, we discuss the method of calculating utility-based lifetime tax incidence.

The Consumption Side

The model includes a representative consumer for each age category within each lifetime income category. All consumers have the same lifetime utility function, with the same parameters, but the function is flexible enough for consumption shares to vary across age and lifetime income categories. That is, consumers who differ either by age or by lifetime income category purchase different bundles of goods. The utility function also allows for labor intensity to vary over the life cycle and for substitution between corporate and noncorporate outputs within the same industry. This latter feature explains the coexistence of the corporate and noncorporate sectors. A diagrammatic summary of the consumption side is provided in figure 2-1.

To compare lifetime levels of well-being and capture intertemporal substitution effects, we model the lifetime utility of consumers with a constant elasticity of substitution (CES) function. The allocation across periods, indicated at the top of figure 2-1, is given by

$$(2\text{-}1) \qquad U = \left[\sum_{t=1}^{T} a_t^{1/\varepsilon_1} x_t^{(\varepsilon_1 - 1)/\varepsilon_1} \right]^{\varepsilon_1/(\varepsilon_1 - 1)},$$

where T is the individual's certain date of death, ε_1 is the intertemporal elasticity of substitution, and x_t is the amount of "composite commodity," a com-

Figure 2-1. *Summary of the Consumption Side*

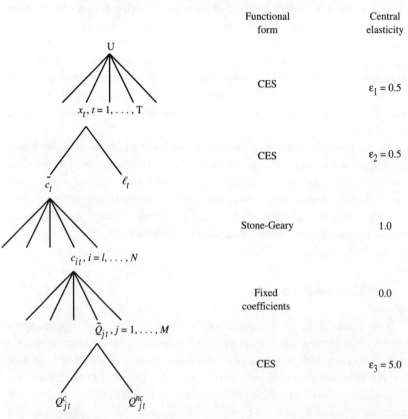

	Functional form	Central elasticity
	CES	$\varepsilon_1 = 0.5$
	CES	$\varepsilon_2 = 0.5$
	Stone-Geary	1.0
	Fixed coefficients	0.0
	CES	$\varepsilon_3 = 5.0$

bination of a composite consumption good and leisure at age t. The weighting parameter, a_t, reflects the consumer's subjective discount rate.[2] To make the model operational, we specify an economic lifetime from chronological age 20 to 79 (so $T = 60$ years), and we use twelve age groups defined by five-year increments. Lifetime utility is determined using 60 years of consumption for each of the twelve lifetime income categories.[3]

The consumer allocates lifetime income across periods to maximize utility (equation 2-1), subject to a lifetime budget constraint given by

2. The derivations of a_t and other parameters are discussed in the chapter on parameterization, chapter 6.

3. The determination of these lifetime income categories is discussed in the chapter on lifetime profiles, chapter 4.

$$(2\text{-}2) \qquad\qquad \sum_{t=1}^{T} x_t[q_t/(1+r)^{t-1}] = I_d \, ,$$

where q_t is the price of the period-t composite commodity,[4] r is the net-of-tax rate of return, and I_d is the present value of lifetime "discretionary" income. The model specifies minimum required purchases of various consumption goods at each age, so discretionary income equals lifetime income minus the cost of required expenditures. Thus the amount of lifetime income available for intertemporal smoothing is only the amount in excess of what is required each period. We interpret the composite commodity, x_t, as "discretionary consumption" of goods and leisure. We define lifetime income as the present value of lifetime labor endowments, plus inheritances, less taxes, plus transfers. We explain the construction of lifetime incomes in chapter 4 and show how we determine consumption-share parameters and minimum-required purchases in chapter 5. Since equation 2-2 is the only constraint facing the consumer, capital markets are perfect. That is, the consumer has unlimited ability to borrow against future income at the same interest rate earned on savings.

The result of the intertemporal optimization problem is a demand for composite commodity at age t given by

$$(2\text{-}3) \qquad\qquad x_t = \frac{a_t I_d}{[q_t/(1+r)^{t-1}]^{\varepsilon_1} \left[\sum_{s=1}^{T} a_s [q_s/(1+r)^{s-1}]^{1-\varepsilon_1}\right]} .$$

At the next level of figure 2-1, we arrive at the labor-leisure choice. For each age t in the consumer's lifetime, the allocation of composite commodity between the composite consumption good and leisure is given by the CES function

$$(2\text{-}4) \qquad x_t = \left[\alpha^{1/\varepsilon_2}\bar{c}_t^{(\varepsilon_2-1)/\varepsilon_2} + (1-\alpha_t)^{1/\varepsilon_2}\ell_t^{(\varepsilon_2-1)/\varepsilon_2}\right]^{\varepsilon_2/(\varepsilon_2-1)} ,$$

where $\bar{c}_t$ is the amount of composite consumption good consumed at t, ℓ_t is the amount of leisure taken at t, and ε_2 is the elasticity of substitution between consumption and leisure. Leisure is labor endowment (E_t) minus time spent

---

4. Composite prices are described later in this chapter, in the discussion of computational procedure.

working (L_t).[5] This allows an endogenous labor supply decision that can be affected by tax policy, thus capturing a distortionary effect of labor taxes.[6] Moreover, by modeling the labor-leisure choice, we capture any differences in tax burdens that may arise because of variations in work intensities across lifetime income categories.[7] For each age t, the consumer maximizes (equation 2-4) subject to the constraint

$$(2\text{-}5) \qquad\qquad \bar{p}_t \bar{c}_t + w\ell_t = q_t x_t \, ,$$

where $\bar{p}_t$ is the price of the age-t composite consumption good, $\bar{c}_t$, and w is the net-of-tax wage rate.[8] This maximization results in the following demands for age-t leisure and the age-t composite consumption good:

$$(2\text{-}6) \qquad\qquad \ell_t = \frac{(1-\alpha_t)(q_t x_t)}{w^{\varepsilon_2}\Big[\alpha_t(\bar{p}_t)^{1-\varepsilon_2} + (1-\alpha_t)w^{1-\varepsilon_2}\Big]} \, ,$$

and

$$(2\text{-}7) \qquad\qquad \bar{c}_t = \frac{\alpha_t(q_t x_t)}{\bar{p}_t^{\varepsilon_2}\Big[\alpha_t(\bar{p}_t)^{1-\varepsilon_2} + (1-\alpha_t)w^{1-\varepsilon_2}\Big]} \, .$$

5. All consumers have the same endowment of time in this model, 4,000 hours a year in the central case, but those with higher earnings are said to own more "effective labor units" in their labor endowment. Thus the labor endowment reflects quality as well as quantity, with one economy-wide wage rate per effective labor unit.

6. Whereas labor supplies are endogenous in this model, labor endowments are exogenous. In other words, we do not specify human capital accumulation. Davies and Whalley (1991) find that incorporating the human capital decision into a general equilibrium model does little to affect estimates of the dynamic welfare costs of capital versus labor income taxes. Their model does not allow for an endogenous labor-leisure choice, however. With endogenous labor supply, a tax on labor may reduce the opportunity cost of schooling and thus increase human capital accumulation. It may also reduce the expected return to the human investment relative to the return on physical capital and thus decrease human relative to physical capital accumulation. A tax on capital applies only to physical capital accumulation and thus increases the present value of the future return on human capital accumulation. Theoretically, the total effect of these taxes on steady-state capital intensity is not clear; thus this issue requires empirical investigation.

7. This model does not require retirement to take place. Instead, the low level of labor supply for elderly individuals is translated into a high preference for leisure, by the parameterization process discussed in chapter 6. Labor income falls significantly in old age, because of both a declining value of labor endowment and the increasing preference for leisure.

8. In a steady state, the net rate of return (r) and the wage rate (w) are constant. Subscripts still apply to age-specific variables such as leisure and commodities that vary over the life cycle. The price $\bar{p}_t$ has a subscript because the weights in the bundle depend on age.

As shown at the third level of figure 2-1, the composite consumption good at each age t is modeled as a Stone-Geary function of the individual consumption goods:[9]

$$(2-8) \qquad \bar{c}_t = \prod_{i=1}^{N} (c_{it} - b_{it})^{\beta_{it}} ,$$

where N is the number of consumer goods (equal to seventeen in our model), c_{it} is the amount of consumer good i consumed at age t, and b_{it} is the minimum required purchase of good i at age t. The share parameters, β_{it}, will vary with age for any individual, reflecting the changing composition of the consumption bundle over the life cycle. Specifying minimum required purchases for each good is especially useful in two respects. First, it allows us to use a single lifetime utility function for all individuals, where actual consumption proportions can vary across income categories. Low-income individuals will purchase amounts more closely approximating the required amounts, whereas higher-income individuals will purchase amounts more closely reflecting the marginal shares of income, β_{it}.[10] Second, the presence of a consumption floor mitigates swings in early consumption. This helps to produce a realistic savings response to changes in the interest rate, while using reasonable measures of the intertemporal rate of substitution.[11]

The consumer maximizes equation 2-8 subject to the budget constraint

$$(2-9) \qquad \sum_{i=1}^{N} p_i(c_{it} - b_{it}) = \bar{p}_t \bar{c}_t ,$$

where p_i is the gross-of-tax price of individual consumption good i. This price is not related to an age-specific bundle but is constant in steady state. The resulting demands for each consumer good at age t are

9. The Stone-Geary function is also known as the linear expenditure system, because of the form of the expenditure relationship implied by such a utility function.

10. Without the minimum requirements, we would have a simple Cobb-Douglas specification where consumption proportions are independent of income level. With the linear expenditure system derived from Stone-Geary utility, as income increases, some goods may increase as a fraction of income while other goods decrease as a fraction of income.

11. See Starrett (1988), who also uses a Stone-Geary form. Isoelastic utility functions, in contrast, lead to higher sensitivity of savings to the interest rate. Starrett points to an example from the Summers (1981) model, with an isoelastic utility function and an intertemporal elasticity of zero. As the real interest rate moves between 4 and 8 percent, consumers switch from borrowing 6 percent of their income to saving 42 percent.

$$(2\text{-}10) \qquad\qquad c_{it} = b_{it} + \frac{\beta_{it}(\bar{p}_t \bar{c}_t)}{p_i},$$

for $i = 1, \ldots, N$.

The fourth level of figure 2-1 illustrates how consumption goods are related to production outputs. In using different sources of data, our classification of producer outputs does not correspond to the classification of goods consumed by households. Therefore, to relate the data, we specify each consumption good as a fixed-coefficient mix of producer goods, $\bar{Q}_j$, $j = 1$, $\ldots$, M (where M equals 19 in our model).[12] These coefficients are given by a "transition" matrix, Z.

Finally, we distinguish between corporate and noncorporate outputs. In the original Arnold C. Harberger model, the corporate output was primarily manufacturing while the noncorporate output was made up of agriculture, services, and real estate. The corporate tax applied to only one sector, and it raised the relative price of that output. Here we wish to capture more detail of the U.S. economy, where a single industry typically comprises both corporate and noncorporate firms. If consumers viewed corporate and noncorporate outputs as perfect substitutes, we would not be able to assign the same technology to both firms producing the same output, because an extra corporate tax would drive the corporate firms out of business. Jane G. Gravelle and Laurence J. Kotlikoff (1989) explain coexistence by introducing different technologies for the same output. Their noncorporate firm has increasing costs and expands only until the extra cost matches the corporate firm's extra tax. In our study, we say that the two sectors produce outputs that consumers perceive as at least slightly different. Even with nineteen industries, the disaggregation is not sufficient to capture differences within an industry between a corporate output and a noncorporate output. In the clothing industry, for example, hand-knit sweaters from small (noncorporate) shops are not the same as machine-produced sweaters purchased from (corporate) department stores. A hamburger from McDonald's is not the same as one from the (noncorporate) corner diner. The two outputs within an industry may be highly substitutable, but they are not perfect substitutes. Specifically, as indicated in the final level of figure 2-1, each $\bar{Q}_j$ is a CES composite of corporate and noncorporate outputs:[13]

12. For example, consumption of "appliances" uses the outputs of the manufacturing, transportation, and trade industries. An excise tax on the manufacturing output does not affect the coefficients used to create the consumer good, but it does affect the price of the consumer good and thus the mix of such goods in consumption.

13. In the housing industry, as discussed later, our corporate-noncorporate distinction is replaced by a distinction between rental housing and owner-occupied housing.

$$(2\text{-}11) \quad \bar{Q}_j = \left[\gamma_j^{1/\varepsilon_3}(Q_j^c)^{(\varepsilon_3-1)/\varepsilon_3} + (1-\gamma_j)^{1/\varepsilon_3}(Q_j^{nc})^{(\varepsilon_3-1)/\varepsilon_3} \right]^{\varepsilon_3/(\varepsilon_3-1)},$$

where Q_j^c is the amount of corporate production of producer good j, Q_j^{nc} is the amount of noncorporate production of producer good j, and ε_3 is the elasticity of substitution between corporate and noncorporate outputs in consumption. Note that equation 2-11 is part of the consumer's utility function. As explained later, we determine the preference weight parameter, γ_j, from the amount of corporate activity in each industry. This explains the coexistence of corporate and noncorporate outputs of the same industry, and it accounts for across-industry differences in the corporate-noncorporate shares of production. These differences in composition are important in a study of tax incidence: corporate-noncorporate tax differences affect producer prices according to industry composition, and these prices affect tax burdens across consumers according to consumption patterns. [14]

Consumers maximize equation 2–11 subject to the constraint

$$(2\text{-}12) \quad p_j^c Q_j^c + p_j^{nc} Q_j^{nc} = p_j^Q \bar{Q}_j,$$

where p_j^c is the price of corporate-produced good j, p_j^{nc} is the price of noncorporate-produced good j, and p_j^Q is the price of composite output, $\bar{Q}_j$. This maximization leads to the following demands for the corporate and noncorporate outputs of industry j:

$$(2\text{-}13) \quad Q_j^c = \frac{\gamma_j(p_j^Q \bar{Q}_j)}{(p_j^c)^{\varepsilon_3}\left[\gamma_j\,(p_j^c)^{1-\varepsilon_3} + (1-\gamma_j)(p_j^{nc})^{1-\varepsilon_3} \right]},$$

and

$$(2\text{-}14) \quad Q_j^{nc} = \frac{(1-\gamma_j)(p_j^Q \bar{Q}_j)}{(p_j^{nc})^{\varepsilon_3}\left[\gamma_j\,(p_j^c)^{1-\varepsilon_3} + (1-\gamma_j)(p_j^{nc})^{1-\varepsilon_3} \right]}.$$

The Production Side

While the consumption side of our model requires intertemporal optimization on the part of consumers, the production side uses annual optimiza-

14. While we were developing this model, Gravelle and Kotlikoff (1988) developed a similar approach. In contrast to their 1989 paper, their 1988 working paper specifies corporate and noncorporate goods as imperfect substitutes. They use both of their models to examine the excess burden of the corporate income tax, and in both cases they find welfare costs much larger than in the standard Harberger model. As discussed later, we find that welfare costs of the extra corporate tax are much smaller than in the standard Harberger model.

tions. That is, we assume that producers' expectations of future prices do not affect their current production decisions. Production is characterized by constant returns to scale, and all industries are perfectly competitive, so each firm makes zero economic profit. These assumptions, while potentially objectionable, are common in the applied general equilibrium literature because they simplify the computational procedure. Output prices can be determined from factor prices, thus minimizing the number of variables involved in the search for an equilibrium.

We model production in a structure similar to that of Don Fullerton and Yolanda Kodrzycki Henderson (1989), in that we draw distinctions between the corporate and noncorporate sectors within each industry and among different types of capital. Such distinctions allow us to capture the effects of differential taxation between the sectors and among capital types. This model improves upon that of Fullerton and Henderson, however, by placing the corporate-noncorporate division at the output level rather than only at the capital level. We provide a diagrammatic summary of the production side in figure 2-2.

Most production processes use not only labor and capital but also the finished outputs of other industries. The use of these "intermediate inputs" implies that relative price changes will have indirect effects on other outputs. We capture these indirect effects by modeling the output of each sector within each industry (that is, for Q_j^c and Q_j^{nc}, $j = 1, \ldots, M$) as a fixed-proportion combination of value-added, VA, and intermediate inputs, A. These components are shown at the first level of figure 2-2. The combination of other outputs used in production is given by a fixed-coefficient matrix whose elements contain the different industries and sectors.[15] For notational simplicity in the text, we suppress the indices for each sector (c, nc) of each industry (j) in the discussion that follows.

As shown at the next level of figure 2-2, each sector's value added is modeled as a CES function of labor and composite capital:

$$(2\text{-}15) \qquad VA = \varphi\left[\zeta L^{(\sigma_1 - 1)/\sigma_1} + (1-\zeta)\bar{K}^{(\sigma_1 - 1)/\sigma_1}\right]^{\sigma_1/(\sigma_1 - 1)},$$

where L is the labor used in that sector, $\bar{K}$ is the composite capital used in that sector, and σ_1 is the elasticity of substitution between labor and compos-

---

15. Each sector of each industry can use as intermediate inputs the outputs of the corporate and noncorporate sectors of any other industry. In other words, corporate firms are not limited to using corporate intermediate inputs, and noncorporate firms are not limited to using noncorporate intermediate inputs. Such a specification is probably realistic, but will tend to dilute the effects of differences between the corporate and noncorporate tax treatments.

Figure 2-2. *Summary of the Production Side*

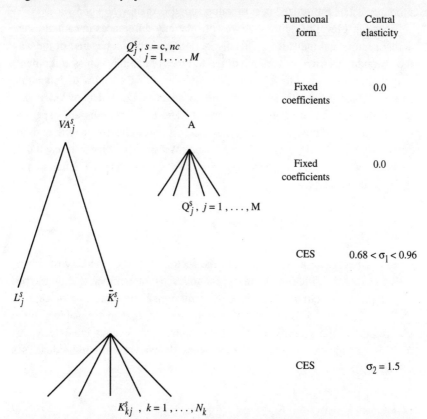

	Functional form	Central elasticity
	Fixed coefficients	0.0
	Fixed coefficients	0.0
	CES	$0.68 < \sigma_1 < 0.96$
	CES	$\sigma_2 = 1.5$

ite capital. This specification will account for varying capital-labor ratios across industries and thus capture any distortion of factor prices that results from the tax system.

Producers choose labor and composite capital to minimize factor costs, subject to the constraint that the "quantity" of value added in equation 2-5 equals one. This minimization leads to the following demands for labor and composite capital per unit of value added:

$$(2\text{-}16) \qquad L/VA \,=\, \varphi^{-1}\left[(1-\zeta)\left(\frac{\zeta\bar{\rho}}{(1-\zeta)w'}\right)^{1-\sigma_1} + \zeta\right]^{\sigma_1/(1-\sigma_1)},$$

and

$$(2\text{-}17) \qquad \bar{K}/VA \,=\, \varphi^{-1}\left[\zeta\left(\frac{(1-\zeta)w'}{\zeta\bar{\rho}}\right)^{1-\sigma_1} + (1-\zeta)\right]^{\sigma_1/(1-\sigma_1)},$$

where $\bar{\rho}$ is the gross-of-tax cost of capital and w' is the gross wage paid by producers. The minimized cost of value added is then $w'L + \bar{\rho}\bar{K}$.

At the last level of figure 2-2, we consider any differences in capital usage across sectors and industries. This distinction is important because of the way the tax code discriminates among different types of capital such as equipment, structures, land, inventories, and intangible assets. Examples of intangible assets include goodwill, acquired through advertising, and knowledge, acquired through research and development. These investments are expensed immediately. The cost of capital across sectors and industries will thus differ according to the mix of capital types used. We specify composite capital in each sector (c, nc) of each industry $(j = 1, \ldots, M)$ as a CES function of different capital types:[16]

$$(2\text{-}18) \qquad \bar{K} = \left[\sum_{k=1}^{N_K} (\psi_k)^{1/\sigma_2} (K_k)^{(\sigma_2-1)/\sigma_2} \right]^{\sigma_2/(\sigma_2-1)},$$

where K_k is capital of type k used in the sector, σ_2 is the elasticity of substitution among the different capital types, and N_K is the number of capital types (equal to five in our model). Producers minimize the total cost of capital, $\sum_{k=1}^{N_K} \rho_k K_k$, where ρ_k is the cost of capital type k in that sector, subject to the constraint that the quantity of composite capital given in equation 2-18 equals $\bar{K}$. This optimization results in the following demands for the individual uses of capital:

$$(2\text{-}19) \qquad K_k = \frac{\psi_k(\bar{\rho}\,\bar{K})}{(\rho_k)^{\sigma_2} \left[\sum_{i=1}^{N_K} \psi_i(\rho_i)^{1-\sigma_2} \right]},$$

for $k = 1, \ldots, N_K$, where quantity K_k and cost ρ_k differ by sector and industry.

Note that the model distinguishes among capital types but not among labor types. Differentiation among labor types, such as skilled versus unskilled labor, might be worthwhile in a model of endogenous human capital accumulation. It is less important in this model, however, because the tax struc-

16. Composite capital is not the same as the total quantity of capital. The model specifies that the total stock of capital is fixed within each period, but capital is homogeneous and malleable so that the mix of capital types can change. We should note that our model ignores adjustment costs like the cost of installing new capital or disassembling old capital. Auerbach and Kotlikoff (1987) and Goulder and Summers (1989) model adjustment costs, but they show that such costs are not very important for long-run results.

ture does not distinguish among labor types in the same way it distinguishes explicitly among capital types. With exogenous, homogeneous labor endowments, taxes distort only the labor-leisure choices of consumers and the labor-capital choices of producers.[17]

Government

The government is involved in activities of three types in this model. First, the government is responsible for payment of certain transfers directly to consumers in each period. These transfers include social security payments, supplemental security income, aid to families with dependent children, and other welfare programs. The PSID data do not include in-kind transfers, and so our model does not account for these. For each lifetime income group, we estimate cash transfer profiles over the life cycle in the benchmark steady state. These transfers are treated as lump-sum payments in the model and ignore the distortionary effects of particular transfer policies. In any simulation, the real value of these transfers is held constant. Thus low-income consumers are protected by increases in their transfer incomes when sales and excise taxes raise product prices.[18] The second type of government activity is production of goods sold in private markets. We refer to activity where a price or fee is charged as "government enterprise." The model treats government enterprise as an additional industry; thus much of the previous discussion on the production side of the model applies here. Although government enterprise does not have a corporate-noncorporate distinction as private industries do, and does not distinguish among capital types, it otherwise operates like the other private industries. It uses primary factors and intermediate inputs, and earns zero excess profits. Instead of an excise tax, however, this industry receives a large subsidy such that its output is sold substantially below cost.

Third, government buys some goods and services for the purpose of free public provision. These goods and services may be nonrival in nature, making them true "public goods," or they may be private in nature. For whatever reasons, government provides these goods without charging prices or fees. These activities are referred to as "general government activities." Revenue

17. Consumers all own the same type of labor, in different quantities. Thus, while we capture differences in productivity through differences in endowments of "effective labor units," we omit any tax distortions in the supply by consumers or demand by producers for skilled labor as opposed to unskilled labor.

18. See, for example, Browning and Johnson (1979).

is collected from the various taxes previously discussed, and income is earned on the government's endowment of capital. Expenditures include purchases of industry outputs and payments for capital and labor services. We model general government as facing gross-of-tax labor and capital prices. The tax rate on labor is based on social security and railroad retirement taxes paid by the government and its employees. The tax rate on capital is based on a weighted average of the capital tax rates faced by industries.[19]

We use a Cobb-Douglas specification to measure a composite of general government's purchases of industry outputs and primary factors. This composite commodity serves four purposes. First, it represents a public good that consumers use. Changes in this composite commodity do not affect any other choices of consumers, so it must be "separable" in utility.[20] Second, however, we usually abstract from changes in government expenditures by keeping constant the level of this composite public good. In this case, there is no need to specify how it enters consumer utility. When tax structures and prices change, in a counterfactual simulation, we select one tax rate to adjust such that government can attain the same level of composite public spending. Third, the Cobb-Douglas function provides a specific index for the price of this composite commodity. This "ideal" price index is very useful for calculating the real revenue necessary to attain the same level of composite public good. Fourth, this specification allows government's purchasing behavior to change with relative prices. Even with an unchanged real value of expenditures, the government has downward-sloping demands. With the Cobb-Douglas form, of course, price elasticities are unity.

With real government expenditures held constant in each period, consumer welfare changes can be measured by simply looking at changes in consumer

19. Governments in the United States do not typically face taxes on corporate income or property. If we modeled only the taxes actually paid on income from capital used by government, the government would face a much smaller tax rate than the private sector faces. The benchmark equilibrium would favor government use of capital, and any subsequent reduction in the private capital tax rate would cause a movement of capital out of the government sector and into the private sector. Such a reallocation of capital might cause large welfare gains, thus contaminating our analysis. To avoid such a problem, we choose to specify the government's effective tax rate on capital as a weighted average of industry rates. Implicitly, government recognizes that the "shadow price" of capital they use includes both the interest they pay and the tax revenue forgone by using that capital in the public sector instead of the private sector. Thus changes in tax policy will not affect the price of government capital relative to that of the private sector.

20. In other words, true consumer utility can be written as a function of two arguments. One argument is U in equation 2-1, interpreted as a sub-utility function of private goods and leisure. The other argument is the composite public good, interpreted as another Cobb-Douglas sub-utility function.

utility.[21] An annual equal-yield feature implies that during a transition period some generations gain and some lose. In our simulations described in chapter 7, we account for such transitional effects in calculating the welfare costs of the various features of the tax system.

International Trade

Our model uses the simple but effective foreign sector specification of Ballard and others (1985). Exports and imports account for differences between the demands of U.S. consumers and the demands facing U.S. industries. The relative prices of traded goods are determined endogenously, and trade balance is required in order to close the model. For each producer good, we specify a foreign import supply function and a foreign export demand function. These functions are written in terms of U.S. prices and incorporate the trade balance constraint.[22]

The model allows "cross-hauling," whereby a given commodity can be both exported and imported, suggesting that the outputs of the foreign sector are imperfect substitutes for the outputs of the domestic sector.[23] In this model, however, we explain cross-hauling by reference to market distances and transportation costs.[24] Lawrence H. Goulder and others' 1983 study finds that allowing imperfect substitutability does not change the model's results very much.

The model does not allow for international flows of primary factors. The effects of capital flows have been investigated in, for example, Goulder, John B. Shoven, and John Whalley (1983) and Goulder and Barry Eichengreen (1989).

21. We specify this equal-yield feature in each period. This can be a problem in the lifetime tax incidence context, since we will want to simulate the replacement of the U.S. tax system with a tax that is proportional on lifetime labor endowments. During a transition, prices will be changing, and thus the equal-yield tax rate will also change. If the tax rate applied to labor endowment changes each year, and if different lifetime income categories exhibit different shapes (not just heights) of endowment profiles, we will not be simulating a proportional tax on lifetime endowments. In the steady state, however, prices are constant, so that this is not a problem.

22. For a presentation of these equations, see Ballard and others (1985, pp. 45–48).

23. This imperfect substitutability is often referred to as the "Armington assumption," after Armington (1969).

24. Ballard and others (1985) provides an example: "it may be perfectly sensible for the United States to export Alaskan oil to Japan and at the same time import the identical product through ports on the East Coast and the Gulf of Mexico, given the cost of delivering Alaskan oil to the eastern United States" (p. 46).

Table 2-1. *Treatment of Taxes in the Model*

Tax	Treatment
1. Corporate taxes (federal and state)	Affect Hall-Jorgenson costs of capital in the corporate sector
2. Property taxes	Affect costs of capital facing both corporate and noncorporate producers and homeowners
3. Investment tax credits	Subsidy to cost of capital for equipment in corporate and noncorporate sectors
4. Depreciation deductions	Cost of capital reduced by present value of depreciation allowances, times applicable marginal tax rates in corporate and noncorporate sectors
5. Social security taxes, unemployment insurance, and workmen's compensation	Ad valorem tax on the use of labor services by industry, with no distinction between employee share and employer share
6. Retail sales taxes	Ad valorem taxes on purchases of consumer goods
7. Excise taxes, other indirect business taxes, and nontax payments to government	Ad valorem taxes on outputs of producer goods
8. Personal income taxes	Progressive linear tax function for each consumer, based on labor and capital income

Treatment of Taxes

Table 2-1 provides a summary of how the model incorporates the features of the U.S. tax system. The treatment is similar to Ballard and others' 1985 model, with some refinements. As in that model, many taxes are specified as ad valorem tax rates applied to the purchases of particular products or factors. Retail sales taxes apply to consumer goods, excise taxes and indirect business taxes apply to producer goods, and social security taxes apply to industries' uses of labor services.

Probably the most difficult part of modeling the U.S. tax system is specifying personal income taxes. Although it would be most realistic to allow a system of graduated marginal tax rates, such a treatment complicates the modeling considerably.[25] In this model we choose to specify income taxes as linear functions of income for each representative consumer, that is, for each age and lifetime income category. The slopes of these tax functions reflect the marginal tax rate, while a negative intercept allows average tax rates to increase with income level. Thus the tax system is not graduated, but it is progressive. The various personal deductions in the tax code are captured in

25. In particular, with each year's marginal tax rate dependent on annual income, lifetime income computation would depend on a series of discount rates that vary not only by time period but according to income level. These complications are addressed in Auerbach, Kotlikoff, and Skinner (1983).

the intercept terms. Specifying a constant marginal tax rate along this tax function greatly facilitates computation, because lifetime income then depends on a single discount rate. For greater simplification, we also use the same marginal tax rate for all individuals. Actual tax payments still depend on circumstances, however, because of the individual-specific intercepts.

To capture specific business tax provisions, we use the Robert E. Hall and Dale W. Jorgenson (1967) notion of investment incentives as refined by Fullerton and Henderson (1989). We specify different cost-of-capital expressions to capture the different tax treatments of the corporate, noncorporate, and housing sectors. Relative discount rates and costs of capital are affected by differences in statutory tax rates, credits, and other tax incentives facing these sectors.

For each sector, we compute nominal discount rates using weights for the sources of finance and using the corresponding required rates of return on each type of finance. These rates of return differ because of taxes, but all are riskless in this perfect-certainty model. We assume that individuals hold debt and equity issued by all three sectors and that arbitrage eliminates any differences in net-of-tax rates of return earned from the different financial instruments. The net real return to holding debt is $r = i(1 - \tau_d) - \pi$, where i is the nominal interest rate, π is the expected inflation rate, and τ_d is the personal marginal tax rate facing debtholders.[26] This net-of-tax return r is one of the economy-wide prices to be announced at each iteration in the search for an equilibrium price vector. Then, from the announced trial value of r, the nominal interest rate can be computed as $i = (r + \pi)/(1 - \tau_d)$.

In the corporate sector, interest costs are deductible at the statutory corporate income tax rate u. Therefore, an investment financed by debt must earn $r_d = i(1 - u)$. This net-of-corporate-tax rate represents the corporation's (nominal) discount rate for debt-financed investment. For retained earnings, the net return r_{re} is the corporation's discount rate. It is taxed again at the personal marginal tax rate applied to accrued capital gains, τ_{re}. Because the individual can arbitrage between debt and equity, the nominal net return $r_{re}(1 - \tau_{re})$ must equal the nominal net return, $i(1 - \tau_d)$. Thus the discount rate on retained earnings is $r_{re} = i(1 - \tau_d)/(1 - \tau_{re})$. Similarly, the nominal net return on new shares r_{ns} is taxed again at the personal marginal tax rate on dividend income, τ_{ns}. The personal return $r_{ns}(1 - \tau_{ns})$ must equal the net return on debt, so the discount rate on new shares is $r_{ns} = i(1 - \tau_d)/$

---

26. As explained earlier, all individuals face the same marginal tax rate on personal income. To capture differences in tax treatments of capital income types in the cost of capital formulas, however, we specify different personal tax rates on interest, dividends, and capital gains.

$(1 - \tau_{ns})$. The corporate sector's overall discount rate is then a weighted average of the three discount rates, where the weights are based on the proportions of corporate investment financed by the three types of mechanisms:

$$(2\text{-}20) \quad r_c = c_d\Big[i(1-u)\Big] + c_{re}\Big[i(1-\tau_d)/(1-\tau_{re})\Big] + c_{ns}\Big[i(1-\tau_d)/(1-\tau_{ns})\Big] ,$$

where c_d, c_{re}, and c_{ns} are proportions of corporate investment financed by debt, retained earnings, and new shares, respectively.

For the noncorporate sector, interest costs are deducted at rate τ_{nc}, the personal marginal tax rate applied to entrepreneurial income. On debt-financed investment, noncorporate firms thus face a discount rate of $i(1 - \tau_{nc})$. Given individual arbitrage, any equity-financed investment must earn a net rate of return equal to the individual's return from holding debt, $i(1 - \tau_d)$. The overall discount rate for the noncorporate sector is then a weighted average of these two discount rates:

$$(2\text{-}21) \qquad r_{nc} = n_d\Big[i(1-\tau_{nc})\Big] + n_e\Big[i(1-\tau_d)\Big] ,$$

where n_d and n_e represent the shares of noncorporate investment financed by debt and equity, respectively.

Homeowners face a marginal tax rate of τ_h, so $i(1 - \tau_h)$ is the appropriate discount rate on debt. Because of arbitrage, as in the noncorporate sector, homeowner equity must return $i(1 - \tau_d)$. Thus the weighted discount rate in housing is:

$$(2\text{-}22) \qquad r_h = h_d\Big[i(1-\tau_h)\Big] + h_e\Big[i(1-\tau_d)\Big] ,$$

where h_d and h_e are, respectively, the debt and equity shares of housing investment.

Given the discount rates facing the corporate, noncorporate, and housing sectors, the gross-of-tax costs of capital are, respectively:

$$(2\text{-}23) \qquad \rho_k^c = \frac{r_c - \pi + \delta_k}{1 - u}(1 - k_k - uz_k^c) + \omega_k - \delta_k ,$$

$$(2\text{-}24) \qquad \rho_k^{nc} = \frac{r_{nc} - \pi + \delta_k}{1 - \tau_{nc}}(1 - k_k - \tau_{nc}z_k^{nc}) + \omega_k - \delta_k ,$$

and

$$(2\text{-}25) \qquad \rho^h = r_h - \pi + (1 - \lambda\tau_h)\omega_h ,$$

where π is the expected rate of inflation, δ_k is the economic depreciation rate of capital of type k, u is the statutory corporate tax rate, k_k is the investment tax credit on capital of type k, z_k^c and z_k^{nc} are present values of depreciation allowances for corporate and noncorporate capital of type k, ω_k is the property tax rate on capital of type k, λ is the fraction of property taxes deducted by homeowners, and ω_h is the property tax rate on homes.[27] Depreciation allowances are specified separately and discounted for each of the five types of capital: equipment, structures, inventories, land, and intangible assets.

These costs of capital directly affect the firms' factor demands. They can also be used to calculate the marginal effective tax rate on any particular assets, that is, the difference between gross-of-tax cost of capital (the relevant ρ above) and the net-of-tax cost (r), divided by the gross-of-tax cost of capital. These marginal rates summarize all taxes on capital, even though investment decisions depend on ρ and saving decisions depend on r. Capital tax revenues are then determined by the difference between the gross return and net-of-tax return on capital, multiplied by the appropriate quantities of capital.

While our model accounts for the different tax treatments of the various financial assets (for example, distinctions among debt, retained earnings, and dividends), it does not allow financial policy to vary with changes in tax policy. In other words, we treat the financial decisions of firms as exogenous. Although changes in tax policy do not affect debt-equity ratios in this model, tax changes will alter the mix of capital types and the capital-labor ratios used by firms.[28]

Overall, the tax system model allows changes in tax law to be readily specified in model-equivalent form. Alternative policies are reflected by specific values for statutory tax rates and other tax parameters. A change in tax policy is simulated by altering one or more of these rates and parameters, subject to the requirement that government raise enough revenue to achieve a constant level of composite public spending. In addition to specific policy

27. Specification of these and other parameters is discussed in chapter 6.
28. Specifying endogenous financial decisions might be desirable but would complicate the model. Slemrod (1983) develops a general equilibrium model with endogenous financial behavior on the part of individuals, in which changes in tax policy affect portfolio choices. Allowing for such shifts in individuals' portfolios may affect the pattern of tax incidence. For example, wealthier individuals may have an easier time avoiding higher taxes (through changes in the composition of their investments) than poorer individuals. Fullerton and Gordon (1983) develop a model with endogenous financial behavior on the part of firms, in which tax policy affects debt-equity ratios. Firms use debt finance until tax advantages are offset by the increasing marginal cost of greater risk of bankruptcy. Also see Galper, Lucke, and Toder (1988), and Berkovec and Fullerton (1992).

proposals or laws, we can address conceptual questions about existing tax law. For example, one way to determine incidence in the entire tax system is to simulate its replacement with a revenue-equivalent proportional tax applied to all incomes.

Equilibrium Conditions and Computational Procedure

This section outlines the mechanics of the model and follows with a more detailed description of the computation of prices and excess demands.

Broadly speaking, general equilibrium in this model is characterized by three conditions: equilibrium in each goods market in each period, equilibrium in the labor and capital markets in each period, and government spending equal to government revenue in each period.[29] To find the equilibrium in each period, the model searches for the vector of prices that satisfies all three. At each iteration, the computations are based on a trial wage rate, market rate of return, and tax scalar. Factor prices are enough to calculate all goods prices, given our assumptions of constant returns to scale, zero profits, and fixed-coefficient input-output matrix. If all tax rates are fixed, then the trial price vector includes a guess for endogenous government revenue.[30] Alternatively, in an equal-yield simulation, the trial price vector includes a scalar for the endogenous tax rate that must adjust to achieve the known revenue target.

The computational order of the model is straightforward. Given the prices of labor and capital and all tax rates, the structure of the model determines all other prices. For an overview of this procedure, we refer to the tree structures in figures 2-1 and 2-2. We begin with factor prices at the bottom of the production structure in figure 2-2 and work our way up through output prices at the top of the tree. These output prices enter the bottom of the utility structure in figure 2-1 and are used to calculate various composite commodity prices. Once at the top of figure 2-1, all the prices for that iteration are known. Then, given incomes and exogenous parameters, demands for goods

29. In principle, one could relax the last assumption and require only that the government budget be balanced in present-value terms. In this case, deficits in some years could be offset by surpluses in others. Our goal is to calculate the incidence of taxation, however, not the incidence of government deficits.

30. See Shoven and Whalley (1973). Briefly, a simultaneity problem is that we need to know tax revenue to determine the level of government transfers and expenditures; thus we need to know tax revenue to know consumer incomes. But we need to know consumer incomes to determine consumer expenditures on goods, and these expenditures affect the level of tax revenue. Simply put, revenue determines incomes, and incomes determine revenue.

and factors are computed from the top of the tree structure back down to the bottom. The factor demands that come out at the bottom of the tree are compared with the fixed-factor supplies for that period, and prices are revised in the appropriate directions to reduce the excess supplies or demands. This process is repeated until factor prices yield quantities demanded that equal quantities supplied.[31]

Turning now to a more detailed description of the price computations, we begin with estimates for the net-of-tax wage rate, net-of-tax rate of return, and total tax revenue. These three elements constitute the price simplex. Given the market rate of return, we determine the discount rates facing the corporate, noncorporate, and owner-occupied housing sectors (r_c, r_{nc}, and r_h), from equations 2-20, 2-21, and 2-22. These discount rates are used in the computation of capital costs by type, given by equations 2-23, 2-24, and 2-25.

Given the costs of the various capital types at the bottom of figure 2-2, we can obtain the cost of composite capital. Because capital demands (in equation 2-19) were derived by minimizing capital costs subject to a quantity constraint on composite capital (given by equation 2-18), we can interpret the Lagrange multiplier as the shadow price, or "cost," of composite capital.[32] Solving for this multiplier, the cost of composite capital is

$$(2\text{-}26) \qquad \bar{\rho}_j = \left[\sum_{k=1}^{N_K} \psi_{jk}\, \rho_k^{(1-\sigma_2)} \right]^{1/(1-\sigma_2)},$$

for each industry ($j = 1, \ldots , M$), and each sector (the ρ_k are ρ_k^c for the corporate sectors, ρ_k^{nc} for the noncorporate sectors, and ρ^h for the owner-occupied housing sector).[33]

31. To locate a general equilibrium price vector, we use a numerical search algorithm. Two methods that have proved successful in other computable general equilibrium models are Merrill's algorithm (1972) and Kimbell and Harrison's procedure (1986). Merrill's algorithm is a faster version of Scarf's grid-search algorithm and is guaranteed to converge. The Kimbell-Harrison iteration procedure involves a very simple revision rule in which prices are changed according to the ratio of quantities demanded to quantities supplied (raised to a power that controls the degree or speed of revision). It is typically faster than Merrill's algorithm, but convergence is not assured. We use the Kimbell-Harrison algorithm for all simulations except the one in which the entire tax system is removed. In this case, the initial iteration computes zero revenue for the denominator of the revision rule. Since the Kimbell-Harrison procedure does not work in this case, we use Merrill's algorithm.

32. The Lagrange multiplier is the term multiplying the constraint in a constrained optimization problem.

33. In the housing industry, instead of specifying corporate and noncorporate sectors, we specify costs of capital for owner-occupied housing versus rental housing. The cost of capital in the rental housing sector is identical to the cost of noncorporate capital. It is owner-occupied housing that receives special tax treatment.

The wage rate from the trial price vector, w, is gross of personal taxes but net of industry-level (payroll) taxes. The gross wage rate paid by producers, w', therefore includes the ad valorem tax rate applied to that industry's use of labor. Given the gross wage rate and the cost of composite capital above, we can compute the price per unit of value added as

(2-27) $$p_j^v = w'L_j/VA + \bar{\rho}_j \bar{K}_j/VA ,$$

for each sector of each industry j. The price per unit of final output at the top of figure 2-2 is then

(2-28) $$p_j = \sum_i p_i^v m_{ij} ,$$

for each sector of industry j, where m_{ij} indicates the use of output i in the production of output j, and where the summation runs across all industries and sectors.[34]

Then, starting at the bottom of figure 2-1, the price of composite output in each industry is based on the prices of the corporate and noncorporate outputs of the industry. Because demands were derived from maximizing equation 2-11 subject to equation 2-12, this price is the reciprocal of the Lagrange multiplier

(2-29) $$p_j^Q = \left[\gamma_j^c (p_j^c)^{1-\varepsilon_3} + (1-\gamma_j^c)(p_j^{nc})^{1-\varepsilon_3} \right]^{1/(1-\varepsilon_3)} ,$$

for producer goods $j = 1, \ldots , M$. At the next level, the prices of the N consumer goods are related to these producer prices according to the coefficients of the Z transition matrix

(2-30) $$p_i = \sum_{j=1}^M p_j^Q Z_{ji} ,$$

where Z_{ji} indicates the amount of producer good j involved in the composition of consumer good $i (i = 1, \ldots , N)$. Next, the price of the age-t composite good for a particular consumer is the reciprocal of the Lagrange multiplier obtained from maximizing equation 2-8 subject to equation 2-9:

(2-31) $$\bar{p}_t = \prod_{i=1}^N (p_i/\beta_{it})^{\beta_{it}} .$$

34. Each of the eighteen private industries contains two sectors, and an additional industry represents government enterprise. Any sector of any industry can use the output of any other sector of any other industry as an intermediate input. Thus equation 2-28 sums thirty-seven producers.

Given the net wage rate w, the price of the composite of goods and leisure at age t is similarly obtained from the maximization of equation 2-4 subject to equation 2-5:

$$(2\text{-}32) \qquad q_t = \left[\alpha_t \bar{p}_t^{\,1-\varepsilon_2} + (1 - \alpha_t) w^{1-\varepsilon_2} \right]^{1/(1-\varepsilon_2)}.$$

We now arrive at the top of figure 2-1 with all prices available. Given factor returns and government transfers, we can compute the present value of lifetime income.[35] Then, given prices and exogenously specified parameters, we can compute sequentially the following demands for each consumer in each period: composite commodity, x_t, from equation 2-3; leisure, ℓ_t, and composite consumption good, $\bar{c}_t$, from equations 2-6 and 2-7; and individual consumption goods, c_{it}, from equation 2-10. By way of the transition matrix Z, we can determine the demands for composite producer goods from the c_{it}. Then we can compute the demands for corporate and noncorporate outputs from equations 2-13 and 2-14. These demands are added to net export demand and government demand to arrive at demands for final outputs. Finally, intermediate inputs are added to determine the total output requirements.

Total demands for capital and labor are found by multiplying this total output by the per-unit factor demands given by equations 2-16 and 2-17. Total implied tax revenue can then be determined, given the output levels of producers and the incomes and consumption patterns of consumers. Excess demands for capital and labor, and "excess revenue," are computed. As previously outlined, these excess demands indicate how the price vector should be altered before the process at the next iteration is repeated. When excess demands become arbitrarily small, an equilibrium is achieved.

Calculating Tax Incidence

We conclude this chapter with a description of our utility-based measures of tax incidence. Our ultimate purpose in computing a general equilibrium is to calculate the welfare effects of a given tax policy on the representative consumers of the model, as compared with a proportional tax on lifetime incomes. The method we use differs from the Joseph A. Pechman and Ben-

---

35. Note that the benchmark equilibrium specifies lifetime incomes according to the estimates described in chapter 4. In simulations of new equilibria, however, the lifetime paths of wages, taxes, and transfers will change. Although the value of labor endowments can change, the lifetime paths of the quantity of labor endowments are exogenous in the simulations.

jamin A. Okner (1974) and Pechman (1985) approach in three important respects. First, by specifying utility functions for our representative consumers, we are able to capture the distortionary effects of taxes. Our computations of welfare changes reflect the fact that the burden of taxation exceeds the amount of dollars actually paid. Second, the pattern of tax incidence is generated within our model. We need to make some assumptions about how taxes are originally levied and about behavior, but the incidence of each tax is then determined endogenously. Finally, we compute lifetime rather than annual tax incidence, because the well-being of an individual may be better reflected by lifetime income rather than annual income.

Within the lifetime model, computing lifetime tax incidence is a straightforward task. Since we have access to lifetime utility functions, we can compute equivalent variations (EVs) based on these functions. To determine the lifetime incidence of a particular tax instrument in the present tax system, we simulate its removal and replacement with a proportional tax on lifetime labor endowments and compare the EVs across the representative consumers.[36] For example, if a tax is progressive over lifetime incomes, we might see that its replacement causes the EVs to be proportionately larger for high-lifetime-income groups than for low-lifetime-income groups. If the replacement causes no change in the efficiency of the tax system, then positive EVs for some groups would have to be offset by negative EVs for other groups. If, on the other hand, the removed tax is more distortionary than the replacement, we might see welfare gains in the form of positive EVs for all income groups. We can also simulate a proposed tax policy change and compare the welfare effects across consumers to see who would gain and who would lose from the change, in a lifetime perspective.

It turns out that the form of lifetime utility in equation 2-1 is conducive to computation of the lifetime EVs. From the optimization of equation 2-1 subject to equation 2-2, the Lagrange multiplier provides the following "lifetime price index" for utility:

$$(2\text{-}33) \qquad P_U = \left[\sum_{t=1}^{T} a_t P_t^{1-\varepsilon_1} \right]^{1/(1-\varepsilon_1)},$$

where P_t is the period 1 price of age-t composite commodity. P_t is equal to $q_t/(1 + r)^{t-1}$, where q_t is the period t price of the age-t composite commodity,

36. Removal of the tax would require concomitant reductions in government spending that would also affect consumers in the model. Instead, replacement of the tax requires specifying the alternative source of revenue.

and r is the real net rate of return. Then the expenditure function takes on the simple form, $E = P_U U$, and the equivalent variation is

(2-34) $$EV = (U^n - U^o) P_U^o ,$$

where U^n is the new lifetime utility level, U^o is the old lifetime utility level, and P_U^o is the price index in equation 2-33 evaluated at old prices. That is, the equivalent variation uses old prices to put a dollar value on the utility change.

CHAPTER THREE

Data Sources

THROUGHOUT this book we make every effort to use detailed, actual data within a rigorous theoretical framework. The previous chapter described the theoretical specification of the lifetime incidence model, and this chapter describes the sources of the data.

Our benchmark data set reflects the year 1984. Income and consumption data come largely from econometric estimations described in chapters 4 and 5. For production, government, and trade sectors, many of the data come from various issues of the *Survey of Current Business* and the *Economic Report of the President*. Other figures derive from unpublished worksheets of the Commerce Department.[1] In addition, some of the numbers are revised versions of the data originally used in Charles L. Ballard and others' (1985) study.

We first present the dimensions of the model by describing the goods and consumer categories included. Next we describe the sources for the consumption-side, production-side, government, and trade data. We include all data that are fed directly into the lifetime tax incidence model. This chapter describes "raw data," the numbers before any consistency adjustments are applied to make the data set one that characterizes an equilibrium benchmark. Those consistency adjustments are described in chapter 6.

Model Dimensions

The model distinguishes among 19 industries (or producer goods), and 17 expenditure categories (or consumer goods). These goods are listed in table

1. We wish to thank Karl Scholz for collecting many of these new data. His figures for 1983 are updated to 1984 for this study.

Table 3-1. *Goods and Capital Assets*

Producer goods (industry categories)	Consumer goods (expenditure categories)	Capital assets
1. Agriculture, forestry, and fisheries	1. Food	1. Equipment
2. Mining	2. Alcohol	2. Structures
3. Crude petroleum and gas	3. Tobacco	3. Inventories
4. Contract construction	4. Household fuels and utilities	4. Land
5. Food and tobacco	5. Shelter	5. Intangibles
6. Textiles, apparel, and leather	6. Furnishings	
7. Paper and printing	7. Appliances	
8. Petroleum refining	8. Apparel	
9. Chemicals, rubber, and plastics	9. Public transportation	
10. Lumber, furniture, stone, clay, and glass	10. New and used cars, fees, and maintenance	
11. Metals, machinery, instruments, and miscellaneous manufacturing	11. Cash contributions and personal care (personal services)	
12. Transportation equipment and ordnance	12. Financial services	
13. Motor vehicles	13. Reading and entertainment (recreation)	
14. Transportation, communications, and utilities	14. Household operations (nondurables)	
15. Trade	15. Gasoline and motor oil	
16. Finance and insurance	16. Health care	
17. Real estate	17. Education	
18. Services		
19. Government enterprises		

3-1. Each of the industries, except for government enterprise, contains a corporate and a noncorporate sector. Thus there are really 37 representative firms in the model, and the 18 private producer goods can each be interpreted as a composite of the corporate and noncorporate outputs in that industry.[2] This disaggregation of production into the specified industries captures important differences in capital-labor ratios and in the corporate-noncorporate ratios. Both ratios affect relative tax rates, since the tax system treats capital income differently from labor income and corporate income differently from noncorporate income.

This model also makes important distinctions among five types of capital

---

2. The data reveal no activity in the noncorporate sectors of motor vehicles and petroleum refining (see tables 3-19 and 3-20). These two industries thus receive full weight on the corporate sector in equation 2-11. Also, as mentioned, real estate is a composite of owner-occupied housing and noncorporate rental housing.

Table 3-2. *Age and Lifetime Income Categories of Consumer Groups*

Age categories		Income categories		Value of labor
Group	Ages	Group	Percentile	endowment (1984 dollars)
1	20–24	1	0–02	<232,757
2	25–29	2	2–10	232,757 − 387,534
3	30–34	3	10–20	387,535 − 481,327
4	35–39	4	20–30	481,328 − 578,051
5	40–44	5	30–40	578,052 − 652,019
6	45–49	6	40–50	652,020 − 714,292
7	50–54	7	50–60	714,293 − 779,414
8	55–59	8	60–70	779,415 − 876,062
9	60–64	9	70–80	876,063 − 987,319
10	65–69	10	80–90	987,320 − 1,218,734
11	70–74	11	90–98	1,218,735 − 1,792,391
12	75–79	12	98–100	>1,792,391

assets that face different tax treatments. As shown in table 3-1, these five are: equipment, structures, inventories, land, and intangible assets. Each reflects differences in rates of economic depreciation, investment tax credits, depreciation allowances, and property taxes.

The most significant innovation in the lifetime tax incidence model is the disaggregation of consumers by age and lifetime income categories. This detail allows us to capture differences in consumption patterns across age and lifetime income categories, and differences in age-wage profiles across lifetime income categories. We specify twelve age categories, each spanning five years, and twelve lifetime income categories. These consumer categories are presented in table 3-2. For lifetime income categories, we start with ten deciles but then subdivide the bottom and top deciles. We thus distinguish the poorest 2 percent of the population and the richest 2 percent.[3] For age categories, we assume that individuals are economically "born" at age 20 and "die" at age 79. Thus an economic lifetime includes sixty annual periods. Consumer utility is evaluated and decisions are made on an annual basis. To save computation time, however, we compute equilibria using a "snapshot" taken every five years.[4]

---

3. We split the top and bottom deciles at the suggestion of Joseph Pechman, who argued that the very top and bottom of the population have quite different income, tax, and transfer paths. Our results confirm that this is indeed the case, especially at the upper end.

4. We calculate equilibria that are five years apart and then interpolate prices for the intervening years. Utility is still based on sixty annual periods. As shown in Ballard (1987), results using this procedure are virtually the same as those from annual calculations.

Consumer Data

As we indicated in chapter 2, the lifetime incidence model reflects a progressive tax structure by specifying a single marginal tax rate combined with a lump-sum grant. The tax is progressive because the average tax rate rises with income, even though the marginal tax rate remains constant. This marginal tax rate is set at 30 percent for all consumers, reflecting the average federal and state marginal tax rate, weighted by wages and salaries, under 1984 tax law.[5]

For each lifetime income category (described in detail in chapter 4), we use econometric estimates from the Panel Study of Income Dynamics to define the lifetime paths of labor endowments, taxes paid, and transfers received. We proceed in this manner: first, all individuals are used together to predict wages from age and other demographic characteristics. Then, for each individual, we calculate lifetime income, using observed real wages for the available years and estimates for other years (based on those demographic characteristics and individual-specific effects). We then sort individuals according to the twelve lifetime income categories. Finally, for each of the twelve categories grouped by lifetime income, we use nonlinear functions of age to estimate wage, tax, and transfer equations. We multiply the wage rate at each age by the assumed number of hours available (for example, 4,000 a year) to obtain a profile for the endowment of effective labor units. We normalize prices such that a unit of labor services receives one dollar in the benchmark equilibrium. Thus differences in wage rates are reinterpreted as differences in endowments, and all individuals receive the same wage per effective labor unit.

Regressions of wages, taxes, and transfers against age, age-squared, and age-cubed provide us with coefficients describing the profiles. Chapter 4 uses these coefficients to plot profiles for selected groups, but this chapter includes the coefficients themselves as necessary input into the general equilibrium model. Table 3-3 shows the estimated coefficients for the path of labor endowments for each lifetime income category. These coefficients are the results of an ordinary-least-squares regression in which the dependent variable is the *log* of the wage rate. Similarly, the coefficients presented in table 3-4 describe the path of federal taxes on labor income, by age, for each lifetime income category. The coefficients in table 3-5 provide the path of government transfers by age for each lifetime income category.

5. Fullerton (1987, p. 32), based on 25,000 individuals.

Table 3-3. *Age-Wage Coefficients, by Lifetime Income Category*

Dependent variable: log wage

Lifetime category	Constant	Age	Age squared	Age cubed
1[a]	−4.0826	0.3100	−0.005853	0.000034089
2	0.7070	0.0464	−0.000729	0.000002334
3	0.2966	0.0716	−0.000954	0.000002584
4	0.6726	0.0503	−0.000271	−0.000003625
5	−0.0257	0.1130	−0.001843	0.000009038
6	1.4868	0.0099	0.000525	−0.000007825
7	3.2849	−0.0968	0.002632	−0.000021403
8	1.3169	0.0476	−0.000577	0.000001887
9	1.3655	0.0548	−0.000793	0.000003798
10	0.3456	0.1232	−0.001993	0.000010156
11	1.1671	0.0914	−0.001464	0.000007333
12[b]	1.2312	0.0948	−0.001016	0.00

Source: Estimated from A Panel Study of Income Dynamics, 1970–87 (data base, University of Michigan, Institute for Social Research). See chapter 4 for a description of the estimation procedure.
a. Poorest.
b. Richest.

Table 3-4. *Age-Labor Tax Coefficients, by Lifetime Income Category*

Dependent variable: labor income taxes

Lifetime category	Constant	Age	Age squared	Age cubed
1[a]	−2,641.108	39.214	2.0678	−0.02827
2	−1,485.826	110.613	−1.0517	−0.00181
3	625.203	−58.106	3.4387	−0.03791
4	3,381.849	−273.668	9.3927	−0.08544
5	−12,215.866	981.298	−19.3911	0.11547
6	812.576	−90.675	6.4435	−0.07352
7	−3,367.044	249.184	−0.8942	−0.02428
8	2,445.158	−217.518	10.2586	−0.09650
9	−8,342.854	669.873	−10.3587	0.04887
10	−10,015.682	543.373	−0.5797	−0.06208
11	−18,112.118	1,111.360	−10.7473	0.00054
12[b]	−154,268.666	8,495.655	−93.3065	0.00

Source: See table 3-3.
a. Poorest.
b. Richest.

The other econometrically estimated inputs to the model are the parameters of demand for consumer goods by age category. As described in chapter 2, we specify a Stone-Geary function for the part of utility that derives from consumer goods. Thus each of the twelve age groups has a minimum-required-purchase parameter and a marginal share parameter for each of the 17 consumer goods, for a total of $12 \times 2 \times 17 = 408$ estimated parame-

Table 3-5. *Age-Transfer Coefficients, by Lifetime Income Category*

Dependent variable: government transfers

Lifetime category	Constant	Age	Age squared	Age cubed
1[a]	18,164.292	−1,101.140	20.5853	−0.11735
2	−2,893.073	245.599	−6.6828	0.06045
3	−8,634.239	682.657	−16.9752	0.13650
4	−6,006.255	491.814	−12.8525	0.10847
5	−5,934.446	475.504	−12.1915	0.10125
6	−5,891.416	494.390	−13.2125	0.11341
7	−8,596.039	688.454	−17.6501	0.14549
8	−13,567.821	1,056.744	−26.1865	0.20789
9	−4252.603	340.856	−8.7625	0.07249
10	−12,561.875	989.103	−24.8874	0.20066
11	−8,448.799	651.563	−16.1451	0.12912
12[b]	366.288	−17.450	0.2004	0.00

Source: See table 3-3.
a. Poorest.
b. Richest.

ters. Using minimum required purchases helps to provide a reasonable savings elasticity and also allows proportions of income spent on the various goods to change as income changes. For each of the twelve age categories, we use data from the Consumer Expenditure Survey (CES) to estimate both sets of parameters. The estimation procedure and results are discussed in chapter 5.

The parameters estimated from the CES provide inputs for gross-of-tax expenditures on consumer goods. We also need information on sales taxes paid. Table 3-6 presents implicit ad valorem tax rates on the 17 consumer goods. To derive these rates, we start with data in Ballard and others (1985) for sales taxes paid and gross-of-tax purchases of consumer goods, scale them to 1984, and compute the implied tax-exclusive tax rates.[6] Note that these rates reflect tax as a fraction of the net price. That earlier model does not differentiate health care and education, so we use the implicit tax rate on services (consumer good 11) for those two goods.

The lifetime incidence model requires some additional vectors of consumption data. Besides expenditures on consumption goods, we need expenditures on leisure. As described later, we assume a maximum number of hours a year (for example, 4,000), subtract actual hours of work, and value

6. The vector of purchases of consumer goods is adjusted to 1984 values by using the ratio of total consumption in 1984 to that in 1973, from the 1985 *Economic Report of the President.* The vector of consumer sales taxes paid is grossed up by using the ratio of total indirect business taxes paid in 1984 to that in 1973, also from the 1985 *Economic Report.*

Table 3-6. *Consumer Purchases and Taxes Paid, 1984*

Millions of dollars

Consumer good	Gross-of-tax purchases	Taxes paid	Implied net tax rate[a]
1. Food	418,623	15,073.6	0.0374
2. Alcohol	60,761	25,562.3	0.7260
3. Tobacco	37,463	16,524.0	0.7890
4. Utilities	110,227	4,103.8	0.0387
5. Shelter	351,336	0.0	0.0000
6. Furnishings	90,466	5,559.2	0.0655
7. Appliances	76,546	4,703.8	0.0655
8. Apparel	194,138	11,929.8	0.0655
9. Public transportation	20,897	83.5	0.0040
10. Automobiles	201,398	9,759.2	0.0509
11. Personal services	334,353	9,726.6	0.0300
12. Financial services	159,431	0.0	0.0000
13. Recreation	112,378	4,799.8	0.0446
14. Nondurables	91,036	4,534.6	0.0524
15. Gasoline	101,359	20,820.5	0.2590
16. Health Care	. . .	. . .	0.0300
17. Education	. . .	. . .	0.0300

Source: Ballard and others (1985), revised as described in the text, using data from the *Survey of Current Business*.
a. Implied tax-exclusive rate = taxes paid/(gross purchases minus taxes paid).

the remaining leisure time at the net-of-tax wage. Using 1984 data from the PSID, table 3-7 indicates average hours worked per week by age category. Notice that this average work week peaks at age 45–49 and falls off sharply at age 65, as would be expected. Thus the leisure-consumption share parameter (as derived in chapter 6) allows work intensity to vary over the life cycle.[7]

Finally, for each lifetime income category, we need data on inheritances and bequests. The model does not consider complicated issues such as multiple offspring, the mobility of individuals across income groups, the timing of inheritances, human capital bequests, or inter vivos transfers. We simply use exogenous bequests to help explain the observed capital stock in a life-cycle context. Therefore each representative individual receives a fixed inheritance at birth and may spend it early in life, but must save sufficient capital by the end of life to leave a comparable bequest (to newborns in the same income group). In fact, to keep the model on a steady-state growth path,

7. As with the consumer goods parameters, the leisure-consumption parameter varies by age but not by lifetime income category. The ratio of total consumption (required plus discretionary) to leisure *will*, however, vary across lifetime income categories, because the leisure-consumption parameter applies to discretionary consumption only. The ratio of total consumption to leisure will decline as lifetime income increases.

Table 3-7. *Average Hours Worked per Week, by Age Category, 1984*

Age category	Average hours per week	Age category	Average hours per week
20–24	33.231	50–54	36.783
25–29	36.930	55–59	30.798
30–34	36.792	60–64	21.410
35–39	38.939	65–69	7.197
40–44	39.116	70–74	3.998
45–49	40.481	75–79	0.915

Source: Computed from data in A Panel Study of Income Dynamics, 1984.

Table 3-8. *Average Value of Bequest, by Lifetime Income Category, 1984*

Dollars

Lifetime income category	Average bequest	Lifetime income category	Average bequest
1[a]	19,290	7	38,992
2	25,720	8	41,538
3	29,275	9	43,958
4	32,587	10	71,219
5	34,977	11	160,140
6	36,885	12[b]	257,200

Source: Menchik and David (1982, table 4, p. 198), with adjustments described in the text.
a. Poorest.
b. Richest.

the required bequest must be enlarged by both technical progress and population growth from the time the inheritance was received.

Fortunately, for our purposes, Paul L. Menchik and Martin David provide an estimate of bequests for ten deciles based on a similar present value definition of lifetime income. Only a few adjustments were necessary to use these estimates in our model.[8] The final 1984 figures for average individual bequests in each of our twelve groups are shown in table 3-8. These bequests are fairly flat across the first ten categories, but increase sharply for the two richest groups.

8. Menchick and David (1982, table 4, p. 198) estimate bequests in 1967 at ten *points* along the distribution of lifetime income. First, we average bequests at adjacent points to represent the intermediate decile. For example, we average the 10th and 20th percentile points to get bequests for our third group. Next we use the pattern of bequests for available deciles to construct appropriate guesses for our first group (the poorest 2 percent), second group (the next 8 percent), and last group (richest 2 percent). Finally, the results are scaled up to 1984 using GNP price deflators from the 1987 *Economic Report of the President*.

Table 3-9. *Bureau of Economic Analysis Categories in Each of Our Producer Good Categories*

Producer good category	BEA commodity numbers	Producer good category	BEA commodity numbers
1	1–4	11	37–58, 62–64
2	5–7, 9, 10	12	13, 60, 61
3	8	13	59
4	11, 12	14	65–68
5	14, 15	15	69
6	16–19, 33, 34	16	70
7	24–26	17	71
8	31	18	72–77
9	27–30, 32	19	78, 79
10	20–23, 35, 36		

Source: Ballard and others (1985, pp. 85–86).

Industry Data

Many of the producer data are drawn from the *Survey of Current Business*, published by the Department of Commerce, Bureau of Economic Analysis (BEA). To capture relevant tax differences, however, we do not require all the BEA's detail in the classification of goods. To save computation time, we aggregate their data to our classification of 19 industries and 17 consumer goods. The specifics of this aggregation, from BEA categories to ours, are indicated in tables 3-9 (for producer goods) and 3-10 (for consumer goods).[9]

Expenditures on consumer goods relate to the output of producer goods through a "transition matrix" shown in table 3-11. The entries are based on a 1977 input-output matrix reported in the May 1984 *Survey of Current Business*. Each of the 19 consumer good categories uses one or more of the 17 producer goods. "Tobacco" in the third column, for example, uses output from industries 5 (food and tobacco), 14 (transportation), and 15 (retail trade).

Table 3-12 shows investment data by industry. For each of the 19 industries, the investment level in the initial data set is given by the sum of private

9. For a verbal description of the BEA consumer goods that fall within each of our consumer good categories, see appendix B of chapter 4 in Ballard and others (1985, pp. 87–88). The only change is that we separate new categories for health care and education by pulling the relevant BEA categories out of services (such as physicians, dentists, private higher education) and non-durable, nonfood household items (such as drug preparations).

Table 3-10. *Bureau of Economic Analysis Categories in Each of Our Consumer Good Categories*

Consumer good category	BEA personal consumption expenditure numbers	Consumer good category	BEA personal consumption expenditure numbers
1	3–6	10	65–69
2	subset of category 1	11	17, 22, 42, 43, 60–62, 88, 91–96, 102
3	7	12	51, 56–69, 72
4	37–39, 41	13	83–86, 89, 97, 104
5	24–27	14	21, 34, 35
6	29, 32, 33	15	40, 70
7	30, 31, 87	16	45–50
8	12, 14–16, 18, 19	17	99–101
9	71, 74–76, 78–81		

Source: Ballard and others (1985, appendix D, table 4.A.2).

fixed-capital formation and the change in net inventories in 1984.[10] For government enterprises, these are set to zero.

We account for indirect effects of taxation through the modeling of intermediate inputs. For this purpose, we need an input-output matrix that indicates how the 19 producer goods are used in the production of each producer good.[11] This matrix, shown in table 3-13, is based on the "Make and Use" tables of the 1980 input-output tables in *Survey of Current Business,* July 1986.[12] The entry in row 4, column 2, for example, indicates the use of producer good 4 in the production of producer good 2. Because the entries correspond to 1980, we use a vector of scalars (shown in the first column of table 3-14), to adjust the 1980 input-output values to 1984 levels. Each scalar represents the ratio of that industry's 1984 GNP to 1980 GNP. These ratios are shown in the first column of table 3-14.

Data on labor use by industry are taken from the July 1986 *Survey of*

10. Both vectors are derived from *Survey of Current Business,* November 1989, table 1 ("The Use of Commodities by Industries, 1984"). Private fixed-capital formation comes from aggregation of entries in column 92 of the table. Change in net inventories is from entries in column 93, where the aggregation reflects the categories shown in our table 3-9.

11. Actually, we need a matrix relating all 37 representative firms to each other (corporate and noncorporate sectors of the first 18 industries, plus government enterprises). Data needed to create such a matrix are not available, however, so we create a 19 × 19 matrix and then expand it to 37 × 37 when we make consistency adjustments to the data set. This procedure is described in chapter 6.

12. The matrix was constructed and documented by Karl Scholz.

Table 3-11. *Transition Matrix Relating Consumer Goods to Producer Goods, 1977*

Millions of dollars

Producer good	Consumer good classification																
	Food 1	Alcohol 2	Tobacco 3	Utilities 4	Shelter 5	Furnishings 6	Appliances 7	Apparel 8	Transportation 9	Automobiles 10	Personal services 11	Financial services 12	Recreation 13	Nondurables 14	Gas 15	Health care 16	Education 17
1	7,854	1,073	0	0	0	0	0	0	0	0	0	0	2,434	19	0	0	0
2	2	0	0	0	0	0	0	0	0	0	0	0	0	20	215	0	0
3	0	0	0	0	0	0	0	0	0	0	0	0	0	0	0	0	0
4	0	0	0	0	0	0	0	0	0	0	0	0	0	0	0	0	0
5	99,861	13,646	8,437	0	0	0	0	0	0	0	0	0	0	0	0	0	0
6	0	0	0	0	0	5,897	7	41,339	0	27	0	0	457	74	0	0	0
7	0	0	0	0	0	44	0	951	0	0	0	0	9,206	4,945	0	588	0
8	0	0	0	0	0	1	775	943	0	0	0	0	0	0	38,592	2	0
9	48	6	0	0	0	0	0	0	0	4,446	179	0	222	12,119	100	5,774	0
10	0	0	0	0	0	10,124	1,146	0	0	47	0	0	0	107	106	0	0
11	0	0	0	0	0	3,719	18,434	5,860	0	1,710	19	0	7,344	2,431	5	1,601	0
12	0	0	0	0	0	31	0	0	0	2,665	0	0	5,423	0	0	0	0
13	0	0	0	0	0	0	0	0	0	46,125	0	0	0	0	0	0	0
14	4,056	554	73	0	0	402	295	297	0	1,730	3,465	0	5,900	672	1,571	108	0
15	52,823	7,218	8,470	62,916	0	18,593	14,904	46,117	15,109	22,758	110	0	14,789	10,512	18,032	8,227	0
16	2	0	0	0	180,773	0	0	0	0	0	1,373	64,155	3	0	0	0	0
17	0	0	0	0	0	0	0	0	0	0	541	0	0	0	0	0	0
18	60,202	8,226	0	275	6,865	0	32	2,331	0	31,441	74,676	0	8,571	0	0	86,990	18,614
19	0	0	0	1,864	0	0	0	0	908	0	2,692	0	803	0	0	0	0

Source: *Survey of Current Business*, May 1984, as compiled by Charles Ballard and Steven Medema.

Table 3-12. *Investment Data, by Industry, 1984*

Industry (producer good)	Private fixed-capital formation	Change in net inventories
1. Agriculture, forestry, and fisheries	0	6,797
2. Mining	536	0
3. Crude petroleum and gas	430	3,884
4. Contract construction	299,921	0
5. Food and tobacco	0	2,372
6. Textile, apparel, and leather	1,556	4,362
7. Paper and printing	0	2,362
8. Petroleum refining	0	155
9. Chemicals, rubber, and plastics	1,089	5,266
10. Lumber, furniture, stone, clay, and glass	11,851	4,491
11. Metals, machinery, instruments, and miscellaneous manufacturing	171,290	27,384
12. Transportation equipment and ordnance	13,745	5,384
13. Motor vehicles	61,981	8,085
14. Transportation, communications, and utilities	7,473	829
15. Trade	41,387	4,088
16. Finance and insurance	0	0
17. Real estate	14,445	0
18. Services	0	0
19. Government enterprises	0	0

Source: Derived from *Survey of Current Business*, November 1989, table 1.

Current Business and unpublished Commerce Department data. Gross and net labor income, labor taxes, and effective tax rates on labor are shown in table 3-15. Labor income gross of tax is the sum of wages and salaries, employer contributions to social insurance, other labor income, and the return to labor of the self-employed. Taxes on labor are the sum of employer contributions to social insurance, plus employee contributions and self-employed contributions.[13] Our input data set includes the second and third columns (taxes on labor, and net-of-tax labor incomes).

Output taxes by industry appear in table 3-16, equal to excise taxes plus indirect business taxes, less property taxes and motor vehicle taxes. Indirect business taxes include public utility, severance, occupancy, license fees, other

13. Data on wages and salaries and self-employed contributions to social security are from the SCB, and data on employer and employee contributions to social security and other labor income come from unpublished Commerce Department sources. These numbers were provided to us by Karl Scholz; however, we modified Scholz's entries for industry 1 to include farm proprietors' income (from the SCB).

Table 3-13. *Input-Output Matrix of Producer Goods, 1980*
Millions of dollars at producers' prices

Supplying industry	Using industry									
	1	2	3	4	5	6	7	8	9	10
1	46,204.4	9.3	2.8	553.4	82,459.3	2,174.1	44.8	2.4	514.0	4,526.9
2	360.3	5,081.2	8.4	2,716.0	188.8	81.2	506.3	321.2	3,879.2	2,660.1
3	346.4	98.7	3,980.8	316.2	133.0	71.8	186.2	126,645.0	4,254.9	167.3
4	2,056.3	277.0	4,821.1	302.6	1,179.9	467.1	901.6	1,004.4	1,365.1	1,005.3
5	13,573.5	7.2	7.7	38.3	48,969.5	549.8	381.8	66.2	1,701.0	84.4
6	266.8	59.0	12.7	1,803.1	100.3	39,986.8	1,188.7	27.7	2,203.6	1,660.9
7	663.8	205.4	125.6	4,470.9	10,042.9	1,599.5	36,779.8	854.1	5,730.3	1,994.8
8	9,208.2	1,630.5	668.7	8,020.0	1,898.6	1,215.8	3,537.5	17,744.7	11,770.4	2,658.6
9	9,048.1	1,002.7	509.3	8,381.4	5,295.0	12,181.5	6,202.9	4,313.2	53,281.4	4,094.2
10	375.9	304.9	26.7	42,768.7	4,078.2	309.4	3,811.9	299.3	1,678.1	22,228.1
11	2,454.0	4,156.6	2,287.3	63,452.6	9,536.3	2,019.9	3,898.7	1,114.0	8,685.3	6,816.7
12	372.0	55.0	23.4	510.2	20.8	28.8	109.3	6.5	48.0	77.7
13	164.3	151.3	19.7	507.2	32.8	17.9	57.7	138.8	72.7	192.9
14	5,580.3	2,298.5	1,358.0	12,610.4	9,976.5	3,594.9	8,921.0	10,281.6	14,605.2	8,437.4
15	9,201.2	1,528.3	597.7	30,301.0	15,286.3	5,444.7	7,407.9	3,261.3	9,294.3	5,591.1
16	2,381.0	428.0	414.8	3,235.9	1,260.3	611.8	889.8	749.2	1,195.9	879.9
17	10,223.0	855.5	6,039.9	889.4	812.7	693.0	1,441.1	344.7	1,896.9	748.8
18	3,684.9	1,501.8	1121.7	26,959.6	7,717.3	3,129.1	5,978.6	2,102.5	9,980.8	3,205.6
19	707.3	383.3	558.3	1,089.7	1,707.8	1,143.5	3,492.7	1,003.8	2,829.3	1,242.8

Table 3-13 (continued)

Supplying industry	Using industry								
	11	12	13	14	15	16	17	18	19
1	45.2	4.8	1.4	38.9	1,034.9	3.9	2,050.7	1,935.3	856.7
2	11,777.6	22.6	47.2	8,999.6	6.5	0.5	13.3	98.1	1,640.7
3	547.1	52.0	31.4	30,246.0	725.6	74.5	105.2	588.8	217.5
4	4,474.4	360.2	237.7	15,017.2	3,619.7	482.8	26,793.0	7,829.3	7,527.0
5	205.9	11.6	20.5	106.8	470.3	9.7	3.8	4,038.4	806.3
6	1,550.8	452.3	1,937.5	308.6	353.8	106.3	8.9	2,392.5	109.1
7	7,907.2	549.2	504.4	2,114.8	11,577.7	4,248.5	1,290.5	13,825.6	505.6
8	6,666.5	782.4	364.6	36,886.7	12,619.3	915.3	868.4	10,013.2	2,403.0
9	21,028.4	1,186.1	4,734.8	2,460.1	1,839.8	103.7	580.0	13,031.0	482.3
10	6,610.0	1,553.8	1,651.8	274.9	948.1	18.4	28.8	1,689.2	96.4
11	204,735.0	21,005.5	27,505.4	8,264.8	3,511.3	759.9	489.5	18,567.7	1,323.3
12	1,527.5	12,674.2	284.9	3,496.0	26.1	36.8	3.7	665.8	115.9
13	1,903.3	569.3	27,709.3	714.6	524.5	28.3	19.7	6,018.8	118.7
14	27,512.0	2,904.7	1,988.2	70,821.4	33,526.2	7,273.9	4,543.7	28,890.6	8,160.9
15	35,692.2	3,193.9	5,391.3	8,708.7	10,291.1	807.1	1,180.1	15,458.0	937.8
16	4,034.1	827.1	338.0	4,232.4	8,088.4	32,469.7	9,426.5	5,794.6	216.3
17	5,337.9	720.5	148.8	4,785.6	23,174.5	4,258.6	26,882.1	26,049.6	684.4
18	18,669.8	3,408.8	2,330.0	16,824.3	53,836.1	13,632.0	7,043.8	53,759.9	1,446.6
19	6,758.1	1,591.5	411.7	8,635.6	15,654.8	4,995.6	2,571.0	12,040.3	1,494.4

Source: Survey of Current Business, July 1986. Each column shows intermediate inputs to that industry; each row shows intermediate uses of that industry's output.

Table 3-14. *Growth, by Industry*

Industry	Ratio of 1984 to 1980 GNP	Ratio of 1984 to 1983 GNP
1. Agriculture, forestry, and fisheries	1.1976	1.2561
2. Mining	1.3900	1.1872
3. Crude petroleum and gas	1.2036	1.0280
4. Contract construction	1.2478	1.1437
5. Food and tobacco	1.3371	1.0457
6. Textiles, apparel, and leather	1.3130	1.0268
7. Paper and printing	1.4499	1.1339
8. Petroleum refining	1.3374	1.0459
9. Chemicals, rubber, and plastics	1.3964	1.0920
10. Lumber, furniture, stone, clay, and glass	1.2965	1.1657
11. Metals, machinery, instruments, and miscellaneous manufacturing	1.2697	1.1416
12. Transportation equipment and ordnance	1.2592	1.1322
13. Motor vehicles	1.4345	1.2897
14. Transportation, communications, and utilities	1.4508	1.0966
15. Trade	1.4063	1.1243
16. Finance and insurance	1.3561	1.0302
17. Real estate	1.5103	1.0954
18. Services	1.5725	1.1282
19. Government enterprises	1.3169	1.0775

Source: *Survey of Current Business*, July 1986, table 6.1.

indirect business taxes, and nontax payments to government. These data are obtained from unpublished worksheets of the Commerce Department's National Income Division (NID). Since the data for labor use, labor taxes, and output taxes by industry reflect 1983 values, we adjust these to 1984 by using the ratio of 1984 GNP to 1983 GNP by industry, as recorded in the second column of table 3-14. The second column of table 3-16 shows output taxes as a fraction of corporate output in each industry, as employed in the model after consistency adjustments described in chapter 6.[14]

Thus we calculate implicit ad valorem tax rates in each industry for labor (observed payroll tax over labor use) and for output (other observed tax over value of output). In contrast, we employ explicit calculations of marginal user costs (in equations 2-23 through 2-25) to account for capital taxation. Table 3-17 displays specific values used for parameters in those formulas. These values are chosen to reflect 1984 tax policy. The constant expected rate of

14. We show only the corporate rates. The nature of our consistency adjustments causes the noncorporate rates to differ very slightly, if at all.

Table 3-15. *Labor Income, Labor Taxes, and Effective Rates, by Industry,*
1983

Millions of dollars

Industry	Labor income gross of tax	Tax on labor	Labor income net of tax	Effective tax rate on net income
All industries	1,804.574	216,733	1,580,207	0.1372
1. Agriculture, forestry, and fisheries	33,370	3,283	30,087	0.1091
2. Mining	13,102	1,266	11,836	0.1070
3. Crude petroleum and gas	21,456	2,187	19,269	0.1135
4. Contract construction	126,663	14,568	112,095	0.1300
5. Food and tobacco	41,002	5,234	35,768	0.1463
6. Textile, apparel, and leather	32,664	4,680	27,984	0.1672
7. Paper and printing	49,946	5,973	43,973	0.1358
8. Petroleum refining	7,133	768	6,365	0.1207
9. Chemicals, rubber, and plastics	52,740	6,098	45,874	0.1329
10. Lumber, furniture, stone, clay, and glass	37,769	4,998	32,771	0.1525
11. Metals, machinery, instruments and miscellaneous manufacturing	207,205	25,154	182,051	0.1382
12. Transportation equipment and ordnance	34,544	3,276	31,268	0.1048
13. Motor vehicles	29,077	3,934	25,143	0.1565
14. Transportation, communications, and utilities	164,715	18,695	146,020	0.1280
15. Trade	356,748	43,367	313,381	0.1384
16. Finance and insurance	115,181	12,919	102,262	0.1263
17. Real estate	19,405	2,521	16,889	0.1493
18. Services	417,588	44,319	373,269	0.1187
19. Government enterprises	44,266	13,493	30,773	0.4385

Sources: *Survey of Current Business,* July 1986, and unpublished data from the Commerce Department.

inflation is $\pi = 0.04$. The personal marginal tax rate on each source of income is calculated as the average of marginal rates for 25,000 individual tax returns, weighted by that source of income. For example, the rate on interest income ($\tau_d = 0.231$) is less than the rate on dividend income ($\tau_{ns} = 0.292$) because interest tends to be earned in lower tax brackets. The rate on accrued capital gains ($\tau_{re} = 0.05$) reflects the exclusion in 1984, deferral advantage, and step-up of basis at death.[15]

15. The "deferral advantage" is that capital gains are taxed only upon realization (sale of the asset), not as gains accrue. A further advantage is the "step-up" of basis at death, which resets the initial value of the capital asset upon transfer at death.

Table 3-16. *Output Taxes, by Industry, 1983*

Millions of dollars

Industry	Output taxes paid	Tax rate[a]
1. Agriculture, forestry, and fisheries	542	0.001
2. Mining	2,005	0.016
3. Crude petroleum and gas	16,131	0.043
4. Contract construction	2,349	0.003
5. Food and tobacco	11,289	0.017
6. Textiles, apparel, and leather	169	0.000
7. Paper and printing	752	0.001
8. Petroleum refining	9,201	0.019
9. Chemicals, rubber, and plastics	1,455	0.002
10. Lumber, furniture, stone, clay, and glass	476	0.001
11. Metals, machinery, instruments, and miscellaneous manufacturing	2,481	0.001
12. Transportation equipment and ordnance	541	0.002
13. Motor vehicles	4,923	0.014
14. Transportation, communications, and utilities	20,353	0.015
15. Trade	85,044	0.067
16. Finance and insurance	8,576	0.016
17. Real estate	17,620	0.020
18. Services	8,450	0.005
19. Government enterprises	0	0.000

Source: Unpublished data from the Commerce Department.

a. Rates take taxes paid as a fraction of output, in the corporate sector, after consistency adjustments described in chapter 6.

In addition, we choose 0.04 for r, the real net rate of return in the benchmark equilibrium. This return is the same for all sources of capital income because of individual arbitrage. Since the return to debt is $i(1 - \tau_d) - \pi$, the initial nominal interest rate must be $i = 0.104$.

The statutory corporate tax rate ($u = 0.495$) reflects the average of state corporate tax rates and deductibility against the 46 percent federal rate. Corporations use debt to finance $c_d = 0.34$ of investment. They also use retained earnings to finance 61 percent and new share issues for only the remaining 5 percent of investment.[16] Since dividend taxes are relevant only for new share issues in this model, the use of these observed financing shares would be consistent with the "new view," that dividend taxes are capitalized into share prices and are not relevant for marginal investment.[17] For our benchmark assumptions, instead, we wish to use the "old view," that dividend taxes

16. King and Fullerton (1984).
17. See Auerbach (1979), Bradford (1981), and King (1977).

Table 3-17. *Tax Parameter Data for Costs of Capital*

Parameter symbol	Description	Value
π	Expected inflation	0.04
u	Statutory tax rate on corporate income	0.495
τ_d	Personal tax rate on interest income (debt-financed investment)	0.231
τ_{re}	Personal tax rate on accrued capital gains (retained earnings)	0.050
τ_{ns}	Personal tax rate on dividend income (new shares)	0.292
c_d	Corporate proportion of investment financed by debt	0.34
c_{re}	Corporate proportion of investment financed by retained earnings	0.33
c_{ns}	Corporate proportion of investment financed by new shares	0.33
τ_{nc}	Marginal tax rate on entrepreneurial income (noncorporate sector)	0.245
n_d	Noncorporate proportion of investment financed by debt	0.34
n_e	Noncorporate proportion of investment financed by equity	0.67
τ_h	Personal marginal tax rate for deductions of homeowners	0.300
ω_h	Property tax rate on residential land and structures	0.01837
h_d	Owner-occupied housing share financed by debt	0.34
h_e	Owner-occupied housing share financed by equity	0.67
λ	Fraction of property tax deducted by homeowners	0.700

Source: Fullerton (1987).

Table 3-18. *Cost-of-Capital Data, by Asset Type*

Capital type	Economic depreciation	Depreciation allowance	Investment tax credit	Property tax rate	Effective tax rate Corporate	Noncorporate
Equipment	0.13	0.340	0.10	0.00768	0.200	−0.138
Structures	0.03	0.135	0.00	0.01126	0.511	0.324
Inventories	0.00	0.000	0.00	0.00768	0.571	0.333
Land	0.00	0.000	0.00	0.01126	0.587	0.371
Intangibles	0.21	1.000	0.00	0.00000	0.074	−0.012

Sources: Fullerton and Lyon (1988); and Hulten and Wykoff (1981).

and capital gains taxes are equally relevant. We therefore split the equity share evenly between retained earnings ($c_{re} = 0.33$) and new share issues ($c_{ns} = 0.33$). Further discussion and a sensitivity analysis appear in chapter 8.

In addition to these economy-wide parameters, the cost of capital formulas require asset-specific parameters. As mentioned earlier, five types of capital are specified in the model: equipment, structures, inventories, land, and intangibles. Intangible capital includes knowledge and goodwill, acquired through research and development, and advertising. Table 3-18 shows parameters that affect the costs of capital for these assets. The rates of economic depreciation in the first column are annual, exponential rates. The first four rates are obtained from estimates produced by Charles R. Hulten and Frank C. Wykoff (1981). The fifth rate of economic depreciation, on intangibles, is a weighted average of the Don Fullerton and Andrew B. Lyon (1988) economic depreciation rates on advertising and research and development.[18] For depreciation allowances, as in the Fullerton and Lyon paper, we use an annual, exponential rate of depreciation on historical cost that is equivalent in present value terms to the complicated system of depreciation allowances found in the actual law. The rate of tax depreciation for intangible capital is effectively 100 percent, because such capital expenses are immediately deducted. In our 1984 benchmark year, an investment tax credit of 10 percent on equipment still applies.[19] The rate for state and local property tax is 0.01126 for land and structures, 0.00768 for equipment and inventories, and zero for intangibles.

The last columns of table 3-18 show effective tax rates in each sector, including the combined effect of corporate taxes, property taxes, and personal taxation of capital income. For each asset, this is calculated as the cost of capital gross of tax, minus the rate of return net of tax, divided by the cost of capital. The rate on corporate equipment (0.200) is less than the rate on structures (0.511), primarily because of the investment tax credit. Both these rates reflect accelerated depreciation allowances at historical cost, eroded in real terms by the 4 percent rate of inflation. Inventories and land receive economic depreciation allowances (at rate zero). Intangibles receive immediate expensing despite a 21 percent rate of economic depreciation. Finally, in this table, effective tax rates in the noncorporate sector are lower than in the corporate sector but reflect similar differences among assets. The negative rates for equipment and intangibles mean that excess deductions and credits more than offset the total tax on these assets.

As described in chapter 2, the lifetime incidence model is able to capture any distortions caused by tax policy in the choice among these five assets. We also capture distortions between the two sectors. Every industry has a corporate sector and a noncorporate sector, each with its own output of the same producer good. In terms of data, however, the labor used in each sector of each industry is not available. Therefore we use the distribution of capital

18. From Fullerton and Lyon (1988), the central rate used for the economic depreciation of advertising is 0.33, and that for research and development is 0.15. Since the value of advertising capital is $165.447 billion, and the value of research and development is $304.979 billion, we obtain a weighted average of 21 percent.

19. Some special structures also received investment tax credits, but we abstract from such detail here. The Tax Reform Act of 1986 repealed the investment tax credit.

between the corporate and noncorporate sector of each industry to determine the distribution of labor and of output between the two sectors. This allocation is discussed further in chapter 6 on parameterization. Figures on corporate and noncorporate capital by asset type in each industry are shown in tables 3-19 and 3-20.[20] These numbers are from various sources, including the *Survey of Current Business,* the Federal Reserve Board's *Balance Sheets of the U.S. Economy,* and unpublished data from Dale W. Jorgenson and Martin A. Sullivan (1981). Because the capital data are from 1983, we adjust them to 1984 levels using the ratio of 1984 GNP to 1983 GNP, from the 1987 *Economic Report of the President* (table B-1). This ratio equals 1.1054.

The matrix of capital assets in each industry can be used to calculate a weighted average of the costs of capital for the five assets for each industry. Resulting effective tax rates are shown in the last column of each table.[21] Within the corporate sector, the tax rate on services is low (0.368) because a high fraction of that industry's capital is tax-favored equipment (52.9 percent). The effective tax rate on agriculture is high (0.531) because that industry uses relatively little equipment (22 percent) and intangibles (1 percent) and relatively more land (64 percent). For real estate, the 23 percent tax rate on owner-occupied housing reflects just the property tax. For other industries, the corporate sector in table 3-19 faces a higher cost of capital than does the noncorporate sector in table 3-20.

In tables 3-17 and 3-18 policy proposals are represented by appropriate changes in tax parameters. The rate of inflation and the shares of investment remain the same as in the benchmark. The model then calculates a new cost of capital for each asset, new prices, and new allocations. Simulation results are discussed in chapter 7.

Government and Trade Data

Recall that government expenditures are modeled by a Cobb-Douglas composite commodity function, defined as a combination of producer goods, labor, and capital. Figures on government purchases are required in order to

20. An exception to the corporate-noncorporate distinction is the real estate industry (17), where the entries under "Corporate capital" in table 3-19 actually represent the amounts of capital used in owner-occupied housing, and the entries under "Noncorporate capital" in table 3-20 represent the amounts used in rental housing.

21. The use of each asset depends on its cost of capital, given by ρ in equations 2-23 to 2-25, and the use of "composite" capital depends on its "price," given by $\bar{\rho}$ in equation 2-26. These tables show effective tax rates, and calculate simple weighted averages, because they are easier to interpret.

Table 3-19. *Corporate Capital and Effective Tax Rates, by Industry, 1983*

| Industry | Percent of total capital | | | | | | Total capital (millions of dollars) | Effective tax rate |
	Equipment	Structures	Inventories	Land	Intangibles			
1. Agriculture, forestry, and fisheries	21.58	5.11	8.94	63.70	0.67		91,146	0.5310
2. Mining	48.05	38.30	11.27	1.56	0.32		54,182	0.4112
3. Crude petroleum and gas	4.73	88.91	3.36	2.65	0.27		186,435	0.5063
4. Contract construction	26.50	1.81	49.93	20.30	1.46		165,207	0.5097
5. Food and tobacco	22.44	16.63	35.57	8.91	16.46		222,718	0.4575
6. Textiles, apparel, and leather	28.86	15.79	40.76	9.00	5.59		74,847	0.4771
7. Paper and printing	40.31	18.92	22.42	11.37	6.97		150,975	0.4332
8. Petroleum refining	20.17	34.54	23.43	15.95	5.91		124,947	0.4885
9. Chemicals, rubber, and plastics	36.35	11.95	23.69	6.31	21.70		302,399	0.3896
10. Lumber, furniture, stone, clay, and glass	31.98	19.56	31.73	10.25	6.48		100,972	0.4617
11. Metals, machinery, instruments, and miscellaneous manufacturing	23.21	13.27	39.66	6.12	17.74		1,010,179	0.4524
12. Transportation equipment and ordnance	8.76	9.47	29.80	4.50	47.47		190,418	0.3826
13. Motor vehicles	29.55	10.11	27.53	4.65	28.17		146,399	0.3883
14. Transportation, communications, and utilities	42.41	49.31	3.79	3.77	0.73		1,301,039	0.4207
15. Trade	12.29	8.32	62.93	12.30	4.17		1,449,432	0.5313
16. Finance and insurance	1.39	15.30	0.61	54.32	28.38		56,568	0.4914
17. Real estate	0.00	74.68	0.00	25.32	0.00		3,286,432	0.2322
18. Services	52.90	29.43	4.12	5.72	7.84		207,395	0.3680

Source: Fullerton and Lyon (1988). For real estate, no. 17, the corporate sector is replaced by owner-occupied housing.

Table 3-20. *Noncorporate Capital and Effective Tax Rates, by Industry, 1983*

Industry	Percent of total capital					Total capital (millions of dollars)	Effective tax rate
	Equipment	Structures	Inventories	Land	Intangibles		
1. Agriculture, forestry, and fisheries	5.09	4.66	9.43	80.14	0.67	2,239,706	0.3489
2. Mining	16.72	73.56	7.24	2.16	0.32	21,315	0.2756
3. Crude petroleum and gas	1.27	88.91	4.60	4.96	0.27	82,165	0.3224
4. Contract construction	21.14	5.37	40.09	31.94	1.46	85,981	0.2800
5. Food and tobacco	10.29	28.65	18.50	26.10	16.46	6,251	0.2696
6. Textiles, apparel, and leather	5.08	11.32	67.01	11.01	5.58	4,650	0.3091
7. Paper and printing	15.82	52.86	8.46	15.89	6.97	8,682	0.2694
8. Petroleum refining						0	
9. Chemicals, rubber, and plastics	24.12	29.84	4.22	20.12	21.71	6,054	0.2004
10. Lumber, furniture, stone, clay, and glass	21.74	49.72	14.76	7.31	6.48	10,960	0.2468
11. Metals, machinery, instruments, and miscellaneous manufacturing	11.07	22.47	28.14	20.58	17.74	22,517	0.2615
12. Transportation equipment and ordnance	5.63	22.62	6.92	17.36	47.47	4,527	0.1887
13. Motor vehicles						0	
14. Transportation, communications, and utilities	23.82	18.92	0.00	56.54	0.73	167,052	0.2832
15. Trade	5.04	15.06	44.60	31.14	4.17	704,386	0.3207
16. Finance and insurance	1.36	55.81	0.00	14.44	28.38	296,363	0.2576
17. Real estate	0.00	74.68	0.00	25.32	0.00	1,382,745	0.3362
18. Services	24.41	50.50	1.03	16.22	7.84	256,658	0.2377

Source: Fullerton and Lyon (1988). For real estate, no. 17, the noncorporate sector is rental housing.

Table 3-21. *Government Purchases, Exports, and Imports of Producer Goods, 1984*

Millions of dollars

Producer goods	Government purchases	Exports	Imports
1. Agriculture, forestry, and fisheries	0	21,828	5,841
2. Mining	288	4,343	2,690
3. Crude petroleum and gas	2,090	2,339	34,786
4. Contract construction	93,271	75	0
5. Food and tobacco	4,151	13,665	15,957
6. Textiles, apparel, and leather	2,203	3,507	29,419
7. Paper and printing	9,992	5,526	8,704
8. Petroleum refining	11,471	8,448	24,432
9. Chemicals, rubber, and plastics	11,139	25,370	22,363
10. Lumber, furniture, stone, clay, and glass	2,808	4,931	12,256
11. Metals, machinery, instruments, and miscellaneous manufacturing	46,405	71,050	117,892
12. Transportation equipment and ordnance	53,204	17,374	6,537
13. Motor vehicles	8,001	17,006	51,067
14. Transportation, communications, and utilities	34,911	22,102	5,556
15. Trade	11,459	21,423	0
16. Finance and insurance	7,052	6,858	866
17. Real estate	9,302	6,519	0
18. Services	40,208	6,812	211
19. Government enterprises	1,369	143	0
20. Labor	371,939	. . .	. . .
21. Capital	276,693	. . .	. . .

Source: *Survey of Current Business*, November 1989, table 1, columns 94, 95.

set parameters for that function. Table 3-21 shows data on government purchases of the 19 producer goods, from table 1 of the November 1989 *Survey of Current Business*.[22] Government purchases of labor and capital services are grossed up to 1984 from data in Charles L. Ballard and others' 1985 study, obtained from the National Income and Product Accounts tables.

Part of the government's income is obtained from rent collected on its endowment of capital services. For the quantity of this endowment, we update the corresponding figure in Ballard and others by applying the growth of total government expenditures. The authors calculated this endowment from the government use of capital by subtracting the net interest paid by federal, state, and local governments. The updated quantity is $255.41 billion. With

22. Government purchases appear in columns 96 through 99 of the table. The aggregation follows table 3-9 in this chapter.

a 4 percent rate of return, the rental income from this stock is slightly more than $10.2 billion.

We also account for taxes paid by government. There are no sales taxes paid on government purchases of producer goods, but we do model government taxes paid on labor and capital services. For general government, the labor tax equals the total tax payments of government on labor, less the estimated labor tax paid by government enterprises. This value is $40.076 billion, updated again from Ballard and others using the rate of growth of government expenditures. The model sets the government's tax rate on capital equal to the weighted average of industry tax rates on capital, for reasons described in chapter 2.

Last, we consider data on international trade, including figures for exports and imports of the 19 producer goods. These figures, also shown in table 3-21, are obtained from the November 1989 *Survey of Current Business*, following the aggregation described in our table 3-9.

The combination of all tables in this chapter represents our entire input file for the consistency adjustments described in chapter 6, and subsequently for the general equilibrium results in chapters 7 through 9. We turn first, however, to complete descriptions of the econometric procedures used to estimate some components of this input file.

CHAPTER FOUR

Determination of Lifetime Incomes

THE MAIN innovation of this study is our focus on the lifetime effect of taxes. In determining the pattern of lifetime tax burdens relative to lifetime abilities to pay, data on the levels and time paths of lifetime incomes play a crucial role in the analysis. We first must determine the levels of lifetime incomes, in order to classify individuals into the appropriate lifetime income categories. We then draw the shapes of lifetime income profiles and look for important differences across categories in the timing of consumption relative to income. Any differences we find in the capital-labor ratios across the lifetime income categories will suggest differences in burdens associated with the various types of taxes.

One difficulty in adopting the lifetime perspective is finding a satisfactory unit of analysis. When using the more familiar "annual" framework, researchers usually examine tax patterns among established households. The "lifetime" of a household is difficult to define, however, because individuals join and leave the household unit at various times. In this study we strike a compromise. We track the lifetimes of individuals, but we account for their spouses' lifetime incomes, as well as their own, in characterizing their abilities to pay.

Very few empirically based studies of lifetime tax incidence exist, primarily because there are little appropriate data. The ideal source would be a panel that covers the entire lifetimes of individuals, but such data are not available. Our approach uses a panel that covers fractions of individuals' lifetimes. Specifically, we use data from the Panel Study of Income Dynamics, covering the years 1970 through 1987. We limit our sample to households whose head and spouse (if any) were unchanged over the 1970–87 period. Thus we have an eighteen-year window of actual data from these individuals' lifetimes.

Other researchers have attempted to determine lifetime incomes. Their studies are typically found in the income distribution literature and are based on labor earnings over the lifetime.[1] In general, these studies have shown that annual and lifetime incomes are not well correlated and that lifetime incomes are more equally distributed than annual incomes. In our work on lifetime incomes, we come to similar conclusions. The lack of correlation between the annual and lifetime income distributions suggests that the lifetime incidence of the various tax instruments might be significantly different from their annual incidence.

Annual and lifetime income distributions differ because annual incomes fluctuate over individuals' lifetimes. An individual who currently earns a low annual income may actually have a high present-value of lifetime earnings. A young person just starting out may be characterized as "poor" in an annual perspective. In the lifetime perspective, the person may have a high income and a high lifetime ability to pay.[2]

As Milton Moss (1978) explains, there are three ways of viewing income changes associated with age. These three "dimensions" of lifetime income are illustrated in figure 4-1, where we assume that the individuals are identical except for age and cohort. The lower curve represents a cross section of annual incomes from year T, for individuals of different ages. The upper curve is a similar cross section from year $T + 1$. First, the cross-sectional dimension (points A and B) compares the annual incomes of age groups alive at a given point in time, thus isolating life-cycle effects. Second, the age-specific dimension (points B and C) looks at individuals within a given age group across different points in time, thus capturing effects of economic growth. Finally, the longitudinal dimension follows a given cohort through time (points A to C). These longitudinal movements are the combined effects of the life-cycle and economic growth factors. For the lifetime tax incidence model, we would like the lifetime income profiles to reflect the pure life-cycle effects on income, since our model separately specifies an exogenous

1. These include Lillard (1977a,1977b), Moss (1978), Irvine (1980), Blomquist (1981), and Friesen and Miller (1983). Creedy (1985) provides a thorough examination of the literature on the dynamics of income distribution. In particular, see his chapters 6 through 9, which discuss age-earnings profiles and the distribution of lifetime earnings. More recently, Fitzgerald and Maloney (1990), using the PSID, found that federal taxes and cash transfers significantly redistribute lifetime incomes. This study is similar to the analysis we describe in this chapter, but it uses a definition of lifetime income (wage rate times hours worked) that reflects labor supply decisions. Our study, in contrast, defines lifetime income according to the time path of wage rates alone. This endowment definition will be discussed further.

2. High lifetime income, however, does not necessarily imply high current ability to pay. A high standard of equity in taxation would require both that current taxes reflect current ability to pay and lifetime taxes reflect lifetime ability to pay.

Figure 4-1. *Dimensions of Lifetime Income*[a]

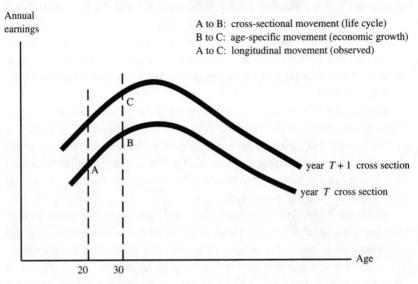

a. Moss (1978, p. 122) has a similar illustration.

rate of economic growth. Panel data, such as those found in the PSID, are ideal in allowing the researcher to isolate these life-cycle effects.

Our definition of "lifetime income" is not the one usually found in the income distribution literature. In our lifetime incidence model, labor supply is endogenous, while consumption and leisure enter the utility function. People can choose to avoid labor- or consumption-based taxes by working fewer hours and decreasing their labor incomes. Two individuals who are paid the same hourly wage have the same ability to pay taxes, in this context, even if one chooses to work fewer hours and thus earns a lower labor income. Therefore, in classifying individuals according to abilities to pay, we require a definition based on the value of lifetime labor endowments rather than lifetime labor earnings. To estimate the paths of endowments, we follow wage rates rather than incomes. Individuals who receive higher wage rates in the data are said to have a larger quantity of effective labor units, given the model's single wage rate. This translation is appropriate, because individuals have the same total amount of time available to them.[3] Throughout this study the

3. We can think of the quantity of labor endowment as the quantity of "effective labor units," where one effective labor unit receives the model's single wage rate. Thus human capital is

phrase "lifetime income" refers to the present value of labor endowment over the lifetime.

In addition to the time paths of labor endowments, we also need the paths of taxes and transfers over individuals' lifetimes. While consumers are categorized according to their before-tax-and-transfer lifetime endowments, they intertemporally allocate their after-tax-and-transfer lifetime endowment. Our estimated tax and transfer paths establish the initial benchmark equilibrium and the parameters for the model's tax and transfer equations. Determining these life-cycle taxes and transfers incidentally allows us to examine the effect of government programs on the distribution of lifetime incomes. Of the studies mentioned in note one, only that of John Fitzgerald and Tim Maloney (1990) attempted such an analysis.

Our primary objectives here are to determine lifetime income categories for a representative sample of U.S. individuals, and describe the time paths of labor endowments, taxes, and transfers by the use of regression functions. Because the PSID data cover only a fraction of individual lifetimes, we use a multistep procedure. First, we estimate general economy-wide wage, tax, and transfer equations. We use the resulting functions to forecast and backcast any missing data for each individual. At this point we have wages, taxes, and transfers for each year in each individual's lifetime, with some of the data observed and some estimated. Next, we compute lifetime incomes and sort individuals into lifetime income categories. We then make several kinds of comparisons. Finally, late in the chapter, we turn to parameters needed for the general equilibrium model. Using actual data only, we estimate wage, tax, and transfer functions for each of the lifetime income categories. These functions expose differences in the shapes of these profiles across categories. These profiles are then incorporated into the lifetime tax incidence model.

Data

For both the initial, economy-wide estimates of wage, tax, and transfer functions and the final estimations by lifetime income category, we use a representative sample of 500 households from the PSID over the period 1970

---

reflected in the quantity instead of the price. In making this translation, we assume that the total time endowment available to an individual is 4,000 hours a year, or about 80 hours a week.

to 1987. We preserve the panel nature of the sample in performing the initial regressions. Tracking individuals over the eighteen-year period allows us to observe several years of data for each individual and aids us in estimating individual-specific determinants. These "fixed effects" improve the accuracy of any constructed paths of wages, taxes, and transfers for the years we do not observe.

For each household we collect variables describing the economic status and demographic characteristics of the head and spouse (if any).[4] With 500 heads and 358 spouses, the total unweighted sample consists of 858 individuals, about 52 percent of whom are female. Of the 142 single-headed households, 52 are male-headed and 90 are female-headed. Whenever any statistical or econometric procedures are performed, the household observations are appropriately weighted to correct for the PSID's oversampling of lower-income households.[5]

For the initial regressions we estimate separate functions for heads and spouses. Because data on taxes and transfers correspond to the household as a whole, we must separate these amounts into a portion attributed to the head and a remainder attributed to the spouse. We take the PSID's estimate of income taxes of the household and we allocate it between head and spouse according to their relative labor incomes.[6] The household's total government transfers received are divided equally between the head and the spouse.[7]

4. In the PSID, the head may be male or female. For a married couple, however, the head is male and the spouse is always female. The spouse may be legally married to the head or simply cohabiting.

5. As previously mentioned, however, we select only households whose head and spouse (if any) were unchanged over the 1970–87 sample period. The random sample of 500 is drawn after this selection. Thus the households sampled all exhibit marital stability, at least over this period. This procedure may inject some bias into the regression results, to the extent that households with greater stability differ from other households in what determines wages, taxes, and transfers. We are not, however, using the initial regressions to make general statements about the importance of a particular demographic variable. We merely use these regression functions to determine, for our particular sample of 500 households, the fitted values for wages, taxes, and transfers for unobserved years.

6. The accuracy of the tax data is less than we would like. The PSID variable on income taxes paid is an estimate of federal income taxes, based on the PSID's computation of household taxable income, a number of "presumed" exemptions, and the filing status of the household. Moreover, the taxes include both capital income and labor income taxes. In our model, capital taxes are collected at the producer level, and individuals face a net-of-all-tax rate of return. We therefore adjust the tax variable by assuming that each household's share of income taxes due to labor income is equal to labor income's share of total taxable income.

7. Total government transfers are the sum of the following: income from aid for families with dependent children (AFDC), supplemental security income, other welfare payments, and social security benefits. In later waves of the PSID (1986 and 1987), these are reported separately for

With each annual wave of the PSID, individuals are asked about values from the previous year. For example, the latest wave we use is dated 1987, but the data on wages, taxes, and transfers correspond to the 1986 calendar year. In all the regressions described in this chapter, we use real values in 1986 dollars.[8]

Initial Fixed-Effect Regressions

In this section we describe the estimation of wage, tax, and transfer functions that are used to construct data for years outside the PSID sample period. All these initial estimations are based on demographic characteristics and individual-specific constant effects.

Log Wage Regressions

We need wage data for each year in these individuals' lifetimes, but we have just eighteen years of observations for each individual. The number of years with positive wages may in fact be less than eighteen. We therefore estimate wage functions that can be used to predict wages that are either unobserved or zero. We estimate separate wage functions for heads and spouses, based on the assumption that the effects of the many demographic variables on wages may differ significantly between primary and secondary earners.[9] Any head or spouse who worked at least one year during the sample period is included in the wage regressions. The result is one sample of 484 heads (out of 500) and another sample of 334 spouses (out of 358). For each individual, we use those years of data for which positive wages are observed.[10] The resulting number of observations on wages of heads is 7,291,

---

the head and the spouse. We preserve that division in our allocation of transfer income between head and spouse. For all other years (1970–85), total transfers are divided equally between head and spouse.

8. We "inflate" values from the 1970–86 waves (1969–85 values), using the GNP deflator.

9. A problem here is that we are considering all spouses to be secondary earners, even if the spouse actually earns the higher salary. The "spouses" sample is a very diverse population. Some spouses work only part time at low-wage jobs and may view their jobs as consumption goods. Other spouses are working at full-time careers. The determinants of wages may differ significantly between these two types of spouses.

10. Excluding zero-wage observations in these initial wage regressions can lead to a form of "sample selection bias" when the estimated functions are used to predict effective wage rates in the zero-wage, unemployed years. People who are unemployed tend to have lower (unobserved)

which implies an average of fifteen years of wage data for each head. The number of observations on the wages of spouses is 3,792, implying an average of eleven years of data per spouse.

We estimate the log of the real wage rate as a function of an individual-specific constant for term, age, education, race, and sex. Our measure of the wage rate is "average hourly earnings," one of the generated variables on the PSID. Average hourly earnings are computed by dividing reported labor income by reported hours of work. The education variable, *educ,* represents the number of years of education. We define variable *white* to equal 1 if the individual is white, 0 otherwise. "Female" equals 1 if the individual is female, 0 otherwise.[11] We allow age to affect wages in a nonlinear manner by including variables for age squared and age cubed. Because we use the fixed-effects model, any time-invariant effects associated with education level, race, or sex are captured in the constant term for each individual. The constant term also reflects the effects of unobserved ability and motivation. To allow these demographic variables to affect the time profile of the wage rate, we interact the education, race, and sex variables with age variables.[12]

Table 4-1 shows initial log wage regression results for the heads and spouses samples. From these results it is immediately apparent that age has a more significant effect on the wages of heads than on wages of spouses. For heads, wages rise and then fall with age.[13] Apart from its influence with the individual-specific effect, education also affects the time profile of wages.[14] For the heads sample, the profile also differs by sex.

---

ability and hence would end up with lower wages than their employed counterparts. This general problem is discussed by Heckman (1979). The selection bias in our particular case is rather insignificant, however, because we account for individual-specific effects. When we perform a two-stage estimation of wages, within a fixed-effects model that accounts for the effect of selection via an "inverse Mills ratio," we find the selection variable to be an insignificant determinant of wages.

11. For the spouses sample, the variable "female" is omitted.

12. For econometric reasons, we cannot include these demographic variables on their own. Education, race, and sex would be perfectly collinear with the individual-specific constant term, because for a given adult individual these variables do not vary over time.

13. To discuss the shape of the age-wage profile, we can calculate how log wages change with age. Let $(b_1, b_2, \ldots, b_9)$ refer to the estimated coefficients as listed (in order) in table 4–1. Then the partial derivative of log wages with respect to age equals $b_1 + 2b_2(age) + 3b_3(age^2) + b_4(educ) + b_5(white) + b_6(female) + 2b_7(age \times educ) + 2b_8(age \times white) + 2b_9(age \times female)$. This gives a slope of the age-log wage function which can vary by age, education, race, and sex.

14. It is difficult to interpret the coefficients on the demographic variables without some effort, because of (1) the inclusion of individual-specific effects, and (2) the interactions of the

Table 4-1. *Initial Log Wage Regressions*[a]

Independent variable	Heads	Spouses
Age	0.122135	−0.289007E-01
	(4.886)	(−0.619)
Age²	−0.160768E-02	0.748786E-03
	(−4.095)	(0.843)
Age³	0.373959E-05	−0.169726E-05
	(1.655)	(−0.279)
Age × educ	−0.140749E-02	0.235030E-02
	(−3.675)	(2.410)
Age × white	−0.108649E-01	0.841494E-02
	(−0.570)	(0.252)
Age × female	−0.389081E-01	. . .
	(−2.788)	
Age² × educ	0.230155E-04	−0.433238E-04
	(3.885)	(−2.607)
Age² × white	0.481060E-04	−0.179074E-03
	(0.248)	(−0.477)
Age² × female	0.407765E-03	. . .
	(3.019)	
Number of individuals	484	334
Number of observations	7,291	3,792
Adjusted R^2	0.681109	0.454177

a. All regressions use real average hourly earnings (base year, 1986) and include individual-specific constant terms. The numbers in parentheses are *t*-statistics.

For both samples, but especially for the spouses, we find that individual-specific, time-invariant effects explain most of the observed variance in wage rates. The fit of the regression for spouses, reflected by the adjusted R-squared of 0.454, is heavily dependent on the inclusion of these constant terms. When the spouses regression is performed without the individual-specific effects, the adjusted R-squared is only 0.094. Although the time-varying components are more important for heads than for spouses, the fairly high adjusted R-squared of 0.681 for heads is also in large part due to individual-specific effects. Without these fixed effects, the adjusted R-squared is only 0.274.

race, sex, and education variables with the age variables. The individual-specific effects in large part capture any time-invariant (constant) effects of race, sex, and education; these are reflected in the height rather than the shape of the age-wage profiles. On the other hand, the coefficients on the interaction terms reflect any effects of race, sex, and education on the shape of the age-wage profile. Therefore, the overall effect of education on log wage rates is determined jointly by the interaction term coefficients and by a portion of the individual-specific constant term.

Tax Regressions

In our incidence study, we classified individuals according to before-tax-and-transfer lifetime labor endowments. Therefore, for the purpose of computing lifetime incomes and sorting individuals into lifetime income categories, we require only the wage functions described above.[15] We still estimate initial, economy-wide tax and transfer functions, however, in order to fill in missing observations of taxes and transfers, and briefly examine the overall, economy-wide effects of government on the lifetime income distribution.[16]

While we use only nonzero observations for the wage regressions described above, we include all observations for the tax and transfer regressions. Thus we have 9,000 observations in our heads sample (18 years × 500 heads) and 6,444 observations in our spouses sample (18 years × 358 spouses).[17]

Table 4-2 shows the results from the initial, fixed-effects tax regressions. Estimates for heads show a significant hump-shaped profile when we relate income taxes to age.[18] Moreover, the shape of the age-tax profile differs depending on the sex of the head; females have less pronounced peaks in their tax profiles.[19] For spouses, age affects income taxes paid, but other demographic variables have insignificant effects on the shape of this age-tax profile. For both the heads and spouses samples, individual-specific effects are very important. The adjusted R-squareds without the fixed effects are 0.132 and 0.089 for heads and spouses, respectively. Inclusion of the fixed effects improves the fit and raises these to 0.660 and 0.500, as shown in the table.

15. Tax and transfer functions are required later for the *final* regressions for each lifetime income category, to set parameters for the general equilibrium model.

16. We could estimate a single "net government transfer" function instead of separate tax and transfer functions. The separation is useful, however, for examining how age and other demographic variables may have different effects on these two forms of government redistribution: income taxes and cash transfers.

17. We choose to estimate these functions using an ordinary-least-squares model (with fixed effects). When there are some observations of zero values, however, an econometrically preferable method would be the Tobin censored regression model (Tobin, 1958).

18. Basically, the large positive coefficient on *age* and the smaller negative coefficient on *age*[2] produce this result, although the age-tax profile strictly depends on all of the coefficients shown (since all involve age).

19. Note that the coefficient on *age* × *female* is negative, thus diluting the positive coefficient on the uninteracted variable, *age*, while the coefficient on *age*[2] × *female* is positive, opposing the negative coefficient on *age*[2].

Table 4-2. *Initial Tax Regressions*[a]

Independent variable	Heads	Spouses
Age	1127.64	−57.8566
	(4.645)	(−0.765)
Age^2	−15.5327	2.94329
	(−4.320)	(2.530)
Age^3	0.633604E-01	−0.316364E-01
	(3.251)	(−4.947)
Age × educ	3.23084	0.786436
	(0.788)	(0.459)
Age × white	85.5223	8.98556
	(0.463)	(0.139)
Age × female	−667.167	. . .
	(−4.691)	
Age^2 × educ	−0.104095E-01	0.111326E-01
	(−0.180)	(0.415)
Age^2 × white	−1.15347	0.205030
	(−0.686)	(0.288)
Age^2 × female	5.53914	. . .
	(4.757)	
Number of individuals	500	358
Number of observations	9,000	6,444
Adjusted R^2	0.660420	0.500089

a. All regressions use real taxes (base year, 1986) and include individual-specific constant terms. The numbers in parentheses are *t*-statistics.

Transfer Regressions

We estimate fixed-effects transfer functions in a manner similar to that used for the tax functions. Results from these regressions are shown in table 4-3. The basic pattern of government cash transfers received over the life cycle is U-shaped, and the steepness of this age-transfer function differs significantly across demographic categories. In the heads sample, for example, individuals who are white or female have less pronounced U-shaped transfer profiles than do their nonwhite, male counterparts.[20] In the spouses sample, on the other hand, those who are white have transfer profiles with a more pronounced U-shape. While the shapes of age-transfer profiles differ signifi-

20. We can evaluate the partial derivative of the transfer function with respect to age, as described in a previous footnote. In this case, however, the differences are apparent by casual inspection of the coefficients. The coefficients on *age* × *white* and *age* × *female* are positive, and those on *age^2* × *white* and *age^2* × *female* are negative. Thus the signs of these coefficients oppose the signs of the coefficients on *age* and *age^2*.

Table 4-3. *Initial Transfer Regressions*[a]

Independent variable	Heads	Spouses
Age	−219.749	31.1804
	(−4.620)	(0.650)
Age²	1.28602	−1.68031
	(1.826)	(−2.277)
Age³	0.155979E-01	0.222043E-01
	(4.085)	(5.472)
Age × educ	−4.06527	0.411395E-01
	(−5.063)	(0.038)
Age × white	84.1296	−86.5621
	(2.325)	(−2.110)
Age × female	214.834	. . .
	(7.709)	
Age² × educ	0.522126E-01	0.186006E-02
	(4.612)	(0.109)
Age² × white	−0.317172	1.21592
	(−0.963)	(2.694)
Age² × female	−2.33428	. . .
	(−10.232)	
Number of individuals	500	358
Number of observations	9,000	6,444
Adjusted R²	0.642179	0.660432

a. All regressions use real transfers (base year, 1986) and include individual-specific constant terms. The numbers in parentheses are *t*-statistics.

cantly across heads with different levels of educational attainment, education is insignificant in explaining the age-transfer profiles of spouses.

Individual-specific effects are relatively less important in explaining transfers than in explaining wages and taxes. The adjusted *R*-squared for the heads sample is 0.499 without fixed effects and 0.642 with these effects. For spouses, the fit increases from 0.489 to 0.660 when fixed effects are added. The relatively smaller significance of individual-specific constant terms suggests that differences across individuals in the level of lifetime transfers are smaller than differences in the levels of wages or taxes.

Determination of Lifetime Incomes and Their Distribution

Given the initial wage, tax, and transfer functions just estimated, we can now construct gross and net lifetime income profiles for our sample of 858 individuals. For each individual we use three types of information in determining lifetime incomes: eighteen years of data from the PSID (1970–87); estimates of the individual-specific constants describing that individual's wage rate, taxes, and transfers; and regression coefficients describing the shapes of age-wage, age-tax, and age-transfer profiles according to demographic characteristics. The first type of information is actual data; the latter two types allow construction of data for those years in each individual's lifetime that fall outside the eighteen-year window of the PSID.

We define an "economic lifetime" as sixty years, from chronological age 20 through chronological age 79. We first determine each individual's year of economic birth and death. We then look for any year in that lifetime for which we do not have data, and we calculate the appropriate real wage rate, taxes, and transfers, using the individual-specific constants and the other coefficients shown in tables 4-1, 4-2, and 4-3. For any year in which the individual is unemployed, we replace the observed zero wage rate with an effective wage rate according to the individual's characteristics.[21] The result of our "fill-in" procedure is a data set that provides the paths of wages, taxes, and transfers over the entire economic lifetimes for each of the 858 individuals in our sample.

We compute lifetime income according to

$$(4-1) \qquad LI_{gross} = \sum_{t=1}^{60} [(w_t \times 4{,}000)/(1 + r)^{t-1}],$$

where t indexes the sixty years within an economic lifetime. The term w_t is the actual or estimated before-tax effective wage rate. We assume that 4,000 hours of time endowment are available each year, based on 50 weeks a year times a maximum of 80 hours a week.[22] The net-of-tax rate of return, r, is set at 4 percent.[23] We then define lifetime income after taxes and transfers as

$$(4-2) \qquad LI_{net} = \sum_{t=1}^{60} \{[w_t \times (1-\tau_t) \times 4{,}000] + T_t\}/(1 + r)^{t-1},$$

21. Because we use individual-specific constants, these characteristics implicitly include any information on wage rates for years in which the individual did in fact work.

22. The size of the time endowment is irrelevant for the determination of lifetime income categories, because we assume the time endowment is the same across all individuals and is the same in every year of one's life. Therefore, our sorting of individuals according to lifetime labor endowments is equivalent to sorting them by the present value of wage rates.

23. The choice of r could affect the sorting of individuals, since a higher discount rate implies a relatively lower lifetime income for individuals whose high-wage years come later in life.

where τ_t is the effective tax rate on wages at age t, and T_t are cash transfers received at age t.[24] These components are determined either from actual data from the PSID or from the fixed-effects functions estimated above. Although the effective tax rate is based on taxes actually paid on the labor supply component of time endowments, our model also values leisure at the same net-of-tax wage rate. Therefore we apply this net wage rate to the full 4,000 hours of time endowment.

These lifetime income measures treat the individual as separate from the rest of his or her household. If we categorized individuals according to the value of their own labor endowments, ignoring that of their spouses, we would have a sample in which secondary earners comprise the bulk of the lifetime poor. Because of pooling of income and consumption within households, such a categorization seems inappropriate. Moreover, it is especially inappropriate given the stability of marriages in our select sample of households. We therefore choose to categorize individuals according to "average household lifetime income." After computing gross and net lifetime incomes for each of the 858 individuals in our sample, if the individual is married we compute "average household lifetime income" (both gross and net) according to

$$(4\text{-}3) \qquad\qquad LI_{avg.} = (LI_{head} + LI_{spouse})/2.$$

If the individual is single, average household lifetime income equals the individual's own lifetime income. After this computation, we have all the information required to sort individuals according to lifetime income categories. We also compute each individual's annual income and average household annual income for 1986 in order to compare the lifetime and annual income distributions. We are particularly interested in comparing the distribution of lifetime incomes with that of annual, transfer-inclusive household incomes, because the latter measure of income was used by Joseph A. Pechman and Benjamin A. Okner (1974).[25]

Table 4-4 presents summary statistics describing age-specific wages, annual incomes, and lifetime incomes. These statistics are based on observa-

24. Net labor income is measured after *labor* income taxes. Both lifetime income measures use the 4 percent net-of-capital-tax rate of return for the discount rate. In our model, all capital taxes are collected from producers.

25. Transfer-augmented annual income is in fact the official measure of income that was adopted after the "War on Poverty" of the 1960s. The definition of poverty began with the idea that an individual's well-being depends on the ability to consume goods and services. It was believed that this ability is best indicated by income, defined to be the pre-tax, post-transfer annual cash income of a family, excluding capital gains or losses. This concept is discussed in Haveman (1988).

Table 4-4. *Lifetime versus Annual Income Variation*[a]

Means in 1986 dollars

Variable[b]	Mean	Standard deviation	Coefficient of variation
Wage at 20	7.177	3.974	0.554
Wage at 49	11.259	9.125	0.810
Wage at 79	6.819	5.014	0.735
Annual income	19,044	35,005	1.838
Annual income plus transfers	20,859	34,462	1.652
Average annual income of household	19,044	24,711	1.298
Average annual income plus transfers of household	20,859	23,816	1.142
Lifetime income of head only[c]	971,746	563,187	0.580
Lifetime income of head after government[c]	906,883	458,723	0.506
Lifetime income of spouse only[d]	588,036	272,992	0.464
Lifetime income of spouse after government[d]	585,577	252,898	0.432
Average lifetime income of household	813,435	371,225	0.456
Lifetime income of household after government	774,319	311,739	0.403

a. 858 observations on heads and spouses.
b. "Average . . . of household" is average of values for head and spouse, if any, and equals the value for head if there is no spouse. Values that are not denoted averages treat the head and spouse as separate individuals. The phrase "after government" corresponds to after taxes and cash transfers.
c. Statistics based on a heads-only sample containing 500 individuals.
d. Statistics based on a spouses-only sample containing 358 individuals.

tions in our sample of 858 individuals, appropriately weighted to get a representative sample of the U.S. population. For each measure, the table shows the mean, standard deviation, and coefficient of variation (standard deviation divided by mean). The mean wage rate is shown for ages 20, 49, and 70, suggesting how the wage profile rises, then falls with age. Wages are higher and more variable in middle age than in youth or old age. Next, we compare the variability of the age-specific wage rates with the variability of annual incomes. These differences suggest that the high variation in annual incomes is largely due to differences across age groups.[26]

26. The annual income measures include individuals of all ages, while the wage measures include only individuals of a particular age. If life-cycle wage variation was unimportant, the coefficients of variation for the annual income measures would be more similar to the coefficients

Lifetime measures remove any differences attributable solely to age; consequently, as table 4-4 shows, variation in lifetime incomes is much lower than variation in annual incomes. The smaller degree of inequality in the lifetime income distribution is one reason lifetime tax incidence results may differ from annual results. Lifetime income is measured before taxes and transfers ("before government"); later we discuss calculations after taxes and cash transfers ("after government").

These results tell us that the lifetime and annual income measures are different, but from a practical standpoint we would like to know how different. If the annual income distribution is not significantly different from the lifetime income distribution, the extra effort involved in lifetime analysis may not be necessary or worthwhile. To assess how much the annual and lifetime measures differ, we do two things: we examine the correlations between annual and lifetime measures and we look at differences between the annual and lifetime categorizations of individuals.

If we consider incomes at the individual level (without taking a household average), the Pearson correlation coefficient between before-tax-and-transfer annual and lifetime incomes is .6754.[27] In contrast, the correlation coefficients between individual lifetime incomes and the individual's wage rates at ages 20, 49, and 79 are, respectively, .9635, .8527, and .8006. The correlations between lifetime and annual incomes are lower than those between lifetime incomes and wage rates because annual incomes include capital income and depend on actual hours worked. Remember that our measure of lifetime income is really a labor endowment measure that is independent of hours worked.

We can also examine the correlation between the income measure used by Pechman and Okner (1974) and the measure we use in our study. Pechman and Okner use the household's transfer-augmented annual income; we use an average of the household's lifetime labor endowment. We find that the correlation coefficient between these measures is .6350. This correlation is low enough to suggest that Pechman and Okner's annual results are not a good "proxy" for lifetime incidence results.

We next look at wage and income categorization and examine some mo-

---

of variation for the age-specific wage measures. One qualification we need to make, however, is that the annual income measures include capital income as well as labor income, so that some of the increased variability may be due to the variability of capital incomes.

27. The Pearson correlation coefficient is a product-moment correlation that takes on values ranging from -1 (perfect inverse correlation) to $+1$ (perfect positive correlation).

Table 4-5. *Wage and Income Percentiles*

1986 dollars

Percentile	Hourly wage at 20	Hourly wage at 49	Hourly wage at 79	Annual income[a]	Lifetime income[b]
10	3.12	4.00	2.75	4,674	409,468
20	4.22	5.35	3.67	6,264	508,570
30	4.99	6.30	4.44	8,642	610,769
40	5.49	7.32	5.08	10,825	688,923
50	6.17	8.98	5.88	14,725	754,721
60	7.22	10.93	6.59	19,015	823,529
70	8.33	13.04	7.76	24,217	925,648
80	9.67	15.72	8.82	29,650	1,043,201
90	12.23	19.80	11.71	40,750	1,287,714

a. Average of annual income plus transfers of head and spouse.
b. Average of lifetime labor endowments of head and spouse.

bility and classification issues. For the percentiles that define decile categories, table 4-5 shows age-specific wage rates, transfer-augmented annual household incomes, and average household lifetime incomes. We sort individuals according to these categories and perform cross tabulations.

We address mobility across wage categories in tables 4-6 and 4-7. In table 4-6 we compare wage-at-20 deciles with wage-at-49 deciles. The first row shows that, of those in the lowest wage-at-20 decile, 72 percent remain in the lowest wage-at-49 decile. Note that many individuals do change their cohort-specific ranking, especially those individuals in the middle of the wage distribution.[28] Only 35.1 percent of individuals remain in the same decile when middle aged as when young. A similar story is told in table 4-7, which compares wage-at-49 deciles with wage-at-79 deciles. Only 30.6 percent of individuals are in the same decile when old as when middle aged. The finding that individuals change their rankings as they age suggests another difference between the lifetime and annual income distributions.

The cross tabulation shown in table 4-8 is our most direct comparison of annual and lifetime income categories. In this table we compare deciles of transfer-augmented, household annual incomes with deciles for average

28. In these cross tabulations, decile 1 is always the poorest decile, and decile 10 is the richest. We show row percentages, with the weighted number of observations in parentheses. We wish to stress that these tables do not illustrate mobility within the full distribution of wages, but only mobility within the distribution associated with one's age group. For example, someone in the top 10 percent of the "wage-at-20" decile is in the top 10 percent of all 20 year-olds, not the top 10 percent of all individuals. Rank changes within an age cohort are likely to be small relative to rank changes within the entire population. Even with no rank changes within an age cohort, individuals would still move across the full wage distribution as long as age-wage profiles are not flat.

Table 4-6. *Wage-at-20 Decile by Wage-at-49 Decile*[a]

Wage-at-20 decile	Wage-at-49 decile									
	1	2	3	4	5	6	7	8	9	10
1	*72.3* (2,081)	16.9 (485)	5.8 (168)	3.8 (109)	...	1.2 (35)	...	...	...	...
2	17.6 (519)	*49.4* (1,461)	6.7 (198)	16.5 (489)	5.5 (164)	1.4 (41)	2.8 (83)	...	...	...
3	4.7 (136)	19.3 (564)	*40.5* (1,182)	2.1 (60)	25.5 (745)	7.2 (211)	0.7 (19)	...	...	...
4	4.7 (101)	8.0 (173)	37.2 (803)	*20.6* (445)	9.3 (200)	17.3 (373)	1.3 (29)	...	1.5 (33)	...
5	1.8 (67)	0.9 (33)	4.5 (165)	49.8 (1,826)	*12.9* (474)	19.4 (712)	9.6 (353)	1.0 (35)	...	...
6	...	2.3 (67)	1.8 (53)	11.2 (324)	23.1 (671)	*13.5* (393)	37.8 (1,097)	7.1 (206)	1.2 (34)	2.0 (57)
7	...	1.2 (34)	...	2.5 (73)	15.5 (454)	12.4 (365)	*10.7* (314)	44.3 (1,301)	12.3 (360)	1.2 (34)
8	...	...	...	1.2 (34)	4.8 (141)	23.9 (704)	9.7 (286)	*26.0* (765)	31.7 (932)	2.7 (80)
9	...	...	...	...	2.6 (77)	1.2 (34)	23.9 (702)	8.5 (249)	*38.9* (1,141)	24.9 (729)
10	...	...	...	...	...	2.3 (68)	1.2 (34)	12.3 (360)	14.7 (431)	*69.5* (2,033)

a. Percent of each wage-at-20 decile falling in the various wage-at-49 deciles; weighted number of observations in parentheses; diagonal italicized.

Table 4-7. *Wage-at-49 Decile by Wage-at-79 Decile*[a]

Wage-at-49 decile	Wage-at-79 decile									
	1	2	3	4	5	6	7	8	9	10
1	*63.6* (1,846)	11.4 (330)	9.0 (261)	6.0 (175)	5.0 (144)	...	2.3 (67)	1.6 (46)	1.2 (35)	...
2	21.4 (604)	*35.8* (1,009)	24.6 (694)	10.5 (295)	4.8 (136)	...	2.8 (79)	...	...	...
3	5.8 (150)	23.4 (601)	*13.2* (340)	19.1 (490)	10.2 (262)	17.9 (460)	1.4 (37)	7.8 (200)	1.1 (29)	...
4	5.6 (189)	10.7 (359)	18.9 (635)	*6.7* (225)	38.9 (1,307)	11.5 (388)	4.4 (147)	2.3 (76)	1.0 (34)	...
5	1.3 (39)	14.7 (431)	15.6 (456)	17.1 (501)	*13.9* (406)	15.3 (448)	12.6 (368)	2.8 (82)	6.7 (195)	...
6	2.4 (70)	5.0 (146)	12.4 (363)	9.8 (289)	24.0 (705)	*8.6* (253)	19.0 (557)	15.0 (441)	1.4 (40)	2.5 (72)
7	...	1.1 (33)	3.9 (114)	3.3 (95)	16.6 (483)	28.6 (833)	*20.2* (590)	11.6 (339)	12.4 (363)	2.3 (67)
8	...	...	2.0 (57)	2.7 (80)	3.5 (101)	16.8 (489)	24.8 (722)	*25.6* (746)	17.9 (521)	6.9 (200)
9	...	...	...	1.2 (34)	3.3 (98)	1.3 (37)	8.9 (262)	27.0 (790)	*43.6* (1,279)	14.7 (431)
10	...	...	...	...	0.8 (23)	1.2 (34)	...	9.2 (269)	14.5 (425)	*74.4* (2,182)

a. Percent of each wage-at-49 decile falling in the various wage-at-79 deciles; weighted number of observations in parentheses; diagonal italicized.

Table 4-8. *Annual-Income-Plus-Transfers Decile by Lifetime Income Decile*[a]

Annual-plus-transfers decile	Lifetime decile									
	1	2	3	4	5	6	7	8	9	10
1	*40.3* (1,166)	12.9 (374)	9.5 (275)	13.9 (403)	14.3 (415)	2.3 (68)	3.7 (108)	...	...	3.0 (86)
2	18.3 (532)	*16.2* (471)	14.9 (432)	2.3 (66)	6.3 (184)	11.4 (332)	10.6 (308)	10.8 (314)	7.9 (228)	1.2 (34)
3	14.8 (432)	24.8 (724)	*14.7* (430)	8.2 (238)	9.1 (264)	9.9 (290)	...	8.1 (236)	3.9 (115)	6.4 (188)
4	9.6 (279)	17.1 (498)	10.0 (293)	7.4 (216)	5.8 (170)	17.0 (497)	10.6 (310)	9.5 (276)	6.8 (200)	6.2 (181)
5	5.7 (166)	22.8 (661)	18.2 (530)	12.6 (366)	9.7 (283)	6.8 (198)	10.4 (303)	6.1 (176)	5.3 (154)	2.3 (68)
6	3.6 (106)	4.1 (122)	17.3 (512)	24.9 (737)	21.7 (644)	7.8 (230)	8.1 (241)	2.4 (72)	7.8 (232)	2.3 (68)
7	2.4 (71)	1.6 (46)	12.6 (364)	22.2 (642)	14.6 (423)	11.5 (334)	8.6 (250)	8.7 (252)	9.2 (268)	8.6 (248)
8	2.3 (66)	1.8 (53)	...	3.0 (86)	9.4 (275)	17.9 (521)	27.1 (790)	*26.3* (766)	12.2 (354)	...
9	2.4 (71)	...	1.3 (39)	6.0 (175)	9.3 (272)	12.0 (350)	17.0 (497)	21.1 (617)	*20.4* (597)	10.4 (304)
10	...	...	...	...	...	2.4 (72)	5.2 (156)	6.2 (184)	27.0 (805)	*59.1* (1,759)

a. Percent of annual-income-plus-transfers decile in the various lifetime income deciles; weighted number of observations in parentheses; diagonal italicized.

household lifetime incomes.[29] The former categorization is the one used by Pechman and Okner (1974), and the latter is the one we use in examining lifetime tax burdens. The first row shows that, of those in the poorest annual income decile, 14.3 percent have lifetime income in the fifth decile, and 3.0 percent have lifetime income in the tenth decile. In general, we find that only 21.1 percent of individuals are in the same annual and lifetime income categories, and only 46.1 percent are in annual and lifetime categories within plus-or-minus-one of each other. If we define "poor" to be in the bottom 30 percent of the population, and "rich" to be in the top 30 percent, then 13.8 percent of the annually poor are lifetime rich. An explanation is provided by the hump-shaped nature of the age-wage profile, which gives many lifetime-rich individuals relatively low annual incomes when they are very young or very old. In contrast, not as many annually rich are lifetime poor; only 2.6 percent of those in the top three annual deciles are in the bottom three lifetime deciles.[30] Table 4-8 makes it clear that classification by annual income and lifetime income are very different. Thus studies examining tax burdens across annual income categories provide little insight into the question of lifetime tax incidence.

The lifetime income measure used in the above comparison is the average household value of lifetime labor endowments before taxes and transfers. It is this before-government measure that we use to sort individuals into lifetime income categories. Since we also estimate initial-stage tax and transfer functions, shown earlier in tables 4-2 and 4-3, we can examine how government taxes and cash transfers affect the lifetime income distribution. For each of our 858 individuals, we construct an age-tax profile and an age-transfer profile, based on that individual's observed taxes and transfers for the years 1970–87, and on an individual-specific effect and demographic characteristics for the out-of-sample years. We then can compute net lifetime income (according to equation 4-2) both for the individual and as an average for the household.

On the basis of the generated tax and transfer profiles, we find that taxes and transfers reduce the variability of lifetime incomes to a slight extent, but this redistribution does little to change lifetime rankings. To see the effect on

29. We also performed cross-tab analysis of before-tax-and-transfer annual incomes with our lifetime income measure and found similar results. That is, the large differences we find in table 4-8 between the annual and lifetime categories are not dependent on the fact that the annual measure includes transfers while the lifetime measure does not.

30. If we define "rich" and "poor" in a more extreme way as the top 10 percent and bottom 10 percent, respectively, then 3.0 percent of the annually poor are lifetime rich, and none of the annually rich are lifetime poor.

Table 4-9. *Gross Lifetime Income Decile by Net Lifetime Income Decile*[a]

Gross lifetime decile	Net lifetime decile									
	1	2	3	4	5	6	7	8	9	10
1	*83.0* (2,399)	15.7 (454)	1.2 (36)	...	...	...	...	...	...	...
2	15.0 (443)	*65.2* (1,924)	19.7 (582)	...	...	...	...	...	...	...
3	...	16.7 (479)	*67.7* (1,946)	15.7 (450)	...	...	...	...	...	...
4	2.5 (72)	...	13.5 (396)	*61.2* (1,792)	22.8 (669)	...	...	...	...	...
5	...	...	...	19.6 (574)	*49.3* (1,444)	29.2 (857)	1.9 (55)	...	...	...
6	...	...	...	1.1 (31)	25.3 (732)	*55.4* (1,601)	18.3 (528)	...	...	...
7	...	...	...	2.3 (68)	2.4 (70)	14.7 (437)	*62.9* (1,863)	17.7 (525)	...	...
8	...	...	...	...	...	1.0 (30)	16.2 (469)	*69.1* (2,000)	13.6 (394)	...
9	...	...	...	...	...	...	...	14.6 (430)	*80.3* (2,371)	5.1 (152)
10	...	...	...	...	...	...	...	...	5.2 (154)	*94.8* (2,782)

a. Percent of before-government lifetime income decile in the various after-government lifetime income deciles; weighted number of observations in parentheses; diagonal italicized.

variability, refer back to table 4-4 and compare lifetime incomes before government with those after government. In the bottom two rows, for example, the average lifetime income of households has a coefficient of variation of 0.456 before government, and 0.403 after government.[31] We show the effect of government on lifetime rankings in table 4-9, which presents a cross tabulation of average household before-tax-and-transfer lifetime income deciles with average household after-tax-and-transfer lifetime income deciles. The table reveals that government sometimes changes the position of an individual in the lifetime income distribution, but not to a significant extent; 68.8 percent of individuals are in the same decile after government as before government, and 98.9 percent are within plus-or-minus-one.[32] Therefore, while government taxes and cash transfers may be bringing lifetime incomes closer together, these programs do not appear to lead to significant amounts of "leap-frogging" in the lifetime categories.

Characteristics and Profiles by Lifetime Income Category

Our final task in this chapter is to split our sample of individuals into before-tax-and-transfer lifetime income categories and estimate category-specific wage, tax, and transfer profiles. These category-specific profiles are used to set parameters for the lifetime incidence model. The decile categories were shown earlier in table 4-5. In addition, we split the top and bottom lifetime deciles into the most extreme 2 percent and the next 8 percent.[33]

Some characteristics of the individuals in the various lifetime income categories are shown in table 4-10. The number of observations, "#obser.," corresponds to the number of person-years, based on actual data (not constructed observations). These samples are used to generate the final wage, tax, and transfer functions by lifetime income category. The characteristics shown in the table are (in order): the proportion white, proportion female, average educational attainment, proportion married, average hourly wage rate, average taxes paid, average cash transfers received, and average before-government lifetime income. The table reveals significant demographic vari-

31. We take a closer look at the effect of taxes and transfers on the value of lifetime incomes later in this chapter, using the final regression functions by lifetime income category.

32. We get a very similar matrix if we cross-tabulate individual before-government deciles with individual after-government deciles.

33. The value of lifetime income corresponding to the 98th percentile is (in 1986 dollars) $1,893,840. The value corresponding to the 2d percentile is $245,931.

Table 4-10. *Characteristics of Lifetime Income Categories*[a]

Category	Percentiles	Observations[b]	Percent white	Percent female	Average education (years)	Percent married	Average (1986 dollars)			Lifetime income
							Hourly wage	Taxes	Transfers	
1	0–2	162 (5,714)	91.1	62.2	9.980	54.9	2.794	692.89	943.34	207,631
2	2–10	745 (24,158)	87.4	43.6	10.006	66.0	4.882	975.88	670.04	353,684
3	10–20	919 (30,772)	95.6	42.5	11.166	84.9	6.458	1,245.92	541.02	464,743
4	20–30	1,158 (36,711)	90.5	45.0	11.232	80.7	8.000	1,974.55	326.51	561,976
5	30–40	1,178 (38,844)	95.5	42.3	12.432	83.1	9.437	2,689.70	347.96	650,656
6	40–50	1,115 (35,250)	91.0	42.7	11.798	85.6	10.356	2,520.85	296.62	725,504
7	50–60	1,093 (38,811)	93.6	42.3	12.771	91.3	11.076	3,278.83	236.57	785,160
8	60–70	1,146 (37,668)	99.9	36.5	12.457	94.6	12.978	4,492.76	164.45	871,752
9	70–80	1,116 (39,296)	92.3	38.9	13.266	90.2	14.275	4,868.02	48.82	980,333
10	80–90	1,170 (38,116)	96.2	34.2	14.181	88.7	17.138	6,495.19	108.04	1,148,530
11	90–98	844 (30,853)	89.4	39.5	15.258	79.0	21.471	9,486.90	158.38	1,496,298
12	98–100	224 (8,694)	100.0	35.4	15.604	85.3	36.577	31,448.43	5.20	2,140,294
All	0–100	10,870 (364,887)	93.5	40.8	12.570	84.8	12.254	4,474.98	274.67	838,326

a. Based on actual data only.　　b. Actual and weighted (in parentheses) number of observations.

ation across these categories. The lifetime poorest are disproportionately non-white, female, and single. Category 1 is 91.1 percent white, 62.2 percent female, and 54.9 percent married. The corresponding figures for the overall sample are 93.5 percent white, 40.8 percent female, and 84.8 percent married. These differences reflect the prevalence of poverty among female-headed, minority households.

In general, as lifetime income increases, the percentage female decreases. The table shows no general racial pattern across the lifetime income categories, but we note that the very richest are entirely white. Education is clearly an important determinant of lifetime incomes; most of those in the top lifetime income decile have college degrees.[34] Table 4-10 also shows that wage rates and taxes increase with lifetime incomes, and cash transfers generally decrease. Moreover, it shows significant differences between the extreme 2 percent and next 8 percent at either end of the lifetime income distribution, in terms of demographic characteristics, wages, taxes, and transfers.

Age alone characterizes the changes in wages, taxes, and transfers for the final regressions in each lifetime income category. We find these life-cycle effects by performing simple ordinary-least-squares estimation of the relevant dependent variable as a function of a constant term and age variables only. For each lifetime income category, a single function is estimated on a sample which includes both heads and spouses.[35]

Wage Functions by Lifetime Income Category

As with the initial wage regression noted earlier, the logarithm of the real wage rate is specified as the dependent variable, and any observations of zero wages are discarded. Regression results by lifetime income category are shown in table 4-11, and these coefficients feed directly into our simulation model.

Plots of some of the age-wage profiles are shown in figure 4-2.[36] The figure indicates that as lifetime income increases, the peakedness of the age-wage

---

34. The education variable measures years of education, so that twelve years is a high school education, and anything more than twelve implies at least some college education.

35. Given the mixed sample and the exclusion of any individual-specific effects, we expect the fit of these final regressions to be inferior to those associated with the initial regressions.

36. In the final wage, tax, and transfer regressions, we include only age and age^2 as regressors for the richest category, and leave out age^3, because this cubed term is highly insignificant relative to the other two terms.

Table 4-11. *Log Wage Regressions, by Lifetime Income Category*[a]

Category	Constant	Age	Age^2	Age^3	R^2
1	−4.082576	0.310038	−0.005853	3.40889E-05	0.05727
	(−5.863)	(7.904)	(8.154)	(7.986)	
2	0.706964	0.046364	−7.28798E-04	2.33421E-06	0.04211
	(3.820)	(3.967)	(−3.067)	(1.499)	
3	0.296617	0.071553	−9.53957E-04	2.58356E-06	0.03754
	(2.589)	(9.310)	(−5.808)	(2.304)	
4	0.672633	0.050278	−2.71207E-04	−3.62471E-06	0.06743
	(6.504)	(7.244)	(−1.819)	(−3.530)	
5	−0.025710	0.113048	−0.001843	9.03842E-06	0.02283
	(−0.201)	(13.395)	(−10.317)	(7.460)	
6	1.486836	0.009928	5.25283E-04	−7.82526E-06	0.04779
	(13.276)	(1.289)	(3.109)	(−6.592)	
7	3.284857	−0.096775	0.002632	−2.14033E-05	0.02532
	(27.155)	(−11.878)	(14.980)	(−17.561)	
8	1.316894	0.047561	−5.76748E-04	1.88653E-06	0.02439
	(10.910)	(5.863)	(−3.289)	(1.545)	
9	1.365456	0.054796	−7.92875E-04	3.79806E-06	0.02770
	(9.535)	(5.404)	(−3.424)	(2.218)	
10	0.345638	0.123182	−0.001993	1.01555E-05	0.04052
	(2.400)	(12.235)	(−8.781)	(6.148)	
11	1.167055	0.091436	−0.001464	7.33255E-06	0.01559
	(7.914)	(9.757)	(−7.588)	(5.708)	
12	1.231150	0.094781	−0.001016	b	0.01429
	(6.385)	(11.259)	(−11.315)		

a. Numbers in parentheses are *t*-statistics.
b. Not included in regression.

profile increases. This suggests that individuals from higher lifetime income categories must engage in more saving in order to smooth their consumption. On the other hand, it is not just the sharpness of the peak, but also the timing that matters. If individuals desire a smooth consumption path that rises with age, less saving is required for those whose wage peak occurs later. Our age-wage profiles indicate that as lifetime income increases across these categories, the peak age first rises and then falls.[37] This timing characteristic

37. The wages peak at the following ages, in ascending order of lifetime categories: 42, 39, 46, 47, 47, 53, 54, 57, 64, 50, 50, and 47. Because the higher lifetime income categories have higher average education levels (see table 4-10), human capital theory would suggest that the lifetime rich should show later peaks in wages. We do not get a uniformly increasing trend. One explanation might be that we are picking up a lot of cross-sectional rather than longitudinal variation. If we were to follow a given individual throughout her lifetime, with positive economic growth her wages might peak at a later age than shown in these profiles. Furthermore, if produc-

Figure 4-2. *Wage Profiles, Selected Groups*

Wage (1984 dollars per hour)

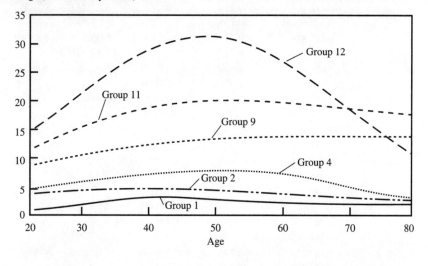

Age

works to increase the savings of lifetime poor and rich individuals relative to middle-income individuals. We later find that both the peakedness and the timing of the wage peak have significant effects on the lifetime incidence of capital-based taxes.

Tax Functions by Lifetime Income Category

As with the initial tax function estimates, the final-stage tax estimates are based on a sample with all actual observations, including those with zero taxes. These tax coefficients, shown in table 4-12, are also included in the general equilibrium model. Plots of some of the age-tax profiles are presented in figures 4-3 and 4-4. The tax profiles are more peaked for the higher lifetime income categories, and figure 4-4 shows a huge difference between the profile for the richest category (12) and the profile for the second-richest category (11). The differences in the peakedness and timing of the peaks are similar to

---

tivity increases affect higher lifetime income individuals more than lower lifetime income individuals, the longitudinal profiles of the higher categories may indeed peak later than those of lower categories, even if the cross sections appear as in figure 4-2. Another possible explanation is that we estimate a wage profile for a sample that includes both heads and spouses. The wage rates of secondary earners are less likely to be correlated with educational levels.

Table 4-12. *Tax Regressions, by Lifetime Income Category*[a]

Category	Constant	Age	Age²	Age³	R²
1	−2,641.108	39.214	2.06783	−0.028269	0.02335
	(−0.928)	(0.245)	(0.705)	(−1.620)	
2	−1,485.826	110.613	−1.05173	−0.001811	0.03740
	(−3.623)	(4.270)	(−1.997)	(−0.525)	
3	625.203	−58.106	3.43873	−0.037905	0.06592
	(1.965)	(−2.723)	(7.539)	(−12.174)	
4	3,381.849	−273.668	9.39272	−0.085443	0.04918
	(6.684)	(−8.059)	(12.880)	(−17.008)	
5	−12,215.866	981.298	−19.39109	0.115467	0.01906
	(−11.095)	(13.480)	(−12.584)	(11.049)	
6	812.576	−90.675	6.44351	−0.073521	0.10406
	(1.904)	(3.090)	(10.007)	(−16.252)	
7	−3,367.044	249.184	−0.89416	−0.024278	0.07172
	(−6.174)	(6.784)	(−1.129)	(−4.418)	
8	2,445.158	−217.418	10.25860	−0.096496	0.04895
	(2.382)	(−3.154)	(6.882)	(−9.293)	
9	−8,342.854	669.873	−10.35869	0.048870	0.02637
	(7.189)	(8.152)	(−5.520)	(3.521)	
10	−10,015.682	543.373	−0.57972	−0.062082	0.04437
	(−5.486)	(4.258)	(−0.202)	(−2.965)	
11	−18,112.118	1,111.360	−10.74730	5.395E-04	0.03409
	(−6.986)	(6.746)	(−3.169)	(0.024)	
12	−154,268.666	8,495.655	−93.30653	[b]	0.04704
	(−15.621)	(19.705)	(−20.287)		

a. Numbers in parentheses are *t*-statistics.
b. Not included in regression.

the differences seen with the wage profiles, because these taxes apply to labor income.

Transfer Functions by Lifetime Income Category

Regression results by category are shown in table 4-13 for age-transfer profiles. Figures 4-5 and 4-6 plot these profiles for several of the categories. Again, the sample includes all actual observations of transfers, including zero observations. Transfers are very large in old age for all lifetime income categories, because of social security payments. Only the lifetime poor see significant transfers when young.[38]

38. The fit of these final transfer regressions is much better than that associated with the final wage or tax functions, because the value of transfers to a head and spouse of the same household

Figure 4-3. *Low-Income Tax Profiles, Groups 1, 2, 4*

Tax paid (thousands of 1984 dollars)

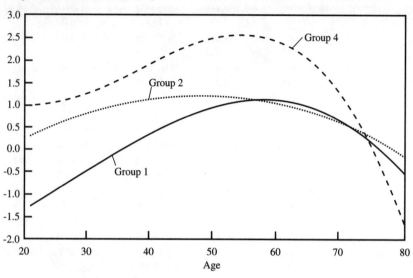

Figure 4-4. *High-Income Tax Profiles, Groups 9, 11, 12*

Tax paid (thousands of 1984 dollars)

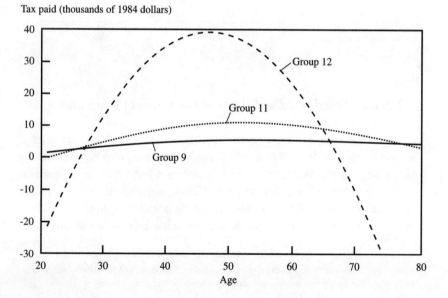

Table 4-13. *Transfer Regressions, by Lifetime Income Category*

Category	Constant	Age	Age^2	Age^3	R^2
1	18,164.292 (18.579)	−1,101.140 (−19.994)	20.5852 (20.422)	−0.117346 (−19.578)	0.38397
2	−2,893.073 (−8.643)	245.599 (11.618)	−6.6828 (−15.549)	0.060451 (21.463)	0.36222
3	−8,634.239 (37.593)	682.657 (44.298)	−16.9751 (−51.545)	0.136497 (60.712)	0.40204
4	−6,006.255 (−38.802)	491.814 (47.342)	−12.8524 (−57.607)	0.108472 (70.577)	0.49455
5	−5,934.446 (−37.277)	475.504 (45.175)	−12.1915 (−54.718)	0.101251 (67.003)	0.49204
6	−5,891.416 (−38.092)	494.390 (46.492)	−13.2125 (−56.626)	0.113406 (69.183)	0.49742
7	−8,596.039 (−52.769)	688.454 (62.746)	−17.6500 (−74.592)	0.145486 (88.639)	0.50355
8	−13,567.821 (−78.327)	1,056.744 (90.777)	−26.1865 (−104.078)	0.207892 (118.622)	0.52336
9	−4,252.603 (−36.970)	340.856 (41.849)	−8.7625 (−47.108)	0.072494 (52.701)	0.16280
10	−12,561.875 (−91.872)	989.103 (103.473)	−24.8874 (−115.496)	0.200663 (127.945)	0.50291
11	−8,448.799 (−40.946)	651.563 (49.691)	−16.1451 (−59.819)	0.129123 (71.838)	0.46763
12	366.288 (18.713)	−17.450 (−20.422)	0.20038 (21.982)	b	0.07112

a. Numbers in parentheses are *t*-statistics.
b. Not included in regression.

Lifetime Distributional Effects of Government Programs

Earlier we examined how government alters the lifetime income rankings of individuals. We found lifetime rankings were not significantly affected by the tax and transfer system. This finding does not imply that these programs fail to redistribute income, but only that lifetime-poor individuals do not jump over some of the lifetime rich. The remaining question is, how does the tax and transfer system affect the levels of lifetime incomes for the different life-

---

is the same. With wages and taxes, a spouse can have a low wage and low labor income taxes but be placed in a high lifetime income category if the head has a high wage.

Figure 4-5. *Low-Income Transfer Profiles, Groups 1, 2, 4*

Transfers received (thousands of 1984 dollars)

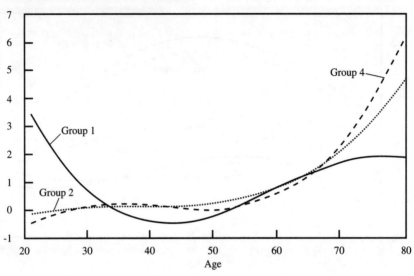

Figure 4-6. *High-Income Transfer Profiles, Groups 9, 11, 12*

Transfers received (thousands of 1984 dollars)

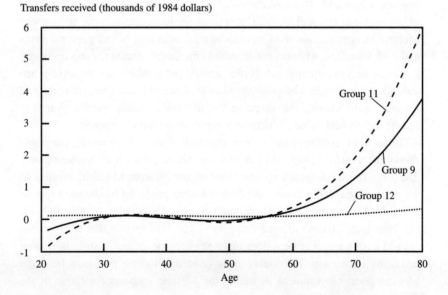

Figure 4-7.   *Net and Gross Income Profiles, Groups 1, 2, 4*

Thousands of 1984 dollars

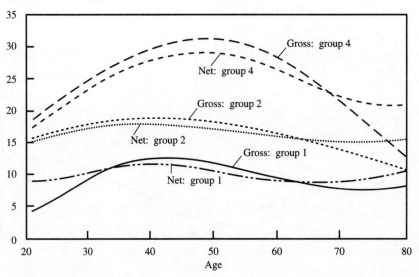

time income categories? We use the final wage, tax, and transfer functions to address this issue.

We get a general picture of the redistribution by plotting lifetime income profiles before and after government. Figures 4-7 and 4-8 illustrate the effect of government tax and transfer programs on life-cycle income for various lifetime income categories. Gross income is measured before personal taxes and cash transfers, whereas net income is measured after taxes and transfers. For most lifetime income categories, annual net transfers are negative when individuals are young and positive when they are old. Government taxes and transfers help smooth the shape of the life-cycle income profile, but they reduce the present value of lifetime income for all but the poorest.

Table 4-14 confirms the stories obtained from the pictures. The table shows the value of gross and net lifetime incomes for each lifetime income category. These computations are based on the estimated lifetime profiles of wages, personal labor taxes, and cash transfers produced by the final regressions. In this interpretation, these numbers describe a representative individual from each lifetime income category. Table 4-14 reveals that the personal tax and cash transfer system does make the lifetime income distribution more equal, by taking larger amounts away from the lifetime rich than from the lifetime poor. Government increases the lifetime incomes for those in the

Figure 4-8. *Net and Gross Income Profiles, Groups 9, 11, 12*

Thousands of 1984 dollars

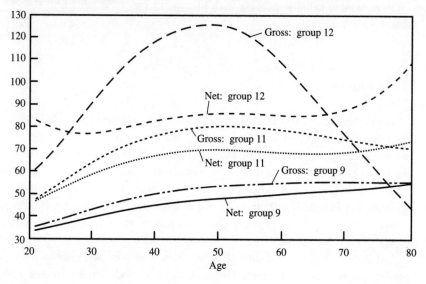

Table 4-14. *Effect of Government on Lifetime Income, by Pre-Tax-and-Transfer Lifetime Income Category*

1986 dollars

Lifetime income category (percentile)	Gross lifetime income	Net lifetime income	Percent change
1(0–2)	196,025	217,014	10.7
2(2–10)	365,520	354,636	−2.98
3(10–20)	447,310	433,053	−3.19
4(20–30)	543,852	514,815	−5.34
5(30–40)	613,736	564,656	−8.00
6(40–50)	704,084	664,877	−5.57
7(50–60)	789,441	734,796	−6.92
8(60–70)	885,365	813,796	−8.08
9(70–80)	1,000,570	910,945	−8.96
10(80–90)	1,129,236	1,028,153	−8.95
11(90–98)	1,450,702	1,305,097	−10.0
12(98–100)	2,041,648	1,734,117	−15.1

poorest category by more than 10 percent, and decreases lifetime incomes for the richest by more than 15 percent.[39] Although net taxes as a percentage of lifetime income usually increase with lifetime income, the table also shows that this increase is uneven.

Conclusion

In this part of our study, we determined lifetime income categories from a representative sample of U.S. individuals, and for each of these categories, we estimated the age profiles of wages, taxes, and transfers. We then incorporated these functions into the lifetime incidence model.

We also wanted to examine how lifetime income distributions may differ from annual income distributions. If these differences are large, the lifetime perspective may provide answers quite different from those of the standard annual tax incidence study.

Initial, economy-wide estimates of the wage functions were necessary to predict wages for out-of-sample years, so that each individual's lifetime income could be computed. We chose to estimate separate functions for heads and spouses and to incorporate individual-specific constant terms. Our estimated regressions describe the real wage rate as a function of age and other observable demographic characteristics, as well as unobservable, individual-specific characteristics. Along with the initial wage regressions, we also estimated fixed-effects tax and transfer functions. Although these functions were not necessary for categorizing individuals, they allowed us to generate tax and transfer profiles and discuss the net effect of government on lifetime incomes.

After using the initial wage functions to fill in any missing data, we computed the present value of labor endowments for each individual. We then assigned each individual to a lifetime income category according to his or her household's average present value of labor endowments. This average of the labor endowments of head and spouse is our notion of "lifetime income" and our measure of an individual's lifetime ability to pay. We cross-tabulated gross and net lifetime incomes and found that government programs do little

---

39. However, these are partial equilibrium calculations for personal taxes only. Here we ignore the possible redistributive effects of other types of taxes as well as government spending, and we do not account for any general equilibrium effects on the income distribution. The results generated from our lifetime incidence model will provide a more complete story.

to alter the lifetime categories of individuals. Taxes and transfers do, however, reduce the inequality in the lifetime income distribution, at least slightly.

We found some interesting differences between the annual and lifetime income distributions. We saw that lifetime income distributions are more equal than annual ones. Much of the higher variability among annual incomes is due to life-cycle variation in incomes. We found that the annual and lifetime income measures are not well correlated and that annual income classifications are very different from lifetime income classifications. In particular, many of the annually poor enjoy high lifetime incomes. Such a finding implies that annual categorization may badly misclassify individuals in terms of lifetime well-being.

We examined some characteristics of the various lifetime income categories and found that the lifetime poor are disproportionately single, female, and nonwhite. Educational attainment and lifetime incomes appear to be highly correlated. The characteristics also show that the extreme tails of the lifetime income distribution are very different from the rest of the population, which reinforces our reasons to split the top and bottom lifetime income deciles in our analysis.

Next, we reestimated the wage, tax, and transfer functions for each of the twelve lifetime income categories, to establish new parameters for our general equilibrium model. We found that wage profiles are more peaked over the life cycle for individuals with higher lifetime incomes. The tax profiles reflect these wage profiles to a large extent. The transfer profiles are similar across the lifetime income categories, and they clearly display a concentration of transfers to the elderly.

Finally, we examined the extent of lifetime income redistribution attributable to government taxes and cash transfers, using our final estimates of tax and transfer profiles by category. Plots of gross and net lifetime incomes revealed that, for most people, net transfers are negative when young and positive when old. When we computed the values of net and gross lifetime incomes, we found that government taxes and cash transfers reduce lifetime incomes for all but the poorest lifetime income category. Because net taxes are a higher percentage of lifetime income for the lifetime rich, government has a small equalizing effect on the lifetime income distribution. Chapter 7 analyzes these redistributions in a general equilibrium setting.

CHAPTER FIVE

Consumption Patterns by Age

THE LIFETIME incidence model groups individuals by present value of lifetime income and several other characteristics. The twelve groups differ not only by capital inheritances and the present value of labor endowments but also by the time paths of wages, taxes, and transfers. For example, as seen in chapter 4, the age-wage profile is much steeper for the lifetime rich than for the lifetime poor. Thus changes in relative factor returns, induced by tax policy, will affect groups differently on the sources side. In this chapter we recognize that groups may differ also by consumption patterns. Thus changes in the relative prices of goods, induced by tax policy, will affect groups differently on the uses side.

Previous models have used the observed consumption patterns of different groups of households to solve backward for the expenditure-share parameters of Cobb-Douglas utility functions. Different consumption patterns therefore imply different utility functions. A problem with this specification is that rich and poor individuals differ not just by the amount of income but in more fundamental respects: even if the poor had more income, they would still behave like poor individuals. Instead, we use a *single* utility function for all individuals in the model. Composite consumption is a Stone-Geary function (equation 2-8). Initial consumption patterns reflect the "minimum required purchases" (*b*), and additional disposable income is spent according to a different pattern of marginal expenditure shares (β). Rich and poor are the same kind of person but purchase different consumption bundles because they have different incomes. We thus avoid the problem of different utility functions while still capturing differential tax burdens on the uses side.

We also capture observed expenditure differences among age groups. That is, the parameters *b* and β depend on age, even though all individuals have the same lifetime utility function. Young people, for example, spend larger fractions of their incomes on alcohol and recreation than older people do. We specify seventeen consumption goods in the lifetime incidence model.

126

Finally, outside the Stone-Geary composition of consumption goods, the labor-leisure trade-off also depends on age. The elderly in the model have a stronger preference for leisure over consumption goods, relative to younger individuals. These leisure-consumption patterns can differ across lifetime income categories as well. Because minimum purchases are required for consumption goods but not leisure, the lifetime poor end up spending larger fractions of their total income on consumer goods than on leisure.

Ideally, in describing differences in consumption patterns across age and lifetime income categories, we would like to have data on consumption for the individuals tracked on the Panel Study of Income Dynamics. Then we would be able to estimate directly any differences in consumed goods across the lifetime income categories constructed in chapter 4. The PSID, however, lacks any detailed consumption data and the available data on expenditures are not in panel form. For this reason, we estimate lifetime incomes using the PSID, but we estimate consumption patterns using a different data set, the Consumer Expenditure Survey.[1] This survey provides the necessary disaggregation by commodity, but it has no data on prices necessary to estimate more complicated functional forms.

Establishing parameters for the consumption-leisure choice is simple, as we show in chapter 6. Consumption pattern parameters, however, are econometrically estimated for a Stone-Geary utility function. We can estimate this from expenditures, without price data. In this chapter, we first discuss the linear expenditure system and outline our procedure. We then discuss the Consumer Expenditure Survey, the aggregation of detailed expenditures, some corrections for underreporting, and econometric procedures. Finally, we present our estimates of the consumption share parameters and minimum required purchases.

The Linear Expenditure System

Our goal is to determine, for each age category, parameters for allocating total consumption expenditures across different consumer goods. These parameters are estimated from CES data, for a Stone-Geary form of utility. The procedure we used to estimate these parameters is similar to A. Thomas King

---

1. To check the fit between these two data sets, one could use the PSID to tabulate available expenditures on particular items such as food and utilities and then compare results with those items from the CES data. This comparison could be based on annual income in both data sets, but lifetime income would be difficult to construct in the CES data.

(1979), except we estimate a full set of parameters for each of twelve age groups.[2] The Stone-Geary sub-utility function, in equation 2-8 of chapter 2, gives rise to demand behavior characterized by the following linear expenditure system (suppressing the age subscript):

$$(5\text{-}1) \qquad \exp_i = p_i c_i = p_i b_i + \beta_i \left(m - \sum_{j=1}^{17} p_j b_j \right),$$

where $\exp_i$ is the expenditure on consumption good i, p_i is the gross-of-tax price of good i, and c_i is the quantity of good i purchased. The individual's total expenditure on consumption, m, is the sum of the seventeen consumption good expenditures, $\sum_{j=1}^{17} \exp_j$. These actual expenditures include minimum requirements as well as discretionary purchases. The term in parentheses in equation 5-1 is discretionary consumption. Equation 2-9 of chapter 2 shows that discretionary consumption is equivalent to $\bar{p}\bar{c}$, the composite price times composite consumption. The parameters b_i and β_i describe the utility function, where b_i can be interpreted as a minimum required quantity of good i. Hence, the term $\sum_{j=1}^{17} p_j b_j$ represents the individual's total minimum required expenditure on all seventeen goods. The parameter β_i then represents the share of expenditures above this minimum that the individual allocates to good i.

This interpretation is useful, but it can also be misleading. In particular, the "minimum" quantities can be negative. The b_i are really just parameters that help characterize preferences in a more flexible manner. If the b_i are all zero, as in the Cobb-Douglas case, then indifference curves are all hyperbolas that asymptotically approach each axis. If the b_i of the good on the horizontal axis is positive, then all indifference curves are shifted to the right. If it is negative, then indifference curves are shifted to the left and may reach the vertical axis. Thus utility may be positive even if consumption of a particular good is zero. We check that no solutions involve negative consumption, but we use positive and negative estimates of b_i to best fit indifference curves within the positive quadrant.

The consumer expenditure survey has age, income, and expenditures on each good, but not prices or "discretionary income." Thus equation 5-1 cannot be estimated directly. It can be rearranged, however, to estimate

$$(5\text{-}2) \qquad \exp_{ih} = \kappa_{ih} + \beta_{ih} m_h + \varepsilon_{ih}, \qquad E(\varepsilon) = 0, E(\varepsilon^2) = \sigma^2,$$

2. The twelve age groups consist of five-year increments, beginning with 20–24 year-olds, and ending with people aged 75–79. We use t to index the sixty years of life, and h to index the twelve age groups.

where

$$(5\text{-}3) \qquad \kappa_{ih} = p_i b_{ih} - \beta_{ih} \sum_{j=1}^{17} p_j b_{jh}.$$

For each of the twelve age groups ($h = 1, \ldots, 12$), we use ordinary least squares (OLS) to estimate equation 5-2 for each of the seventeen consumer goods ($i = 1, \ldots, 17$). We thus perform 204 separate regressions. Estimates of β_{ih} are taken directly from the coefficients on m, and these estimates are used in equation 5-3 with the estimated κ_{ih} intercepts to solve for the b_{ih} (as described further below). The results provide 408 estimated parameters for utility.

This procedure requires several assumptions. First, it requires that the error term ε is uncorrelated with m_h, or estimates of β_{ih} will be biased. Second, it requires that all individuals face the same prices. Estimates may be biased, for example, if elderly individuals are concentrated in Florida and face prices that differ from those in other regions of the country. Third, we estimate a single set of preferences for each age group, as is consistent with our model.

In particular, we do not try to describe expenditures on particular goods as functions of demographic variables such as education and marital status. Since our model does not include those characteristics, we want only to capture differences in consumption patterns across age categories. Through the β_{ih}'s and b_{ih}'s, we also capture differences in consumption patterns across income levels.[3]

To obtain the b_{ih} from equation 5-3, we must address two problems. First, the equation uses only the product $p_i b_{ih}$, so the b_{ih} are not identified separately from the prices. This problem is easily handled with our adoption of the units convention. We define a unit of each commodity as the amount that costs one dollar. Then each expenditure amount represents a quantity, and all prices are 1, as in our benchmark equilibrium. Second, for each age group h, the seventeen equations given by equation 5-3 are not independent; since expenditure shares must sum to one, we have only sixteen independent equations. Yet we have seventeen unknowns (each of the $p_i b_{ih}$). This problem requires an additional identifying restriction.

For example, we could set the value of $\sum_{j=1}^{17} p_j b_{jh}$, the cost of the bundle

3. Of course, by directly capturing differences in consumption patterns across age and lifetime income categories, we indirectly capture differences associated with the other demographic variables. For example, lifetime income and education are highly correlated, and younger individuals are more likely to be single.

of minimum requirements. Since the β_{ih} and κ_{ih} have been estimated, equation 5-3 would then identify the seventeen different b_{ih}. Alternatively, we could set the value of just one of the $p_i b_{ih}$. In that case, the sum of minimum expenditures is determined. In his earlier estimation, King uses several different approaches. First, he computes an implied $\Sigma p_j b_j$ by setting the $p_i b_i$ for a good which he believes to have $p_i b_i = 0$ (alcoholic beverages). Second, he sets $p_i b_i$ for a good believed to have low positive $p_i b_i$ (financial services). Third, King tries using a reasonable own-price elasticity for one particular good (fuel) to compute the necessary implied value of the corresponding $p_i b_i$. All three cases yield a similar value for $\Sigma p_j b_j$, close to \$2,500 for 1973. So in the end, instead of setting one of the $p_i b_i$, he simply sets the sum of these equal to that intermediate value of \$2,500.

We also choose to set a plausible dollar figure for the sum of minimum required purchases. Our choice is $\sum_{j=1}^{17} p_d b_{jh}$ \$8,000, a reasonable figure relative to the income levels used in our model. In addition, this choice is approximately the same as King's value adjusted for growth and inflation.[4] This sum is assumed to be the same for individuals of all ages. We then use equation 5-3 to solve for the implied $p_i b_{ih}$ for each of the seventeen goods within each of the twelve age categories. The final step interprets each $p_i b_{ih}$ as the estimate of b_{ih}, assuming all consumers face the same price vectors and normalizing the quantities so that all prices equal one.

This procedure is applied to each consumer good for individuals in each of the twelve age groups. Thus two parameters for seventeen goods were estimated for the sub-utility function characterizing each age group (a total of $2 \times 17 \times 12$, or 408 parameters).

The Consumer Expenditure Survey

We use data from the 1984–85 CES. The data set consists of two parts. In a quarterly "Interview Survey," households provide information on their income and expenditures over the previous three months. A different sample

---

4. When the bundle of minimum required purchases costs \$8,000, some of our b_{ih} are slightly negative. As was discussed, negative b_{ih} are not a problem in our model so long as the total expenditures on each consumer good are positive. To obtain b_{ih} that are all nonnegative, we could set the smallest b_{ih} equal to zero. In this case, the sum of minimum required purchases would have to be greater than \$10,000. A problem then arises for the poorest income categories, because the present value of minimum required purchases over the lifetime exceeds the value of lifetime income. Thus we kept the sum of b_{ih} equal to \$8,000.

of households participate in a "Diary Survey," keeping very detailed records of purchases over a two-week period. The Interview Survey, which forms the primary basis for these estimations, relies on a rolling sample. During any quarter, about 25 percent of the respondents are interviewed about their expenditures for the first time, and this group is then interviewed for three additional quarters.[5]

To examine annual expenditure patterns, it is necessary to aggregate data from several quarters. We take two waves of households and follow each through four quarters (the complete cycle of interviews for each household). Our first wave was interviewed each quarter of 1984, and our second wave was interviewed from the second quarter of 1984 through the first quarter of 1985. We thus use five quarters of CES data. We then follow King's procedures in eliminating households with incomplete income reporting, less than a full year's participation, and those receiving food stamps. The final sample includes 1,629 households.

King also notes that some households report almost no expenditure on food or shelter. He believes these are elderly people dependent on other households, but he elects to include them as discrete consumer units on the grounds that they represent only a small proportion of the total observations. In our sample, these households account for less than 2 percent of the total. For consistency with earlier work, we include them as well.

The expenditure data in the CES are collected at the household level, but the rest of our model uses lifetime incomes and parameters for sub-utility functions that are defined at the individual level. To reconcile the expenditure data with the model specification, we divided the values derived from the CES data by the number of adults (those over 18 years of age) in the household. Thus each reference individual was attributed only a share of the household's total expenditures.[6]

---

5. The samples are overlapping; in any one quarter, some households are interviewed for the first time, and others are interviewed for the second, third, or fourth time.

6. This procedure does not adjust for economies of scale in household consumption. For an overview, see Deaton and Muellbauer (1980, pp. 192–213). This problem will not affect the β_{ih} coefficient in equation 5-2, however, since the amount of total expenditures for the individual, m_h, will still be the total of amounts spent on the different x_{ih}. That is, the shares of total expenditures will be unchanged when all expenditures are divided by the same number. On the other hand, the choice of the divisor does affect the estimate of the minimum required purchase, through its effect on the intercept κ_{ih} estimated in equation 5-2. If we underestimate the consumption of individuals when we divide household consumption by the number of adults (ignoring economies of scale), we will underestimate the b_{ih}'s. In other words, if there are economies of scale, our b_{ih}'s may be biased downward.

Aggregation of Detailed Expenditures

Although the CES provides aggregated information on expenditures for broad classes of consumption goods, these categories differ from the seventeen goods we defined in our study. Therefore the values for expenditures on each of our seventeen classes of consumption goods have to be aggregated from the detailed expenditures file of the Consumer Expenditure Survey. To allocate these detailed expenditures into our seventeen categories, we use table 3-10 in chapter 3 and the similar aggregation found in Ballard and others.[7] This list also forms the basis for the transition matrix that links these seventeen consumer goods to the nineteen producer goods.

We made the following modifications to reported expenditures for several of the seventeen commodity groups.

Financial Services

Households report a number of explicit expenditures on financial services (for example, financing charges and costs of safe deposit boxes), but financial institutions provide a number of other services without explicit charge. These costs are therefore not reported in the CES. Following King, an imputed value for these implicit financial service expenditures is assigned to each household. This imputed value is calculated, using the National Income and Product Accounts (NIPA) convention, as 0.03 times the household's financial assets (savings and checking accounts, stocks, and U.S. bonds reported for the last day of the month before the household's final interview). A large number of households failed to respond to questions concerning at least one category of their financial assets, so these have to be imputed based on family after-tax income.

Insurance costs are also included in financial services. Since households have some expected return on their insurance premiums, not all of these

7. The consumption categories defining King's fifteen commodities can be found in Ballard and others (1985, pp. 110–11). For the present seventeen categories, we separate medical care and education. Medical care includes four of the detailed categories previously grouped with services: "physicians," "dentists," "other professional medical services," and "privately controlled hospitals"; and two previously classed as nonfood nondurables: "drug preparations and sundries," and "ophthalmic products and orthopedic appliances." The education commodity includes detailed categories called: "private higher education," "private elementary and secondary education," and "other private eduation and research," all of which are included in the services commodity of King (1979) and Ballard and others (1985).

Table 5-1. *Average Annual Expenditure on Appliances, by Income and Family Size, 1984–85*

Income (dollars)	One or two members	Three or four members	Five or more members
Less than 6,000	120.12	237.86	319.66
6,000–11,999	167.33	225.79	93.86
12,000–17,999	219.80	211.20	150.54
18,000–23,999	339.81	199.20	219.74
24,000–29,999	365.66	263.33	283.61
30,000–35,999	312.93	347.99	378.31
36,000–47,999	612.37	400.44	314.38
48,000 and over	632.69	571.36	532.12

Source: Consumer Expenditure Survey.

should be counted as net expenditures. Again, according to the NIPA convention, 25 percent of insurance premiums are treated as net expenditures on insurance.

Durables

Households may purchase durable items infrequently, but they receive services from these items over longer periods. Thus reported expenditures on these goods largely reflect the timing of purchases rather than the actual consumption services of durables. To provide a better measure of the flow of services provided by each of these goods, we first tabulate average expenditure outlays by household income and certain other characteristics. The results of these tabulations are shown in tables 5-1 through 5-3.[8] The characteristics used for each durable are those noted in King's study, with some refinements. For appliances, in table 5-1, we group households according to annual income and family size. For furniture, in table 5-2, we distinguish among annual income categories, dwelling size (number of rooms), and whether the household owns or rents its housing. Finally, for motor vehicles, in table 5-3, we distinguish among annual income categories and the number of earners in the household. Then the tabulated average expenditure on that durable for a given cell is attributed to all individuals in that cell, as a proxy

8. For all households, we use the income and family characteristics reported during the household's final quarterly interview. The expenditures that form the basis of the tabulations are still divided by the number of adults in the household.

Table 5-2. *Average Annual Expenditure on Furniture, by Income, Tenure, and Number of Rooms, 1984–85*

Dollars

Income	Up to three rooms	Four or five rooms	Six or more rooms
	Owners		
Less than 6,000	452.34	177.66	268.73
6,000–11,999	210.43	134.54	238.78
12,000–17,999	157.78	134.32	219.64
18,000–23,999	671.23	357.75	208.30
24,000–29,999	239.80	226.32	284.78
30,000–35,999	332.95	332.38	346.69
36,000–47,999	1,187.69	443.72	399.13
48,000 and over	732.14	521.73	685.23
	Renters		
Less than 6,000	64.83	52.22	13.04
6,000–11,999	96.88	108.19	48.20
12,000–17,999	200.01	123.13	156.22
18,000–23,999	195.15	174.13	160.35
24,000–29,999	767.29	319.54	288.41
30,000–35,999	361.01	246.96	85.78
36,000–47,999	178.07	296.25	195.74
48,000 and over	74.00	437.60	120.98

Source: Consumer Expenditure Survey.

for expenditures on the flow of services provided by these durables. The motor vehicles figure is augmented by expenditures such as rentals and automobile repair and maintenance to obtain the total flow of services consumed from motor vehicles.[9]

Similar treatment was considered for durable components of the recreation category, such as boats, but these tabulations make sense only as a proxy for consumption flows if all households can be expected to purchase the durable at some time. Since this assumption did not seem appropriate for durable recreation goods, and since expenditures on these goods appear infrequently in the data, these costs were simply treated as direct outlays.

9. Expenditures on furniture and appliances are not augmented by extra rental or repair expenditures, for two reasons. First, as a result of the way the detailed categories are divided among commodities, automobile repair is included in the motor vehicles commodity, and furniture and appliance repair expenditures are included under services. Second, since rentals of furniture and appliances seem more likely to substitute for purchases, it seemed inappropriate to use these rentals as additions to durable purchases. Instead, rental expenditures for appliances and furniture are treated as separate expenditures in the tabulations.

Table 5-3. *Average Annual Expenditure on Motor Vehicles, by Income Group and Number of Earners, 1984–85*

Dollars

Income	No earners	One earner	Two or more earners
Less than 6,000	143.57	1,160.55	1,637.07
6,000–11,999	244.34	997.99	566.73
12,000–17,999	760.55	542.01	872.68
18,000–23,999	1,154.94	1,507.35	1,243.08
24,000–29,999	1,260.69	1,292.49	1,041.77
30,000–35,999	1,242.15	1,953.07	1,075.44
36,000–47,999	1,874.91	2,442.91	1,708.20
48,000 and over	1,892.99	2,582.47	1,730.78

Source: Consumer Expenditure Survey.

Shelter

Homeowners' expenditures on shelter are based on the rental equivalents for their houses, as calculated in the Consumer Expenditure Survey.[10] The CES reports several other categories that seem to be homeowner expenditures, such as property taxes, homeowner's insurance, and material costs for home repairs. For rental property, however, these expenditures would be paid by the landlord. The equilibrium rental price would cover the landlord's property taxes, insurance, and repairs. Thus the reported rental equivalents for homeowners should already incorporate an average of these costs. To avoid double counting, we ignore the homeowners' direct expenditures of this form.

Services

To correspond to the BEA definition of this category, we rely on quarterly data from the detailed expenditure files of the CES, and on values for contributions to religious, political, educational, and other organizations reported in the consumer unit's final quarterly interview in the "family" file.

Nonfood Nondurables

This commodity includes goods such as cleaning supplies, stationery, and pet food. Few expenditures in this category are included in the Interview

10. Although King reports that he has to impute this value for some homeowners, this value was available for virtually all homeowners in 1985. Thus no imputations were necessary for this analysis.

Survey; the CES primarily collects information on these purchases through the Diary Survey, which targets this type of high-frequency purchase. Unfortunately, a different sample of consumer units is used in the Diary Survey than in the Interview Survey, and there is no convincing way to link the two. We chose to tabulate expenditures by diary households according to their after-tax income, the age of the reference person, and family size for 1984. These expenditures are then attributed to the interview households in each cell. This procedure is also used for the "nonprescription drugs and sundries" component of the medical care commodity.

Corrections for Underreporting

Interviews for the Consumer Expenditure Survey require households to report expenditures on a large number of specific types of goods and services for the three-month period preceding the interview. Not surprisingly, analyses of the interview data suggest inaccurate reporting by households, especially underreporting of potentially sensitive expenditures such as tobacco and alcohol.[11] Raymond Gieseman (1987) compares recent CES reported totals with control totals from the Personal Expenditure Component of the NIPA. His results, summarized for 1984 in table 5-4, suggest underreporting for almost all types of commodities in the CES. To take into account these disparities, and to follow King's procedure, we use the proportions listed in table 5-4 to scale up reported expenditures. Strictly speaking, this procedure is appropriate only if all interview respondents tend to understate expenditures, rather than if some respondents omit them altogether.

Econometric Procedure

Through aggregation of the detailed expenditure data, we obtain values for each household's expenditures on each of the seventeen consumption commodities. As just described, these values are scaled up for underreporting and adjusted down to obtain individual-equivalent values. The total expenditure variable, m_h, was created by summing the individual's seventeen expenditure values. To find the parameters describing the linear expenditure system for each of the twelve age groups, we estimate equation 5-2. For each age group, these equations create a situation of "seemingly unrelated regressions," since

11. Houthakker and Taylor (1970); and Gieseman (1987).

Table 5-4. *Reported 1984 CES Expenditure Totals as a Proportion of NIPA Estimated Totals*

Category	Value	Category	Value
1. Food	0.75	10. Automobiles	0.96
2. Alcohol	0.48	11. Personal services[b]	0.88
3. Tobacco	0.68	12. Financial services[c]	1.00
4. Utilities[a]	0.97	13. Recreation	0.64
5. Shelter[a]	1.00	14. Nondurables	0.79
6. Furnishings	0.81	15. Gasoline	0.96
7. Appliances	0.68	16. Health care[d]	1.00
8. Apparel	0.56	17. Education[d]	1.00
9. Public transportation	0.84		

Source: Adapted from Raymond Gieseman, "The Consumer Expenditure Survey: Quality Control by Comparative Analysis," *Monthly Labor Review*, March, 1987, pp. 8–14, esp. p. 11.

a. Housing is taken to be accurate, since these expenditures are based primarily on rental equivalents calculated by the Bureau of Labor Statistics and not reported by interview respondents. Gieseman reports a value of 0.96 only for the combination of "rent, fuel and utilities." We have increased this value to 0.97 for utilities, since Gieseman additionally gives a 0.99 value for telephone expenditures.

b. The value for services applies only to the direct expenditure component of service expenditure. A value of 1.00 is presumed for the contributions component.

c. Financial services is also taken to be accurate, even though Gieseman suggests a much lower number. Our imputation for implicit financial service charges presumably eliminates most of the underreporting which he observes.

d. For medical care and education, no proportions are available. Therefore these ratios are arbitrarily set to one.

the error terms for a single group of individuals are unlikely to be independent across the seventeen regressions. Least-squares estimators are unbiased, but often inefficient. When the independent variables are the same, however, as they are in these regressions, the least-squares estimators remain efficient.[12] Thus we perform least-squares estimation on weighted observations, using the population weights for the sample provided by the Bureau of Labor Statistics.

Parameters of the Linear Expenditure System

The β_i share parameters are taken directly from the regression coefficients. To obtain minimum required purchases, b_i, we transform the estimated intercept terms according to equation 5-3.

For comparability with King's results, however, we first run regressions for households rather than individuals and for all ages rather than for twelve separate age groups. Table 5-5 presents King's parameters for 1972–73 and our new estimates for 1984–85. For marginal expenditure shares, shown in the first two columns, we can compare results directly. For minimum expenditures however, results are in nominal magnitudes. For comparison with King's 1972–73 values, we derive "adjusted" minimum expenditures by tak-

12. See, for example, Kmenta (1971, pp. 517–29).

Table 5-5. *Comparison of Linear Expenditure System Parameters for 1984–85, with King's Parameters for 1972–73*[a]

	Share (β_i)		Minimum expenditure($p_i b_i$)		
Category	1972–73	1984–85	1972–73	Adjusted, 1984–85	Actual, 1984–85
1. Food	0.1508	0.1565	816	555	1832
2. Alcohol	0.0273	0.0293	−3	22	73
3. Tobacco	0.0073	0.0058	122	71	234
4. Utilities	0.0928	0.0406	282	307	1013
5. Shelter	0.1440	0.1448	842	724	2388
6. Furnishings	0.0278	0.0239	122	76	251
7. Appliances	0.0079	0.0257	99	144	375
8. Apparel	0.0889	0.1141	9	−32	−106
9. Transportation	0.0156	0.0293	−15	−57	−188
10. Automobiles	0.0788	0.0869	338	435	1435
11. Personal services	0.2046	0.1595	−581	−319	−1052
12. Financial services	0.0843	0.0396	59	93	306
13. Recreation	0.0745	0.0533	−114	28	92
14. Nondurables	0.0211	0.0095	241	154	509
15. Fuel	0.0290	0.0341	237	229	754
16. Health care	. . .	0.0273	. . .	142	470
17. Education	. . .	0.0197	. . .	41	−135

Source: 1972–73 parameters from King (1979).

a. As the basis for his b_i values, King uses a total minimum expenditure ($\Sigma p_i b_i$) of $2,500 in 1972–73. For our "actual" b_i estimates, in the last column, we use a total minimum required expenditure of $8,000. This difference approximately reflects growth in nominal GNP between the two periods. For the "adjusted" b_i values, to compare with King, we scale down actual 1984–85 estimates by the ratio of 1972 to 1984 GNP.

ing our "actual" estimated 1984–85 values times the ratio of nominal GNP in 1972 to nominal GNP in 1984. For most of the goods, results for 1984–85 appear similar to those for 1972–73. The discretionary expenditure shares are quite similar in the two periods, especially for food (0.1508 and 0.1565) and for housing (0.1440 and 0.1448). On the other hand, expenditures on appliances appear to have increased since 1972–73, both in minimum requirements (in real terms from 99 to 114) and as a share of discretionary income (from 0.0079 to 0.0257). A change in the share parameter for services (from 0.2046 to 0.1595) may be attributed to the fact that we separate education and medical care from the services category.

Finally, to obtain the necessary parameters for our model, we switch from households to individuals and run seventeen separate regressions for each of the twelve age categories. From these 204 regressions we obtain the 408 parameters presented in tables 5-6 and 5-7.[13]

13. The first age group includes fifty-three observations, but every other age group has well over a hundred. These regressions intentionally omit many explanatory variables, so the R^2 are

Table 5-6. *Annual Minimum Required Purchases, by Age Group, 1984–85*

Dollars

Category	Age group					
	20–24	*25–29*	*30–34*	*35–39*	*40–44*	*45–49*
1. Food	1,336.35	1,295.95	1,387.98	1,392.31	1,381.98	1,327.56
2. Alcohol	136.69	193.42	0.03	−172.27	84.65	−122.96
3. Tobacco	156.19	143.96	189.77	181.61	175.05	226.88
4. Utilities	425.37	635.47	585.23	622.37	589.93	657.56
5. Shelter	1,140.26	1,248.54	1,197.09	1,452.15	1,136.68	1,050.00
6. Furnishings	265.77	330.51	368.30	472.91	396.02	391.84
7. Appliances	525.86	520.16	597.98	647.77	663.28	643.06
8. Apparel	379.42	67.53	84.48	395.56	190.39	233.40
9. Transportation	31.12	−45.07	−64.04	−50.30	−80.77	−143.98
10. Automobiles	2,366.82	2,070.11	2,354.71	2,475.56	2,316.02	2,526.50
11. Personal services	245.14	37.72	−165.25	−348.48	−168.71	44.16
12. Financial services	146.27	101.22	183.61	163.93	133.31	145.10
13. Recreation	177.04	334.54	192.31	127.29	128.57	63.55
14. Nondurables	191.47	294.73	254.70	406.50	305.18	268.42
15. Fuel	440.69	678.86	521.37	578.42	526.24	451.89
16. Health care	34.16	56.22	259.37	−241.57	206.97	240.36
17. Education	1.39	36.13	52.36	−103.75	15.20	−3.31

Category	Age group					
	50–54	*55–59*	*60–64*	*65–69*	*70–74*	*75 +*
1. Food	1,337.12	1,336.66	1,507.64	1,446.22	1,232.67	1,282.03
2. Alcohol	34.27	6.09	66.91	−6.96	53.71	27.88
3. Tobacco	203.43	230.30	143.53	103.87	127.56	54.27
4. Utilities	557.52	683.08	792.66	620.52	700.73	691.29
5. Shelter	1,456.35	1,075.54	1,458.16	1,534.36	1,715.78	1,978.31
6. Furnishings	461.41	407.90	409.99	400.93	386.59	325.05
7. Appliances	642.16	595.95	534.22	431.15	462.52	364.82
8. Apparel	88.71	−40.43	25.64	204.14	310.12	247.12
9. Transportation	−35.28	−108.79	−627.42	−109.37	88.66	49.55
10. Automobiles	2,557.65	2,468.82	2,013.79	1,434.71	1,395.25	850.35
11. Personal services	−320.05	112.39	14.09	154.55	−104.35	362.36
12. Financial services	45.20	102.19	346.23	242.26	171.16	379.52
13. Recreation	110.77	68.28	187.96	188.62	89.45	158.38
14. Nondurables	193.58	291.44	284.14	342.55	305.10	284.21
15. Fuel	588.32	563.10	493.31	502.13	318.43	323.66
16. Health care	183.82	240.20	306.88	465.51	746.27	620.57
17. Education	−105.00	−32.74	42.31	44.80	0.34	0.62

Table 5-7. *Estimated Expenditure Share Parameters, by Age Group, 1984–85*

	Age group					
Category	20–24	25–29	30–34	35–39	40–44	45–49
1. Food	0.12726	0.12528	0.12082	0.14769	0.14239	0.14193
2. Alcohol	0.07362	0.03059	0.04591	0.06275	0.02216	0.04617
3. Tobacco	− 0.00385	0.00255	0.00021	0.00156	0.00157	− 0.00183
4. Utilities	0.05167	0.03309	0.04752	0.03776	0.04367	0.02976
5. Shelter	0.21444	0.19367	0.16491	0.16101	0.17431	0.15868
6. Furnishings	0.02047	0.03446	0.04045	0.02573	0.04147	0.04625
7. Appliances	0.01407	0.04371	0.03731	0.02976	0.03806	0.04154
8. Apparel	0.09692	0.12375	0.12631	0.08589	0.10763	0.10705
9. Transportation	0.02502	0.02849	0.02464	0.01982	0.02272	0.03778
10. Automobiles	0.07056	0.12342	0.10304	0.09339	0.13097	0.13101
11. Personal services	0.06550	0.10358	0.13374	0.12758	0.11431	0.08684
12. Financial services	0.03086	0.05065	0.03023	0.03473	0.04079	0.03810
13. Recreation	0.07298	0.03919	0.06261	0.05753	0.04767	0.05028
14. Nondurables	0.01228	0.01092	0.01472	0.00746	0.00912	0.01643
15. Fuel	0.05818	0.00722	0.02466	0.02090	0.02516	0.03350
16. Health care	0.06511	0.04946	0.01918	0.06431	0.02044	0.02406
17. Education	0.00491	− 0.00002	0.00375	0.02211	0.01756	0.01244

	Age group					
Category	50–54	55–59	60–64	65–69	70–74	75 +
1. Food	0.11571	0.12574	0.11228	0.12613	0.14762	0.10120
2. Alcohol	0.02642	0.03765	0.02422	0.03722	0.03464	0.01973
3. Tobacco	0.00336	0.00328	− 0.00052	0.00052	− 0.00064	− 0.00060
4. Utilities	0.02738	0.02499	0.00715	0.04044	0.04389	0.04825
5. Shelter	0.13010	0.18246	0.17556	0.15509	0.17496	0.29508
6. Furnishings	0.03816	0.04636	0.04099	0.03459	0.03054	0.02504
7. Appliances	0.03855	0.03904	0.02932	0.03246	0.02331	0.02452
8. Apparel	0.11279	0.12476	0.10880	0.08387	0.02047	0.03289
9. Transportation	0.02121	0.02997	0.14687	0.06406	0.01411	0.02601
10. Automobiles	0.12087	0.11889	0.09685	0.14234	0.12254	0.10120
11. Personal services	0.15743	0.09306	0.14904	0.10819	0.21052	0.14819
12. Financial services	0.06129	0.05332	0.02668	0.07269	0.07063	0.07684
13. Recreation	0.04293	0.06349	0.03278	0.03627	0.03494	0.01853
14. Nondurables	0.01678	0.00418	0.01089	0.00569	0.00277	0.00681
15. Fuel	0.02134	0.01546	0.01298	0.02882	0.05661	0.02477
16. Health care	0.03025	0.01744	0.02313	0.03037	0.01215	0.04841
17. Education	0.03544	0.01992	0.00297	0.00125	0.00096	0.00314

Comparing these parameters across age groups suggests a life-cycle pattern of consumption expenditures for certain types of goods. For example, expenditures on alcohol and recreation are largest when individuals are young, both as shares of discretionary income and as minimum requirements. Changes in the number of adults in the household have already been taken into account, but child-rearing activities might explain a midlife bulge in the expenditure shares of certain commodities such as furniture, appliances, and education. Furthermore, retirement may account for other changes. For example, airline travel comprises a large component of the transportation commodity. The share for this good is unusually high for young retirees (ages 60–64) but falls off precipitously for the very old. For services, however, the minimum requirement and to some extent the expenditure share increase in old age. This commodity includes leisure-related costs like movie and sports admissions. The share for medical care does not seem to change with age, but the minimum required purchase of medical care shows a pronounced increase in old age. On the other hand, some of the seventeen goods exhibit no obvious life-cycle pattern. For example, the parameters describing food and nondurable expenditures are basically constant across the different age categories.

These parameters also reveal how spending can depend on income. To set aside differences among age groups, consider the new estimates in the last column of table 5-5. Spending will increase the fastest as a fraction of income for goods with minimum expenditures near zero, or even negative, such as clothing, transportation, services, recreation, and education. Spending will be relatively high at low-income levels for goods with relatively large minimum required purchases relative to the marginal share, such as food, tobacco, utilities, housing, and fuel.

Chapter 6 describes how we mesh these preference parameters with other data to establish a benchmark equilibrium and a steady-state path. Succeeding chapters use all these behavioral parameters to simulate the effects of tax changes on equilibrium prices and quantities.

---

not always high. They generally lie between 0.2 and 0.6, but a couple of age groups have as many as four of their seventeen regressions with R^2 less than 0.10. The commodities for which these equations are least well estimated are tobacco and education. The R^2 most often exceed 0.5 for other goods such as food, shelter, apparel, and services.

CHAPTER SIX

Calibrating Parameters and Adjusting the Data Set

IN CHAPTER 3 we described the various components of the data we use in the lifetime incidence model. Chapters 4 and 5 showed how we estimated particular parameters. In this chapter, we describe how we combined the various data of chapter 3 with the parameter estimates of chapters 4 and 5 to generate the remaining parameters required to complete the entire model.

The general equilibrium nature of our model prevents us from using all observed data directly, because in so doing, we would discover that quantities supplied are typically not equal to quantities demanded. For example, data on production of a particular good will not be exactly consistent with other data on the consumption of that good. To generate counterfactual simulations, we must begin from a consistent, benchmark equilibrium, where parameters and data combine to characterize an economy in which each good and factor market is in equilibrium. We meet this consistency requirement by adjusting the data set. The adjusted data can then be used to solve for the remaining necessary parameters.

This chapter first discusses the procedures we use to obtain a consistent benchmark equilibrium data set. Then, given the equilibrium data and any estimated or exogenously specified parameters, we describe the nonstochastic calibration techniques we used to determine the remaining parameters.

Calibration is a procedure often used in the applied general equilibrium literature. On the one hand, these models are too large to be estimated in a full system of simultaneous equations. On the other, single-equation methods would lead to a benchmark equilibrium solution that does not match either observed data or adjusted consistent data. For these reasons we use calibration to close the model: we solve for remaining parameters such that the use of all these parameters together leads to an equilibrium solution that exactly replicates the consistent equilibrium data set. We emphasize, however, that this procedure improves upon previous general equilibrium tax models by using econometric estimates to determine lifetime income and consumption patterns.

Obtaining a Consistent Data Set

Before we calibrate parameters, we must ensure that quantities demanded equal quantities supplied for every good and factor market. Because the actual data typically violate this condition, we must either adjust the demand levels to equal the observed supply levels or adjust the supply to meet the demand. In this section we describe these adjustments in the order in which they are undertaken.

Starting with data on the capital stock by type for each industry's corporate and noncorporate sectors, we determine the distribution of total capital use between the corporate and noncorporate sectors within each industry. Having no data for shares of corporate versus noncorporate labor or output in each industry, we assume that capital-labor ratios are the same for both sectors within each industry, and use the same data. Given that production functions are homogeneous of degree one in inputs,[1] the relative corporate-noncorporate use of an input must equal the relative corporate-noncorporate output of the industry.

In the labor market, we take as given the data on value of labor used by industry and government. The sum of these labor demands gives us aggregate labor for the benchmark year. For individuals, we use data from the Panel Study of Income Dynamics to estimate paths of lifetime labor endowments, taxes, and transfers, as described in chapter 4. The shapes of these profiles are taken as given for a representative individual from each lifetime income category in the benchmark data set. PSID data also provide labor-leisure ratios at each age, and constant population growth gives us the fraction of each group at each age level. Thus we can obtain the value of labor supplied at any one point in time.

We must then scale up from individual labor supplies to aggregate labor use. To do this, we first multiply labor supply for each representative consumer by the relative proportion of such consumers in the economy.[2] This

1. A production function that is homogeneous of degree one has the characteristic that an increase in all inputs by a given proportion increases output by the same proportion; that is, production exhibits constant returns to scale.

2. The first and twelfth lifetime income categories each contain 2 percent of the population, the second and eleventh lifetime income categories each contain 8 percent of the population, and all other lifetime income categories each contain 10 percent of the population.

weighted-average consumer is representative of the entire U.S. economy. We then take aggregate labor demand and divide by that one representative individual's labor supply. The result implies that we have 124.6 million adult individuals. We also have proportions in each age and income category. We can thus derive the number of individuals in each category, and we can multiply this by the individual tax and transfer profiles (shown in tables 3-4 and 3-5) to obtain aggregate personal taxes paid and aggregate transfers received. Using the same numbers for individuals in each lifetime income category, we can scale individual capital endowments (inheritances), presented in table 3-7, to reflect aggregate amounts.

We describe below how we calculate the present value of income from each group's capital inheritance, labor endowment, personal taxes paid, and transfers received. To get discretionary income, however, we need to subtract minimum required purchases for the group. In fact, all demand calculations require aggregate demands for each age and income category. Recall from chapter 5, however, that we estimated preference parameters for an *individual* in each age group. We therefore take minimum required purchases, b, and multiply by the number of individuals in each category. This aggregate minimum expenditure can be subtracted from income to get discretionary income. Then the share parameters, β, can be applied to aggregate discretionary income to get aggregate demands. With aggregate minimum requirements and unchanged share parameters, we effectively derive aggregate demand functions from the estimated individual demand functions.

We now have annual incomes and minimum expenditure amounts for all age and income groups alive in 1984, but we also need corresponding amounts for a given cohort across all ages. We use the steady-state growth rate to project forward or back through time.[3]

Now we can compute the present value of aggregate lifetime discretionary income for each representative group, given the appropriately adjusted capital endowments, minimum required purchases, and profiles of labor endowments, taxes, and transfers. This procedure is fairly complex. We first com-

3. For each cohort alive in the benchmark equilibrium, we account for the effects of population and technical progress by grossing up or scaling down the annual discretionary income amounts. For a person who is currently 40 years old, for example, annual income at age 30 was lower than the current income of a person who is currently 30. Given an annual economic growth rate of g, equal to 0.01 in this case, the 40-year-old's income at age 30 equals $(1 + g)^{-10}$ times the current 30-year-old's income. Similarly, a person who is currently 25 years old will earn a higher income at age 30 than people who are currently 30 years old. The 25-year-old's income at age 30 equals $(1 + g)^5$ times the income of the person who is now 30. In adjusting the benchmark data set, we use this procedure whenever lifetime incomes must be computed.

pute the intertemporal share parameters, a_t, given a specified rate of time preference, δ. For our standard set of parameters, we set δ to 0.005.[4] Then the a_t are determined according to

$$(6\text{-}1) \qquad a_t = [1/(1+\delta)]^{t-1}/\sum_{s=1}^{T} [1/(1+\delta)]^{s-1},$$

for $t = 1, \ldots, T$, and where $T = 60$. These parameters are defined from the beginning of economic life at age 20 until the date of death at age 79. These sixty parameters sum to one.

Lifetime discretionary income is allocated across periods to maximize lifetime utility, resulting in amounts of a "composite commodity" consumed in each period of an individual's lifetime (called x_t in equation 2-3 of chapter 2). A simultaneity problem arises in determining this composite commodity in each period. One amount of x_t is implied by the top-down approach of equation 2-3 when we apply the a_t shares to the value of lifetime income.[5]

We cannot yet undertake this calculation, however, because equation 2-3 requires the price q_t, which depends on the weight parameter α_t (in equation 2-32). A different level of x_t is implied by the bottom-up approach of equation 2-4 in which the composite commodity x_t is composed of leisure ℓ_t and composite consumption $\bar{c}_t$ according to the parameter α_t. We have "data" for the observed amount of leisure,[6] but not yet values of $\bar{c}_t$ or α_t. If $\bar{c}_t$ were merely data on consumption, we would follow the standard calibration technique. We would have benchmark prices as well as observed quantities of $\bar{c}_t$ and ℓ_t, and we would solve equations 2-6 and 2-7 for α, which must satisfy

$$(6\text{-}2) \qquad \alpha_t = (\bar{p}_t^{\varepsilon_2}\bar{c}_t) / (\bar{p}_t^{\varepsilon_2}\bar{c}_t + w_t^{\varepsilon_2}\ell_t),$$

4. Even though $\delta > 0$ indicates impatience on the part of consumers, we set the net-of-all-tax rate of return, r, equal to 0.04. Since this r exceeds δ, the amount of composite commodity, x_t, rises with age.

5. The demand for x_t in equation 2-3 involves the intertemporal elasticity of substitution, ε_1, assumed exogenous to the model. For our standard parameterization of the model, we set ε_1 equal to 0.50. This parameter is chosen in conjunction with others to try to reflect choices in the literature, to generate the observed capital stock, and to try to produce reasonable savings elasticities. As shown in table 8-1 in chapter 8, the savings elasticity is 1.3 in this case. We vary ε_1 in sensitivity analysis, as described in that chapter.

6. From the PSID, we have average hours worked per week, by age category (table 3-7). In the central case, we assume that the total endowment of time is 4,000 hours a year, but we vary that assumption in the sensitivity analysis of chapter 8. We multiply hours by the wage rate at that age, for each group, to calculate the endowment of effective labor units and the supply of effective labor units. This units convention guarantees that every individual receives the same wage rate per effective labor unit ($1, in the benchmark). The difference between the endowment and the supply of effective labor units is our "data" for the amount of leisure at each age.

where ε_2 is the elasticity of substitution between consumption and leisure. This elasticity is set at 0.50 for standard parameters of the model, but it is varied in sensitivity analysis.[7] These α_t's vary by age, but not by lifetime income category, because both the consumption amount $\bar{c}_t$ and the leisure amount ℓ_t vary only by age.[8]

We cannot observe sub-utility levels $\bar{c}_t$ from consumption data, but we can still use equation 6-2 as a necessary relationship between $\bar{c}_t$ and x_t. This observation returns us to the sub-utility calculation in equation 2-4. We have data on ℓ_t, an assumption for the value of ε_2, and a specific relationship between $\bar{c}_t$ and α_t. We cannot solve these equations analytically. However, a guess for $\bar{c}_t$ can be used in equation 6-2 to solve for α_t, and these can be used together in the bottom-up approach of equation 2-4 to find x_t. The same value of α_t also can be used in equation 2-32 to get q_t, and in the top-down approach of equation 2-3 to find another x_t. The difference between the two calculations of x_t is then used to adjust the guess on $\bar{c}_t$.

In other words, since these equations cannot be solved analytically, we use an iterative numerical procedure. When the x_t match, we have mutually consistent values for leisure ℓ_t, composite consumption $\bar{c}_t$, the weight parameter α_t, the composite commodity x_t, and its price q_t. We also then know how lifetime endowment is allocated between leisure and consumption in different periods.

Next, from available prices and quantities of composite consumption x_t and leisure ℓ_t, we can use equation 2-5 to calculate the value of other consumption expenditures $(\bar{p}_t\bar{c}_t)$. This dollar amount is allocated among the seventeen consumption goods according to the demand parameters (the β's and b's) estimated from the Consumer Expenditure Survey. We use demand functions 2-10 to calculate the individual c_{it} amounts of each good at each age for each lifetime income category. These demands can be added across the income categories to get aggregate demand for each consumer good. We then apply the tax rate for each consumer good (shown in table 3-6) to the aggregate level of expenditure on each good to obtain the value of sales and excise taxes paid.

We can now calculate savings in each period and capital stock accumulation from available figures on annual discretionary incomes, initial capital endowments, and expenditures in each period of life. Annual discretionary

7. The central value of 0.5 is near the center of the range of elasticities consistent with estimated labor supply elasticities, as discussed more below.

8. Note that this model does not specify a particular retirement date. Instead, each age group has its own preference for leisure, which may increase sharply in later years.

income is equal to the value of labor endowment, plus government transfers, minus taxes, minus the value of minimum required purchases. This discretionary income plus the return on the current stock of capital can be used either toward purchase of that period's composite commodity, x_t, or toward savings, which augments the individual's capital stock. The new capital stock then enters next period's consumption-savings problem, and this computation continues until the end of economic life. We use this procedure to determine capital stocks for each of the sixty years in the economic lifetime for each lifetime income category. Note that these capital stocks are determined from within the model framework, with the assumption of life-cycle optimization, and will remain during counterfactual simulations. Thus savings and capital stocks will respond to a change in tax policy.

These calculations for the capital stocks held by individuals do not yet match the total industry and government use of capital, as is necessary to describe a benchmark equilibrium in the capital market. The value of capital supplied is simply the net rate of return, r (set equal to 0.04), times the total value of the capital stock held by individuals. We take the single ratio of aggregate capital holdings to aggregate capital demands, and we use it to scale up or down the vector of industry and government demands for capital.

Life-cycle savings in this model depend entirely on the shape of the estimated earnings profile relative to the slope of the desired consumption profile, as determined by parameter choices. In the central case, we assume 0.04 for the net rate of return, 0.005 for the rate of time preference, and 0.5 for the intertemporal elasticity of substitution. With all these assumptions, life-cycle savings yield \$339.4 billion of capital income. In addition, our specification of bequests (table 3-8) accounts for \$265.6 billion of capital income. An implication is that bequests account for 44 percent of the capital stock, a figure that is quite consistent with Laurence J. Kotlikoff and Lawrence H. Summers (1981) and Kotlikoff (1988). Total capital income is \$605.0 billion, as against expenditures on capital of \$574.5 billion. The ratio, 1.053, is used to scale up capital expenditures. We also adjust data on total investment to equal total savings.[9]

The next step is to compute the benchmark amount of tax revenue. Both

9. Investment data are presented in table 3-12. Total investment equals the sum of net private fixed-capital formation and the change in net inventories. The values of private fixed-capital formation shown in table 3-12 are gross amounts; to obtain net values we multiply by 0.3329, the average ratio of net investment to gross investment during 1976–85, as noted by the 1987 *Economic Report of the President*. Total savings in the model are \$150.2 billion, and total net investment in 1984 was \$283.8 billion. Thus we multiply the net investment vector by the ratio, 52.9 percent.

initial data on payroll taxes paid by industry (table 3-15) and output taxes
paid by industry (table 3-16) are taken as fixed for the benchmark. Implied
tax rates are calculated as taxes paid divided by labor or by output, respectively. Income taxes are provided by the adjusted data on individual tax profiles. Consumption taxes are calculated by applying the appropriate tax rates
(table 3-6) to the amounts of consumer goods purchased. The only remaining
sources of revenue are taxes on capital. We model capital taxes as if collected
only at the producer level, so income taxes paid by individuals reflect taxes
based on labor incomes only. We then determine capital tax collections from
adjusted data on industry uses of capital stocks by type, multiplied by the
difference between the computed gross-of-tax cost of capital and net return to
capital for each capital type:

$$(6\text{-}3) \qquad T_K = \sum_{j=1}^{18} \sum_{k=1}^{5} [(\rho_k^c - r)K_{jk}^c + (\rho_k^{nc} - r)K_{jk}^{nc}],$$

where j indexes the eighteen private industries (other than government enterprises), k indexes the five capital types, ρ_k^c and ρ_k^{nc} are the gross-of-tax costs
of corporate and noncorporate capital of type k (defined in equations 2-23
through 2-25), and K_{jk}^c and K_{jk}^{nc} are the amounts of corporate and noncorporate
capital of type k used in industry j.[10] This total revenue from capital taxation
is added to the other sources of tax revenue.

We also make consistency adjustments in government budget balance and
trade balance. For government budget balance, we adjust government purchases of producer goods (table 3-21) so that the total of these purchases
equals the sum of tax revenue, plus income from government endowments,
minus transfers paid, minus government purchases of capital and labor. For
trade balance, we sum up the values of exports and of imports (table 3-21)
and then adjust the export vector so that total exports equal total imports.

Since we have already established consistency between purchases of consumer goods and levels of disposable income, we can now calculate levels of
producer good purchases from the transition matrix in table 3-11. The resulting vector of producer goods by industry is then divided between corporate
and noncorporate sectors within each industry, using the ratios of corporate
to noncorporate capital. These ratios are also used within each industry to
divide corporate and noncorporate portions of government expenditures, exports, imports, and investment.

10. The amounts of corporate and noncorporate capital are shown in tables 3-19 and 3-20 of
chapter 3. Recall, however, that in the real estate sector (17) the distinction is between owner-
occupied and rental housing, instead of between corporate and noncorporate producers.

We need to make a final consistency adjustment to production data to reflect zero profits for each sector within every industry. The zero profits condition implies that for each representative firm receipts must equal expenditures. Receipts include final demand for the products, such as consumer demand for producer goods, government demand, and net exports. Receipts of the firm also include any intermediate demands for the goods as inputs to the production of other goods, as reflected by the sum of a row in the input-output matrix. Expenditures by the firm include the components of value added, such as the gross-of-tax costs of labor and capital, plus output taxes. Expenditures also include the cost of any outputs of other industries used as intermediate inputs, as indicated by the sum of a column in the input-output matrix. To match these sums, we adjust the entries in the input-output matrix using an iterative procedure developed by Michael Bacharach (1971). We do not adjust final demands or value added, but the elements of the rows and columns of the input-output matrix are adjusted alternately. Once the rows are adjusted, the next column adjustment throws off the row sums. This iteration continues until every row-sum plus final demand is close to the corresponding column-sum plus value added.

Calibration of Other Parameters

Given the estimated parameters for lifetime incomes and consumption patterns and the implied data set just described, we can now calibrate other parameters that are needed for the model. The equations that determine these parameters are based on the optimization problems described in chapter 2. Some of these calibration procedures require an additional parameter, to be specified exogenously, as summarized in table 6-1.

As discussed, savings behavior depends heavily on assumptions about the rate of return r, rate of time preference δ, and intertemporal elasticity of substitution ε_1. These are chosen in concert so that the model-generated savings replicates other data on capital stocks. We vary each assumption, however, when we perform sensitivity analysis in chapter 8. For any given set of assumptions for these exogenous parameters, we can then determine all remaining parameters.

The consumption side starts with estimated expenditure parameters b and β, plus parameters a and α from equations 6-1 and 6-2. Next, the optimum combination of corporate and noncorporate goods in sub-utility equation 2-11 results in demand equations 2-13 and 2-14. We assume that the consistent-

Table 6-1. *Various Elasticities and Other Parameters Used in Standard Parameterization of the Model*

Parameter	Description	Value used
r	Net-of-all-tax rate of return	0.040
δ	Rate of time preference	0.005
π	Expected inflation	0.040
(sum = "g" in text)	⎰Rate of population growth	0.005
	⎱Rate of technical progress	0.005
ε_1	Intertemporal elasticity of substitution	0.5
ε_2	Elasticity of substitution between consumption and leisure	0.5
$b\varepsilon_3$	Elasticity of substitution between corporate and noncorporate outputs of same good	5.0
σ_1	Elasticity of substitution between capital and labor	see table 6-2
σ_2	Elasticity of substitution across capital types	1.50
...	U.S. price elasticity of export demand	-10.00
...	U.S. price elasticity of import supply	0.465

benchmark equilibrium amounts are optimal, given prices. Therefore demand equations can be solved "backward" to find the share parameter γ_j as a function of consistent-benchmark data on corporate and noncorporate outputs:

$$(6\text{-}4) \qquad \gamma_j = \frac{(p_j^c)^{\varepsilon_3} Q_j^c}{(p_j^c)^{\varepsilon_3} Q_j^c + (p_j^{nc})^{\varepsilon_3} Q_j^{nc}},$$

where the p_j^c's and p_j^{nc}'s are prices of corporate and noncorporate outputs of the same industry, the Q_j^c's and Q_j^{nc}'s are the quantities of these outputs produced, and ε_3 is the elasticity of substitution between corporate and noncorporate outputs. We are unaware of any estimates of such an elasticity. We choose to set ε_3 to 5.0 in the standard parameterization of the model in order to capture the idea that these goods are similar to one another within each industry. In the benchmark equilibrium, the net-of-tax prices of all goods are equal to one. The output tax rates (table 3-16) provide gross-of-tax prices. With these prices and the quantities of corporate and noncorporate outputs, the computation of the γ_j is straightforward.

On the production side, calibrated parameters include the share parameter on labor versus composite capital, the scale parameter for value added in production, and the share parameters for the five capital uses. The order of determination is from the highest level of disaggregation to the lowest, since each level's parameters help determine composite goods for the next level.

Starting at the disaggregate level for uses of capital in each sector of each industry, we need the costs of capital for the five capital types (equations 2-23 through 2-25). Given these costs, the optimum combination of capital types in sub-production function 2–18 results in factor demand equations 2-19. These demand equations can be solved backward to find the share parameters Ψ as a function of calculated capital costs ρ_k, $k = 1, \ldots, 5$, and data on capital of type k in industry j, K_{jk} (as shown in tables 3-19 and 3-20 of chapter 3):

$$(6\text{-}5) \qquad\qquad \psi_{jk} = \frac{\rho_k^{\sigma_2} K_{jk}}{\displaystyle\sum_{i=1}^{5} (\rho_i^{\sigma_2} K_{ji})} \, ,$$

where σ_2 is the elasticity of substitution among the five capital types. In the absence of empirical estimates of σ_2, we assume that this elasticity does not vary across industries or sectors. We set it to 1.50 in the standard parameterization. The costs of capital depend on various features of the tax code, features that are modeled using the tax parameters shown in table 3-17. These parameters are altered when a counterfactual change in tax policy is simulated, as we will describe in chapter 7. We alter some of these assumptions in the sensitivity analysis in chapter 8. Because the costs of capital differ between the corporate and noncorporate sectors, and because corporate and noncorporate usage of capital differs, we calculate a share parameter for each capital type, sector, and industry.

With these share parameters, we can compute the cost of composite capital, $\bar{\rho}_j$, using equation 2-26 for each sector. We can also calculate the quantity of composite capital, $\bar{K}_j$, using equation 2-18 for the corporate and noncorporate production in each industry j. These costs and quantities will differ between the corporate and noncorporate sectors of the same industry. We assume that this quantity, $\bar{K}_j$, is the desired amount of composite capital, given its price, $\bar{\rho}_j$. Similarly, the observed data on labor use, L_j, is the desired amount of labor, given its gross-of-tax price, w'. The optimum combination of productive factors in the value-added production function 2-15 implies factor demand functions 2-16 and 2-17, so the latter can be solved backward to find the share parameter ζ_j, as a function of available prices and quantities:

Table 6-2. *Value-Added Elasticities of Substitution between Composite Capital and Labor*

Industry	Sigma$_1$	Industry	Sigma$_1$
1. Agriculture, forestry, and fisheries	0.6759	11. Metals and machinery	0.7373
2. Mining	0.7949	12. Transportation equipment	0.8159
3. Crude petroleum and gas	0.7949	13. Motor vehicles	0.9228
4. Construction	0.7949	14. Transportation, communications, and utilities	0.7949
5. Food and tobacco	0.7117	15. Trade	0.7949
6. Textile, apparel, and leather	0.9025	16. Finance and insurance	0.7949
7. Paper and printing	0.9033	17. Real estate	0.7949
8. Petroleum refining	0.7830	18. Services	0.7949
9. Chemicals and rubber	0.9603	19. Government enterprises	0.7949
10. Lumber, furniture, stone, clay, and glass	0.9123		

Source: Caddy (1976). His work compiled hundreds of estimates from various sources.

$$(6\text{-}6) \qquad \zeta_j = \frac{w'L_j^{1/\sigma_1}/\bar{\rho}_j \bar{K}_j^{1/\sigma_1}}{1 + (w'L_j^{1/\sigma_1}/\bar{\rho}_j \bar{K}_j^{1/\sigma_1})} ,$$

where σ_1 is the exogenously specified elasticity of substitution between capital and labor in production. A large literature on these elasticities indicates that they differ by industry. We use the central-tendency value for each industry's elasticity, wherever estimates differ. The weighted average of all available estimates is 0.7949. For industries without existing estimates, we assume that σ_1 equals this weighted average for the other industries. The final employed values for these elasticities are presented in table 6-2. Since no estimates separate the corporate and noncorporate sectors, we assume the same elasticity for both.

With these labor-capital share parameters, we have all components of value added except for the scale parameter φ_j. The value-added production function 2-15 can be inverted to solve backward for this scale parameter as

$$(6\text{-}7) \qquad \varphi_j = \frac{w'L_j + \bar{\rho}_j \bar{K}_j}{\left[\zeta_j L_j^{(\sigma_1 - 1)/\sigma_1} + (1 - \zeta_j)\bar{K}_j(\sigma_1 - 1)/\sigma_1 \right]^{\sigma_1/(\sigma_1 - 1)}} ,$$

where the numerator is value added, and the denominator can be calculated from available information.

For government purchases of goods and factors, as described in chapter 2, we specify a Cobb-Douglas composite function. This composite commodity can be interpreted as a public good that is separable in the individual consumer's utility function. To set parameters for this Cobb-Douglas function, however, we need only to solve for the share parameters. We take government expenditures on each of the particular goods and factors, as observed in the benchmark data (table 3-21), and divide by the total. These share parameters remain the same in tax policy simulations, but the revenue (government's "income") can change. Thus additional revenue would be spent in the same proportions. Also, price changes cause quantity adjustments. For "equal-yield" replacement policies, we require that government's composite commodity be kept at the same level. Thus if the price of a good purchased by government tends to rise, a larger amount of nominal revenue is required.

Trade is modeled in a simple manner by specifying import supply and export demand in terms of U.S. prices, using the same form as Charles L. Ballard and others.[11] With the constraint of trade balance, specifying one own-price elasticity defines a relationship between the two U.S. price elasticities. As an estimate of the own-price elasticity of foreign demand for U.S. exports, incorporating trade balance conditions, we use − 1.4, as suggested by Robert M. Stern, Jonathan Francis, and Bruce Schumacher (1976). For the same elasticity without trade balance conditions, we use − 10, to capture the idea that foreign demand for U.S. exports should be highly sensitive to price. By implication, the own-price elasticity of foreign supply of U.S. imports must be 0.465, and the same elasticity incorporating trade balance must be 0.40. The only other parameters needed for the trade equations are constant terms. With benchmark prices of unity, the constant terms in the import and export functions are simply the values of imports and exports found in the benchmark data set, given in table 3-21.

At this point, calibration is complete. We have a carefully crafted combination of estimated parameters, prices of one, observed quantities, and derivations for any remaining parameters. This combination was designed so that the benchmark consistent data set is replicated by a "forward" solution of the model: when we use these estimated and calibrated parameters together with labor endowments and unchanged 1984 tax rules, we find an equilibrium in which all prices are 1.0 and all quantities match the benchmark data.

11. See Ballard and others (1985, pp. 45–48, 139) for a discussion of the trade equations and of the relationship between the price elasticity of export demand and the price elasticity of import supply.

CHAPTER SEVEN

Simulations and Results

NOW THAT we have described the model, collected the data, and estimated the parameters, we are ready to conduct simulations. We can address two types of questions. We can use the model to simulate specific policy questions, such as specific tax changes associated with the Tax Reform Act of 1986. Such simulations do not factor in changes in all economic variables, but they can isolate the likely effect of a tax policy change if all other variables (such as the rates of inflation and unemployment) are constant. Specific policy simulations are described later, in chapter 9.

We can also use the model to address conceptual questions, by simulating the wholesale removal of an entire tax instrument. The repeal of a whole tax system may not represent a viable policy option, but results indicate the overall effects of the tax removal. These results include all counterfactual prices, quantities, and lifetime utilities of each group. The burden of the tax is indicated by the gain from removing it.

In this chapter we conduct some of these conceptual experiments to evaluate the lifetime incidence associated with different taxes. With the removal of each tax instrument, we specify the replacement tax the government uses to collect the same revenue as before. Then we measure gain or loss by the lifetime equivalent variation. The EV is the amount that could be paid to the group at the beginning of life, in current prices, that would be "equivalent" in terms of utility to a whole lifetime under the tax alternative. In other words, the EV is the amount of money necessary to achieve the new utility at the old prices. This gain from the removal of the tax represents our measure of the burden of the tax. We can also calculate the lifetime incidence of the entire U.S. tax system.

We begin by describing the policy parameters for each tax change. Next, as a basis for comparison, we present some detailed results from a benchmark simulation of 150 years with no change in any tax. Then we present the results of each simulation and compare the counterfactual results with benchmark results. All the simulations in this chapter are based on one "standard" set of parameters. In chapter 8 we change some of the model's parameters one at a time, recalculate incidence, and compare results.

Tax Parameters for Each Simulation

In this section we specify which tax rates are set to zero, or which other parameters are altered to simulate the removal of each tax. We cannot just remove a tax, however. If tax revenues were to fall, we would also have to specify how government expenditures would be reduced. This "balanced-budget" incidence calculation would measure the combined effects of the tax and expenditure change. For expenditures that do not change, we have to specify how government will recoup the revenue loss. This "differential" incidence calculation measures the combined effects of the tax removal and its replacement.[1] There is no way to isolate the impact of the tax removal alone.

Our analysis takes a differential incidence approach. For each tax removal, we first replace the revenue with a proportional tax on all individuals' lifetime labor endowments. The rate of endowment tax is calculated to raise the same amount of real revenue as in the benchmark equilibrium.[2] Because the present value of lifetime labor endowment includes the value of leisure, this replacement tax is equivalent to a proportional tax on all commodities that enter the utility function. Thus a proportional tax on this comprehensive measure of welfare represents a benchmark against which other tax instruments can be judged progressive or regressive. In addition, since the replacement tax does not distort any labor-leisure or consumption choices, it represents a lump-sum tax against which we can measure the excess burden of each tax instrument. It is not a viable policy option, but it is a useful hypothetical alternative for judging the efficiency of the actual U.S. tax system.

We do not apply the replacement tax to inheritances, so the tax on labor endowment is not a tax on all endowments. Given that different lifetime income categories have different capital inheritances, our choice for the replacement tax base can affect our results on lifetime tax incidence. A tax on inheritances would not be neutral, however. It would cause continually

1. Musgrave (1959) describes these different ways of calculating tax incidence.
2. Recall that government expenditures effectively enter consumer utility through a separable Cobb-Douglas sub-utility function. We assume government raises enough revenue to attain the same sub-utility as in the base case. Thus if the prices of goods purchased by government rise, the actual dollar revenue will also have to rise.

shrinking bequests and inheritances over time unless consumers saved more during their lifetimes to leave a bequest that makes up for the extra inheritance tax. This extra savings would effectively reverse some of the distorting effects of the current taxes on income from capital. The inheritance tax would provide welfare gains by removing some distortions in this model, so the distortions associated with the replaced taxes would seem more pronounced. Thus we use the more neutral replacement tax on labor endowments only.

In addition, however, we use an alternative replacement tax. The labor endowment tax is a nondistorting lump-sum tax replacement, but it is not very feasible. We use a tax on value added as a more realistic tax replacement. This VAT does distort labor-leisure choices in this model, but it provides an interesting additional set of results for comparison.

When each existing tax system is removed, an initial transition period affects young and old differently. The distributional effects across generations are seen in our figures showing the gain or loss to each annual cohort (from those who are old at the time of the change to those born in future years). The distributional effects between future rich and poor households are seen in our tables of welfare gains to each lifetime income group in the steady state. Overall effects on rich and poor, and old and young, are captured in a measure of "efficiency gain." In general, when an existing distortionary tax is replaced with a lump-sum endowment tax, this efficiency gain is positive.

We should consider two other points relating to this measure of efficiency. First, for the steady-state generation, we simply add the equivalent variations of all income groups to obtain an overall measure of welfare gain. While the gain over the lifetime for any individual is appropriately measured by the equivalent variation, it is much more difficult to measure in the aggregate. Implicitly, as a social welfare function, this procedure places equal weight on a dollar to the rich and a dollar to the poor.

Second, this steady-state welfare gain is not a pure efficiency measure, because it includes redistribution to later generations from current generations that may lose when the tax change is imposed.[3] Indeed, the figures in this

---

3. If the elderly take much leisure, for example, the replacement of almost any tax with an alternative tax on the total endowment of time will impose a windfall loss on those alive at the time of the change. With a fixed total revenue, the extra tax on the elderly allows a lower tax on new generations. Auerbach, Kotlikoff, and Skinner (1983) address this problem by introducing a "lump-sum redistribution authority" that collects enough extra tax on future generations to finance payments to older generations. Those alive at the time of the tax replacement are held to no change in utility, so these transfers must be calculated endogenously. Given their perfect foresight model, the authors must solve simultaneously for lump-sum tax and payment amounts in each year of the equilibrium sequence. Gravelle (1991) suggests a simpler plan that does not

chapter show gains to steady-state generations and losses to transitional generations. For an overall measure of "efficiency," we simply take the present value of all equivalent variations discounted at the net rate of return. This procedure implicitly puts lower weight on later generations, but the discounting is necessary to obtain a finite sum for a sequence that is growing over time because of technical progress and population growth. To avoid having a measure of efficiency that would increase with the number of individuals, we discount by population growth to calculate this present-value EV for the size of the population alive at the time of the change.

The difference between the steady-state welfare gain and the overall efficiency gain indicates how much of the steady-state gain is attributable to effects in the transition.

Finally, we note that our main results do not depend on ambiguous aggregations, transitional losses, or pure efficiency measures. Our primary interest is in the distributional effects of tax policy as reflected in the separate steady-state EV calculations. Tax incidence depends not on overall gains or losses but on each group's gain or loss relative to those of other groups. The distribution of equivalent variations across the lifetime income categories tells us about the regressivity or progressivity of the removed tax compared with that of a proportional endowment tax. Given this standard, if the replacement with the proportional tax causes lifetime poor individuals to enjoy welfare gains that are larger than those of rich individuals, the replaced tax is said to be lifetime regressive.[4]

We described the benchmark policy parameters in chapter 3. To generate simulations, we remove each tax and replace it with a proportional tax on labor endowments. The changes resulting from each tax removal are summarized in table 7-1 and described here:

Personal taxes. To eliminate personal taxes, we first change the marginal income tax rate from 0.30 to zero. Also, the coefficients describing income taxes collected from individuals (in table 3-4) are set to zero. These generate the different intercepts of the linear income tax function for each group. Finally, we set to zero the noncorporate investment tax credit and some specific

---

require calculating a perfect foresight transition, but isolates pure efficiency effects by comparing steady states that do not penalize transitional generations.

4. Economists typically measure relative effects, dividing the tax burden by household income. A tax is said to be regressive if this ratio decreases with income. Following this convention, we focus on equivalent variations relative to lifetime incomes as our measure of lifetime tax incidence. We also report the absolute size of equivalent variations.

Table 7-1. *Parameter Modifications for Each Tax Removal*

Type of tax	Modification for removal
Personal taxes	All personal marginal tax rates (τ_d, τ_{re}, τ_{ns}, τ_{nc}, τ_h, τ) are set to zero, tax coefficients (for the intercepts of each linear tax schedule) are set to zero, and noncorporate investment tax credit rates are set to zero
Sales and excise taxes	Sales tax rates on the seventeen consumer goods are set to zero, and output tax rates on the thirty-nine producer goods are set to zero
Labor-use taxes	Industry labor-use tax rates are set to zero, and government tax rate on labor use is set to zero
Property taxes	Property tax rates on residential property and on the five business types of capital are set to zero
Corporate taxes	Statutory corporate tax rate and corporate investment tax credit are set to zero
Entire tax system	All of the above

personal tax rates that affect the cost of capital (see table 3-17 for tax rates on receipt of interest, capital gains, dividend income, entrepreneurial income, and homeowner deductions).

Sales and excise taxes. We remove these by simply setting to zero all sales tax rates on the seventeen consumer goods (in table 3-6) and output tax rates on the thirty-seven outputs of producer goods (derived from table 3-16). The former are generally imposed by the fifty states, and the latter are mostly federal-level excise taxes. Our model has only one level of government, however, and all these taxes apply to commodities.

Payroll taxes. Our vector of tax rates on each industry's use of labor (in table 3-15) represents the industry-discriminating features of social security payroll taxes, unemployment compensation taxes, and public workman's compensation. Government also pays payroll tax on its use of labor. These taxes are eliminated by setting to zero the tax rates on use of labor by all industries and by government.

Property taxes. The cost of capital formulas in chapter 2 includes the rate of property tax on each type of capital. We change the property tax rate on residential land and structures from 0.01837 to zero. Table 3-18 also shows positive property tax rates on four of the five business assets (equipment, structures, land, and inventories); only intangible capital escapes property tax in the benchmark. This tax system is removed by setting all these tax rates to zero.

Corporate taxes. The corporate income tax is modeled by a set of parameters in the cost of capital formula (equation 2-23). The statutory corporate tax rate, u, is 0.495 in the benchmark, to reflect both the 46 percent federal rate and an average 6.55 percent state rate that is deductible against the federal tax. This rate is changed to zero. Also, the investment tax credit for corporations, k, is set to zero. Other provisions for depreciation are irrelevant, since the present value of allowances, z, is multiplied by the statutory corporate rate in the formula. With these changes, the cost of corporate capital is equal simply to the corporate discount rate,[5] minus expected inflation, plus the property tax rate.

Entire tax system. To measure the effects of removing all these tax instruments, we cannot simply add up the effects of removing each. That is, because of interactions in a second-best economy with multiple distortions, the combination is not equal to the sum of the parts. Therefore we combine all the above changes into a single counterfactual experiment, effectively removing all sources of tax revenue and requiring that all revenue be generated from the lifetime endowment tax. Results of this simulation provide a picture of the lifetime incidence in the entire U.S. tax system.

Other simulations. Many previous efforts calculate the effects of intersectoral tax differences by simulating the removal of the "surtax" on the corporate sector relative to the noncorporate sector. In our model, this level playing field would be achieved through the full integration of corporate and personal taxes. Under the partnership method, for example, all corporate-source income would be fully taxed, once, at the personal level. This reform is considered in chapter 9, along with other specific policy reforms such as the Tax Reform Act of 1986 and the introduction of a value-added tax. For now, however, we note that the removal of the corporate surtax is different from the removal of the entire corporate tax system. This chapter simply removes each tax system.

The Benchmark as a Basis of Comparison

We first present some pertinent results from the base case, a sequence of 150 years with no change in tax policy. Then, for each simulation, we ex-

---

5. Corporate tax rate changes may affect the discount rate itself. With a fall in the corporate tax rate, there is a rise in the after-tax interest rate, which is the discount rate on debt-financed investment.

Table 7-2. *Summary of Base-Case Results in Initial and 150th Year*

Millions of 1984 dollars unless otherwise specified

Item	Initial period	Year 150
After-tax income[a]	4,375,152	18,583,848
Sales taxes paid	231,788	984,645
Personal taxes paid	387,621	1,646,289
Transfer income	92,754	393,990
Value of labor supplied[b]	4,065,008	17,266,353
Value of capital supplied[c]	605,010	2,569,793
Value of leisure[d]	756,338	3,213,250
Output per unit of labor	4.082	8.414
Effective tax rate on capital		
Corporate sector	0.4655	0.4655
Noncorporate sector	0.3278	0.3278
Owner-occupied housing	0.2321	0.2321
National income	5,708,255	24,246,045
Total government revenue[e]	1,657,647	7,040,833
Exports (= imports)	338,577	1,438,144
Capital stock	19,832,231	84,251,436
Capital-labor ratio[f]	4.879	4.879
Rental-wage ratio[g]	0.040	0.040

Source: Output of the model, using all data and assumptions described throughout the book.
a. Capital income plus labor income, minus personal income taxes (before transfers).
b. After payroll tax but before personal tax.
c. Net of all taxes.
d. Valued at the wage rate net of all taxes.
e. Tax revenue plus government's capital endowment revenue.
f. Capital stock divided by quantity of labor supplied.
g. Equals rate of return net of all tax, since wage rate equals one.

amine the changes in national income, capital stocks, labor supply, goods prices, and other important variables. We chose to create thirty equilibrium simulations, five years apart, since all the counterfactuals manage to reach a steady state within 150 years of the policy change.

For the base case, table 7-2 summarizes some of the aggregate results. The first column indicates $4.375 trillion of after-tax income in the first period, plus another $756 billion of leisure not supplied to the market. Personal taxes are $387 billion. Prices and effective tax rates are constant in this benchmark sequence, while dollars grow by a combination of technical progress and population change. Thus the second column for the 150th year shows values that are 4.25 times the first column entries for income, taxes paid, capital, labor, and leisure. The output per unit of labor, however, grows from 4.08 to 8.41.

Table 7-2 also shows that the ratio of capital stock to labor supplied is 4.88. To compare this figure with others used in the literature, we first note that the net rate of return is 0.04, the overall effective tax rate is about one-

Table 7-3. *Base-Case Capital Stocks and Leisure, by Lifetime Income Category, 150th Year*

Millions of 1984 dollars

Lifetime income category[a]	Capital stocks	Leisure	Ratio of capital income to labor income
1[b]	362,539	6,931	0.153
2	3,066,082	117,050	0.199
3	3,290,692	208,546	0.136
4	4,669,427	273,850	0.162
5	3,518,761	314,671	0.104
6	4,575,462	391,529	0.121
7	7,841,299	447,221	0.194
8	4,799,392	510,236	0.098
9	5,493,590	586,857	0.099
10	6,799,266	693,445	0.109
11	13,864,287	768,637	0.224
12[c]	5,976,569	271,384	0.290

Source: Output of the model, using all data and assumptions described throughout the first six chapters.

a. Recall that the number of individuals in the different categories varies. Categories 1 and 12 contain 2 percent of the population each, categories 2 and 11 contain 8 percent each, and all other categories contain 10 percent each.

b. Poorest.

c. Richest.

third, and thus the gross return to capital is about 0.06. The implied ratio of capital income to labor income is $4.88 \times .06 = 0.29$, so capital's share of total income is 0.23 in our benchmark sequence. This share is very close to the "historical share" of 0.25 used by Lawrence H. Summers (1981) and Alan J. Auerbach and Laurence J. Kotlikoff (1987).[6]

Table 7-3 shows accumulated capital and steady-state leisure for the twelve lifetime income groups. The first two columns provide the basis for percentage changes shown later. We also want a summary capital-labor ratio for each group, to help explain distributional effects of factor price changes. A complication here is that this ratio changes with age. For the third column, we simply add all ages in each group to get total capital income and total labor income. Their ratio summarizes the net effect in our model of estimated wage profiles, life-cycle behavior, and other specified parameters. It does not change smoothly across the groups, primarily because the profiles are based

6. As described in earlier chapters, the capital stock is determined within our model by the life-cycle framework, bequests, and our choices for parameters. In the standard case, we chose parameters so that the capital stock replicates other production data. Thus the capital share replicates "historical" figures. If we were to use a lower intertemporal rate of substitution or a higher rate of time preference, the benchmark sequence would have less capital. The next chapter considers various sensitivity cases with different parameter configurations and sometimes different capital shares.

Table 7-4. *Initial Period Base-Case Values of Annual Discretionary Income (DI) and Savings, for Each Income Group*

1984 dollars per person

Age	Group 1 DI	Group 1 Savings	Group 2 DI	Group 2 Savings	Group 3 DI	Group 3 Savings	Group 4 DI	Group 4 Savings	Group 5 DI	Group 5 Savings	Group 6 DI	Group 6 Savings
1	1,249	−649	9,265	1,403	9,275	−1,927	12,715	−1,999	13,786	−3,121	19,842	−1,197
2	1,882	−50	10,553	2,551	12,057	655	15,937	960	17,017	−192	22,251	836
3	3,180	1,103	11,717	3,115	14,582	2,325	19,142	3,043	20,386	1,887	25,013	1,993
4	4,199	1,982	12,437	3,252	16,431	3,344	21,810	4,621	23,141	3,390	27,664	3,086
5	4,330	2,061	12,488	3,089	17,327	3,934	23,525	5,934	24,847	4,634	29,854	4,702
6	4,126	1,675	12,447	2,293	17,819	3,351	24,633	5,630	25,979	4,144	31,882	4,711
7	3,337	771	11,833	1,205	17,421	2,276	24,429	4,536	26,011	3,154	32,838	4,395
8	2,570	−69	11,077	145	16,640	1,064	23,289	2,830	25,492	1,984	32,873	3,620
9	2,009	−617	10,267	−610	15,691	192	21,396	1,038	24,669	1,277	31,908	2,800
10	1,785	−1,135	9,458	−2,632	14,740	−2,487	18,944	−3,683	23,623	−2,376	29,829	−2,524
11	1,825	−1,015	8,548	−3,215	13,828	−2,933	16,094	−5,920	22,265	−3,031	26,595	−4,882
12	2,478	−455	7,965	−4,183	13,613	−3,697	13,751	−8,984	21,208	−4,916	23,203	−9,306

Age	Group 7 DI	Group 7 Savings	Group 8 DI	Group 8 Savings	Group 9 DI	Group 9 Savings	Group 10 DI	Group 10 Savings	Group 11 DI	Group 11 Savings	Group 12 DI	Group 12 Savings
1	31,644	7,615	26,416	−994	31,869	333	31,864	−5,393	53,590	1,961	94,762	21,835
2	30,395	5,937	30,354	2,453	35,080	2,980	38,687	763	60,431	7,878	93,331	19,099
3	30,706	4,415	33,765	3,774	38,296	3,791	45,152	4,386	66,846	10,355	95,724	15,929
4	31,843	3,772	36,235	4,214	40,921	4,080	50,132	6,607	71,719	11,405	99,436	14,240
5	33,334	4,606	37,646	4,876	42,722	5,019	53,157	8,615	74,695	12,971	102,700	15,511
6	35,321	4,289	38,633	3,233	44,219	3,491	54,772	6,655	76,311	9,634	104,724	10,540
7	36,601	4,116	38,663	1,606	44,746	2,111	54,536	4,166	75,935	6,137	103,916	5,322
8	36,924	3,513	38,363	251	44,830	980	53,439	1,633	74,466	2,678	101,173	−231
9	35,757	2,512	38,080	156	44,705	1,073	52,264	717	72,574	1,143	97,914	−2,986
10	32,615	−4,337	37,912	−4,240	44,278	−4,219	51,431	−5,864	70,366	−9,029	95,274	−16,875
11	27,380	−8,572	37,858	−3,152	43,328	−3,856	51,236	−4,507	67,820	−9,425	94,535	14,577
12	21,387	−15,742	38,933	−3,421	42,710	6,020	53,202	−4,368	66,444	−13,332	98,975	−13,713

on twelve separate regressions. In general it follows a U-shaped pattern, declining to 0.098 for the eighth group and rising to 0.290 for the highest lifetime income group.

For further disaggregation, table 7-4 shows discretionary income (available after minimum required purchases) and savings (based on life-cycle behavior) for each age category within each income group. In any row, the difference between these two numbers is composite consumption of leisure and goods (in excess of minimum required purchases). The table thus shows the outcomes of combining wage profiles from coefficients in table 3-3, minimum required purchases from table 5-4, and all other assumptions in the model. Note that while discretionary income usually rises and then falls with age, composite consumption always rises with age. The rate of time preference is lower than the net rate of return, so individuals desire smoothly rising consumption. Given our estimated hump-shaped earnings profiles, savings is often negative when individuals are young, positive when they are middle aged, and negative again when they retire. Although not shown in the table, leisure itself increases steadily with age for all groups.

Comparing lifetime income categories in table 7-4, we notice that most groups start with one or two five-year periods of borrowing, whereas some groups start with positive savings. These differences reflect the separately estimated wage profiles in table 3-3 and figure 4-2. Groups with earnings that peak late in life tend to borrow more early in life. Finally, we note that dissaving in retirement leaves each group with exactly enough capital to give a bequest that has grown at the economy-wide growth rate since their inheritance was received.

Counterfactual Results Compared to the Benchmark

When we simulate the removal and replacement of a tax, we generate a "counterfactual" sequence. Welfare effects are discussed later, but table 7-5 starts with some other counterfactual steady-state results for each tax replacement. It shows percentage changes from the base-case results of table 7-2. Table 7-5 shows that all simulations lead to higher capital stocks and capital-labor ratios. All (except the removal of payroll taxes) lead to higher output per unit of labor and higher national income. These increases reflect the "efficiency" of replacing a distorting tax with a lump-sum tax on endowments.

As for the payroll tax replacement, starting from the bottom of the column, we see a higher gross wage (lower rental-wage ratio), unchanged capital-labor

Table 7-5. *Percentage Changes in Summary Results for Steady State with Removal of Various Taxes*

Item	Removal of taxes					
	Personal	Sales and excise	Payroll	Property	Corporate	All
After-tax income[a]	15.78	−1.71	−1.98	1.69	−0.01	18.50
Sales taxes paid	2.88	. . .	−6.08	−0.96	−0.48	. . .
Personal taxes paid	. . .	24.74	16.66	4.20	2.12	. . .
Transfer income	−2.54	−9.23	−6.82	−2.50	−1.18	−21.00
Value of labor supplied[b]	2.52	0.79	0.62	−0.22	−0.21	3.47
Value of capital supplied[c]	33.52	−0.38	−6.80	16.75	2.90	49.57
Value of leisure[d]	29.31	−2.96	−2.34	0.83	0.79	24.19
Output per unit of labor	2.65	0.34	−0.02	1.18	0.99	5.43
Effective tax rate on capital						
Corporate sector	−64.25	0.30	0.60	−14.03	−9.58	. . .
Noncorporate sector	−41.37	0.76	2.44	−42.86	.00	. . .
Owner-occupied housing	26.50	2.07	6.81	−126.80	.00	. . .
National income	5.46	1.10	−0.06	1.21	0.78	9.10
Total government revenue[e]	−0.64	−2.28	−6.33	−0.24	−0.71	−9.41
Exports (= imports)	−4.09	−4.66	−7.20	−1.16	−1.56	−17.52
Capital stock	15.89	1.55	0.63	7.19	2.20	30.82
Capital-labor ratio[f]	13.05	0.76	0.02	7.44	2.42	26.44
Rental-wage ratio[g]	10.48	−2.38	−7.60	6.68	.00	6.50
Replacement tax on endowment (millions)	2,094,104	1,308,089	751,028	414,980	33,761	5,526,465
Replacement tax rate (tax as percent of lifetime endowments)	9.58	8.55	4.91	2.71	0.22	25.29

a. Capital income plus labor income, minus personal income taxes (before transfers).
b. After payroll tax but before personal tax.
c. Net of all taxes.
d. Valued at the wage rate net of all taxes.
e. Tax revenue plus government's capital endowment revenue.
f. Capital stock divided by quantity of labor supplied.
g. Equals rate of return net of all tax, since wage rate equals one.

ratio, but slightly higher capital stock. Therefore labor supply is slightly higher. These increases are reflected in the positive efficiency gain discussed later. Since labor is numeraire,[7] however, the higher relative wage means that *other* prices are falling. When the gross wage is fixed by assumption, the lower relative prices of outputs mean that nominal income falls. This example highlights the problem with national income accounting, and the reason we use utility-based calculations such as the equivalent variation.

7. That is, the gross price of labor is kept constant under all simulations, and all other prices are adjusted to attain the equilibrium outcomes.

The incidence literature in the tradition of Arnold C. Harberger (1962) places great importance on the "functional" distribution of income between labor and capital. Harberger's incidence results were presented in terms of the relative returns to those factors, expressed as the rental-wage ratio, r/w. (In our model r is the return net of all taxes, whereas w is the wage net of payroll tax and gross of personal tax.) Removal of property taxes raises the net rate of return r, and thus the rental-wage ratio (r/w). The tax is borne more than proportionately by capital in this functional distribution.

Removing personal taxes lowers the wage w (gross of personal taxes), and thus raises r/w. Removing payroll taxes raises the wage w (net of payroll tax), and thus lowers r/w. This tax on labor is borne by labor. Similarly, removal of consumption-based taxes reduces r/w. That is, sales taxes also are borne predominantly by labor.

Interestingly, the removal of the corporate income tax has no effect on relative rates of return. In terms of the "functional distribution," where Harberger found that the corporate tax was generally borne fully by capital, we find that it is borne proportionately by both factors. We should note, however, that all the changes in the corporate tax column of table 7-5 are small: the corporate tax in our model raises little revenue and usually has little effect, because any positive tax on the income from equity-financed investment is almost entirely offset by investment tax credits, accelerated depreciation, and interest deductions on debt-financed investment.[8]

For the replacement of the entire tax system with the proportional endowment tax, table 7-5 shows an increase in the rental-wage ratio of 6.5 percent. This result indicates that capital rather than labor tends to bear the larger burden of the existing tax system. The point of our research, however, is to improve on this measure of incidence: a major problem with this older literature's emphasis on the functional distribution is that most individuals have *both* labor income and capital income. Capital income is associated more with age than with lifetime income category. Below, we express tax incidence as the gain or loss to each lifetime income group, using a measure that incorporates the "uses-side" effects of goods prices as well as "sources-side" effects of factor prices.

Next, consider the effective tax rate on capital in the three sectors. Table

8. The base year is 1984, so the corporate tax reflects the generous accelerated depreciation and investment tax credit provisions of the Economic Recovery Tax Act of 1981. Corporate tax revenue in our model is based on these low effective marginal tax rates, but actual revenue was also reduced considerably by the 1981 act. According to figures in the 1987 *Economic Report of the President*, table B-78, corporate tax revenue fell from more than 15 percent of total federal revenue in the 1970s to about 10 percent by 1984.

Table 7-6. *Effects of Tax Removal on Effective Marginal Tax Rates on Capital Assets*

		Removal of taxes					
Sector	Base case	Personal	Sales and excise	Payroll	Property	Corporate	All
Corporate							
Equipment	0.200	−0.334	0.198	0.194	0.072	0.413	0.00
Structures	0.511	0.284	0.514	0.519	0.431	0.442	0.00
Inventories	0.571	0.347	0.572	0.575	0.532	0.413	0.00
Land	0.587	0.379	0.588	0.592	0.532	0.442	0.00
Intangibles	0.074	−0.460	0.075	0.077	0.072	0.338	0.00
Overall	0.466	0.166	0.467	0.468	0.400	0.421	0.00
Noncorporate							
Equipment	−0.138	0.148	−0.142	−0.154	−0.411	−0.138	0.00
Structures	0.324	0.203	0.327	0.335	0.164	0.324	0.00
Inventories	0.333	0.148	0.335	0.340	0.236	0.333	0.00
Land	0.371	0.203	0.374	0.380	0.236	0.371	0.00
Intangibles	−0.012	0.000	−0.013	−0.013	−0.012	−0.012	0.00
Overall	0.328	0.192	0.330	0.336	0.187	0.328	0.00

7-2 shows that this rate is 0.47 in the corporate sector, 0.33 in the noncorporate sector, and 0.23 for owner-occupied housing. Table 7-5 shows that removing most types of taxes would reduce the corporate rate relative to the other effective tax rates and thus work toward leveling the playing field among the corporate, noncorporate, and housing sectors. Removing property taxes causes the distortion to increase, however, since it most reduces the lowest effective tax rate (on owner-occupied housing).

For more detail, table 7-6 displays effective tax rates by asset within each sector. The corporate sector rate in the base year is only 0.20 for equipment because of the 10 percent credit, and only 0.07 for intangible assets because of expensing. Rates exceed 0.50 for other assets such as structures, inventories, and land. These disparities are basically unaffected by most of the tax removals, but they are virtually eliminated by the corporate tax removal. In this way the corporate tax affects the prices of equipment- or intangible-intensive outputs relative to the prices of other outputs. It thus has both distributional and efficiency effects, even though the revenue implications are small.

For the twelve lifetime income groups, effects of each tax removal on capital stocks and leisure are shown in table 7-7. These percentage changes start from the benchmark magnitudes in table 7-3. The figures indicate that the major tax instruments in the United States tend to depress capital formation and discourage labor supply (increase leisure) for almost every group. The effect of each particular tax differs in magnitude. Variations in the percentage changes for capital stocks among groups can be attributed to variations in their capital holdings, which in turn result from variations in the estimated time pattern of earnings (compared with the time pattern of desired consumption).[9] Variations in the percentage changes in leisure reflect the differences in labor intensity across these groups.

Replacing the various taxes with an endowment tax also has direct and indirect effects on the relative prices of goods and leisure. Table 7-8 presents consumer goods prices (net of sales taxes) in the initial equilibrium period and in the steady state (the 150th year). All such prices equal 1.0 in all periods of the base sequence. Note that the removal of these distortionary taxes tends to lower the steady-state prices of consumer goods. That is, the effect of each tax is to raise consumption prices (the wage is numeraire). The reason in each case is different, but the price of the consumer good always reflects the cost of factors and taxes, with no leftover profits. For example, the property tax was shown to reduce the net rate of return (r/w in table 7-5) by 6.7 percent, but it raises the required gross-of-tax rate of return and thus raises product prices. It especially raises the price of housing services in table 7-8. In contrast, the payroll tax was shown to reduce the net wage and thus raise r/w in table 7-5. Product prices in this case reflect a fixed wage, w, a higher return to capital, r, and the higher payroll tax.

For the sake of later discussion, notice which goods in table 7-8 experience the largest price increases because of taxes. Typically the prices that rise the most because of taxes (fall the most with removal) are those corresponding to goods with relatively high minimum required purchases, such as food, alcohol, tobacco, housing, and gasoline. This result suggests one reason that tax burdens on the uses-side tend to fall more heavily on the lifetime poor: distortionary taxation inflates the prices of "necessities" more than "luxuries" like services and education. That is, the bundles of goods consumed by the lifetime poor are subject to higher tax rates than those consumed by the lifetime rich. The fact that consumption of goods becomes more costly relative to the net wage rate explains why we see, in table 7-7, that most of these taxes increase leisure and reduce labor supply.

So far we have discussed the prices of goods relative to leisure, but taxes also affect the relative prices of composite commodities (goods and leisure)

9. Some groups do not have to save as much as other groups in the benchmark sequence because their wage profiles peak later in life. See figure 4-2 and accompanying discussion of the estimated wage profiles.

Table 7-7. *Effects of Tax Removal on Percentage Changes in Capital Stocks and Leisure in Steady State*

Lifetime income category	Personal		Sales and excise		Payroll		Property		Corporate		All	
	K	L	K	L	K	L	K	L	K	L	K	L
1	−26.46	−30.70	3.06	9.23	2.02	3.55	2.46	5.11	2.17	5.94	−15.65	−16.81
2	7.62	−12.21	0.90	−0.94	1.64	−1.58	4.31	1.69	2.23	1.50	19.77	−11.78
3	17.27	−13.18	3.10	−1.98	1.42	−1.94	7.59	0.78	2.83	1.05	36.39	−14.94
4	15.04	−11.36	1.40	−2.41	1.39	−2.09	6.44	0.88	2.56	0.97	30.43	−13.90
5	36.35	−9.27	4.63	−2.63	1.15	−2.11	11.37	0.46	3.56	0.86	62.23	−12.59
6	28.00	−11.78	3.01	−2.97	1.13	−2.26	10.82	0.55	3.42	0.78	50.88	−15.31
7	17.67	−9.91	−0.05	−3.01	1.32	−2.34	7.05	1.11	2.67	0.86	31.99	−13.10
8	23.34	−10.02	3.99	−3.24	0.60	−2.35	14.77	0.43	4.01	0.69	54.28	−14.24
9	29.66	−9.48	3.61	−3.33	0.57	−2.35	14.87	0.46	4.06	0.69	59.69	−13.85
10	28.41	−9.42	4.00	−3.34	0.29	−2.45	14.02	0.49	3.59	0.63	56.55	−13.89
11	12.40	−7.86	0.95	−3.14	0.36	−2.62	7.59	1.33	2.11	0.70	27.43	−11.59
12	27.33	−3.05	0.08	−3.04	0.67	−2.64	6.52	1.78	2.01	0.79	37.50	−6.69

a. K = capital stock; L = leisure.

Table 7-8. *Effects of Tax Removal on Prices of Consumer Goods*[a]

| | | Removal of taxes | | | | | | | | | | |
| | | Personal | | Sales and excise | | Payroll | | Property | | Corporate | | All | |
Consumer good	Benchmark tax rate	Initial period	150th year	Initial period	150th year	Initial period	150th year	Initial period	150th year	Initial period	150th year	Initial period	150th year
1. Food	0.0374	1.004	0.957	0.950	0.945	0.935	0.933	1.002	0.978	0.993	0.985	0.886	0.810
2. Alcohol	0.7260	1.004	0.957	0.950	0.945	0.935	0.933	1.002	0.978	0.993	0.985	0.886	0.810
3. Tobacco	0.7890	1.002	0.951	0.935	0.930	0.934	0.932	1.003	0.978	0.988	0.980	0.865	0.785
4. Utilities	0.0387	0.995	0.954	0.949	0.945	0.933	0.931	1.004	0.984	0.995	0.989	0.879	0.816
5. Shelter	0.0000	1.085	1.008	0.957	0.950	0.936	0.933	0.969	0.934	1.005	0.993	0.952	0.813
6. Furnishings	0.0655	0.997	0.959	0.945	0.942	0.923	0.921	1.005	0.988	0.985	0.980	0.858	0.803
7. Appliances	0.0655	0.994	0.958	0.949	0.946	0.931	0.929	1.006	0.990	0.984	0.979	0.868	0.815
8. Apparel	0.0655	0.997	0.960	0.946	0.942	0.931	0.929	1.005	0.988	0.986	0.980	0.867	0.813
9. Transportation	0.0040	0.996	0.954	0.950	0.946	0.932	0.930	1.004	0.984	0.995	0.989	0.879	0.816
10. Automobiles	0.0509	0.996	0.965	0.953	0.950	0.932	0.931	1.005	0.990	0.990	0.986	0.879	0.832
11. Personal services	0.0300	1.003	0.979	0.972	0.970	0.934	0.933	1.001	0.990	0.997	0.993	0.909	0.871
12. Financial services	0.0000	1.007	0.984	0.964	0.961	0.935	0.934	1.001	0.990	0.998	0.994	0.906	0.867
13. Recreation	0.0446	0.998	0.961	0.956	0.952	0.933	0.931	1.005	0.987	0.990	0.984	0.883	0.827
14. Nondurables	0.0524	0.996	0.959	0.948	0.945	0.931	0.930	1.006	0.988	0.988	0.983	0.872	0.817
15. Gasoline	0.2590	0.999	0.958	0.918	0.914	0.933	0.931	1.003	0.984	0.986	0.980	0.844	0.782
16. Health care	0.0300	1.001	0.976	0.968	0.966	0.935	0.934	1.002	0.990	0.995	0.992	0.904	0.865
17. Education	0.0300	1.002	0.980	0.974	0.971	0.936	0.935	1.001	0.991	0.997	0.994	0.912	0.876

a. Net-of-tax consumer prices. These prices equal 1.0 in the benchmark.

Table 7-9. *Prices of Composite Commodity (Goods and Leisure), by Age Category*

| Age category | Base case | Removal of taxes | | | | | |
		Personal	Sales and excise	Payroll	Property	Corporate	All
1	4.903	5.157	4.405	4.631	4.801	4.852	4.262
2	4.613	4.865	4.250	4.358	4.525	4.566	4.129
3	4.841	5.088	4.413	4.571	4.753	4.790	4.276
4	5.012	5.264	4.549	4.733	4.920	4.961	4.408
5	4.767	5.016	4.389	4.502	4.679	4.717	4.256
6	5.051	5.298	4.594	4.768	4.960	4.997	4.438
7	5.027	5.279	4.623	4.746	4.945	4.976	4.485
8	4.829	5.081	4.423	4.560	4.738	4.779	4.285
9	4.342	4.585	4.025	4.103	4.262	4.299	3.921
10	4.871	5.120	4.466	4.600	4.785	4.822	4.330
11	4.188	4.437	3.844	3.960	4.111	4.149	3.765
12	4.056	4.321	3.783	3.837	3.963	4.022	3.704
Ratio of most expensive to least	1.245	1.226	1.222	1.243	1.252	1.242	1.211

at different points in the life cycle. These prices differ by age category in the benchmark steady state (table 7-9), because the mix of goods purchased when one is young is not the same as the mix purchased when one is old. In particular, the weight on leisure is highest for the oldest groups. When the personal tax is removed, the prices of these composites rise, primarily because the price of leisure rises. For all other simulations the prices of composite commodities fall (that is, taxes raise prices). The last row of the table indicates the ratio of the most expensive composite commodity to the least expensive. For all simulations except the removal of the property tax, this ratio is lower than in the benchmark, indicating that taxes increase price disparities. For an overall evaluation of intertemporal price distortions, however, we would need to use the net rate of return to compare the present prices of composite consumption in different periods.

Lifetime Tax Incidence under Standard Parameters

Tables 7-10 through 7-14 show the distribution of U.S. tax burdens across the twelve lifetime income categories. Recall that individuals are classified by the present value of labor endowments before taxes and transfers. All of these tables have the same format, first showing the distributional incidence for the steady-state generation and then the overall effect for the steady-state generation (as a percent of lifetime income and as a percent of the revenue from the tax). The last two lines use the present-value sum of all welfare changes to all generations. The overall steady-state calculations may include gains that come at the expense of transition generations, so the present-value calculation is meant to summarize the net gain or loss for examining issues of efficiency.

The equivalent variation in column 1 of each table derives from equation 2-34 and is shown in billions of 1984 dollars. Because the lifetime income categories differ in population, column 2 adjusts the EV to show the burden per person in each group.[10] The result is still an absolute dollar figure, and one may wish to judge the size of these burdens relative to some other measure, such as income or utility. In particular, we wish to define a tax as "proportional" in its incidence if the average tax burden as a fraction of income is equal across all income categories.

A remaining problem is to define income. Since our study focuses on lifetime tax incidence, the third column of these tables shows the EV as a percent of the present value of lifetime income. This denominator includes all endowment income plus transfers minus taxes, and it equals the present value of all spending on goods and leisure. The ratio can be interpreted as the percentage increase in welfare for each person in the group.[11] In addition, these percentage gains in the third columns of tables 7-10 to 7-14 are used to generate the stacked-bar graph of figure 1-4 in chapter 1.

Incidence of Personal Taxes

As shown in table 7-10, personal taxes are lifetime progressive. Removing personal taxes and replacing them with a proportional endowment tax gives richer individuals larger welfare improvements than poorer individuals, both

10. Recall that we subdivided the top and bottom deciles. Thus lifetime income categories 1 and 12 each constitute 2 percent of the population, categories 2 and 11 each constitute 8 percent, and all the other categories each contain 10 percent. The total adult population in this model is 124.6 million.

11. Equivalent variation as a percent of lifetime utility could be misleading. Because lifetime utility depends on consumption *in excess* of minimum required purchases, the ratio of utility to income may be quite low for poor individuals. Thus a tax that took the same fraction of everyone's income could take a very high fraction of the poor group's utility. All taxes look very regressive by such a measure, so we report only the EV as a percent of lifetime income.

Table 7-10. *Incidence of Personal Taxes under Standard Parameters for Steady-State Generations, at 1984 Levels, Compared with a Proportional Labor Endowment Tax*[a]

Lifetime income category	EV (billions of dollars)	EV in dollars per person	EV as percent of lifetime income
1	−0.60	−12.248	−4.31
2	−0.21	−1,062	−0.23
3	−1.27	−5,177	−0.92
4	0.57	2,319	0.35
5	3.60	14,712	1.99
6	0.06	265	0.03
7	3.83	15,661	1.64
8	4.13	16,880	1.60
9	6.14	25,114	2.13
10	7.47	30,563	2.26
11	13.68	69,911	3.92
12	10.69	218,521	9.00
Total	48.10	19,667	2.02
Steady-state EV as percent of revenue	. . .	. . .	9.83
Efficiency measures[b]			
As percent of lifetime income	. . .	. . .	0.68
As percent of revenue	. . .	. . .	3.14

a. Positive gain from removal = the burden of the tax. The lifetime equivalent variation (EV) shows the gain in billions of 1984 dollars for each income group in the new steady state. We divide by the number of individuals in each group to get EV per person (in 1984 dollars.) We divide by the present value of lifetime labor endowments to get the percentage gain in the last column. Efficiency measures at the bottom of the table take the present value of lifetime gains for transitional generations as well as those in the steady state.

b. Present value of EV for all generations as percent of: present value of all lifetime income, or present value of revenue from this tax.

in absolute and relative terms. This result implies that as lifetime incomes increase, the burdens of personal taxes rise more than proportionally. Remember that individuals in this model have different linear personal tax schedules, with different intercepts but the same marginal tax rate. The personal tax system in this model is not "graduated" in the sense of increasing marginal tax rates, but it is "progressive" in the sense of increasing average tax rates that reflect the benchmark data on taxes paid by each group. These results show that on a lifetime basis, the general equilibrium economic incidence is also progressive.

As indicated in the first column of the table, the total lifetime welfare cost to each annual cohort is $48 billion in the steady state (at 1984 levels). This figure is certainly a large dollar magnitude, but in part it just reflects the large size of the U.S. economy. It can be better interpreted relative to other large numbers like population, income, and tax revenue. The second column shows that this $48 billion steady-state gain amounts to $19,667 per person. The appropriate measure for judging the size of this lifetime equivalent variation is the present value of lifetime income. Therefore the third column shows that this gain is 2.02 percent of lifetime income. To indicate something about the welfare characteristics of each tax instrument, the following line shows that the EV is 9.8 percent of the personal income tax revenue just replaced by the endowment tax.

This steady-state gain is not a pure efficiency gain, because it omits effects on transitional generations. In particular, future generations benefit at the expense of older generations. This intergenerational transfer is easy to understand: the replacement with the endowment tax (a tax on consumption and leisure) increases the burden on older individuals who have already paid income taxes throughout their working years and are now taking retirement leisure. Since more revenue is collected from those old at the time of the change, less needs to be collected from the young and future generations. Part of the steady-state gain therefore reflects this intergenerational redistribution.[12]

To disentangle these redistributions from net gains in economic efficiency, we take the present value of EVs to all annual cohorts. Affected cohorts include those who started economic life fifty-nine years before the change through those born in all years after the change. Because this measure accounts for early losses as well as future gains, it can be interpreted as a net efficiency gain. For the removal of the personal income tax, this present-value efficiency gain to all generations is 0.68 percent of the corresponding present value of all lifetime incomes. The difference between the 2.02 percent steady-state gain and the 0.68 present-value gain simply reflects losses to transitional generations.[13]

---

12. Auerbach (1989) and Gravelle (1991) discuss a conceptual derivation of a "pure" efficiency effect that uses special lump-sum transfers to protect transitional generations from loss. See note 3. One problem is that their counterfactual simulations do not correspond to any viable policy option. Here we simply impose the tax change, trace the transition, and take the present value of gains and losses.

13. Our lifetime efficiency cost as a fraction of lifetime income can be compared to other measures of annual efficiency cost over annual income. For example, the efficiency cost of Harberger (1966) is often expressed as 0.5 percent of GNP. That figure relates to corporate tax distortions in the allocation of capital between sectors, whereas our 0.68 percent figure relates to personal income tax distortions in the allocation of time between labor and leisure, and in the allocation of consumption among time periods.

Table 7-11. *Incidence of Sales and Excise Taxes under Standard Parameters for Steady-State Generations, at 1984 Levels, Compared with a Proportional Labor Endowment Tax*[a]

Lifetime income category	EV (billions of dollars)	EV in dollars per person	EV as percent of lifetime income
1	0.37	7,635	2.69
2	1.55	7,921	1.70
3	1.87	7,649	1.35
4	1.96	8,008	1.19
5	1.97	8,050	1.09
6	1.90	7,752	0.90
7	2.08	8,526	0.89
8	1.92	7,857	0.74
9	1.96	8,030	0.68
10	2.31	9,429	0.70
11	3.17	16,226	0.91
12	1.22	24,940	1.03
Total	22.29	9,114	0.94
Steady-state EV as percent of revenue	. . .	. . .	7.29
Efficiency measures[b]			
As percent of lifetime income	. . .	. . .	0.28
As percent of revenue	. . .	. . .	2.11

a. Positive gain from removal = the burden of the tax. The lifetime equivalent variation (EV) shows the gain in billions of 1984 dollars for each income group in the new steady state. We divide by the number of individuals in each group to get EV per person (in 1984 dollars.) We divide by the present value of lifetime labor endowments to get the percentage gain in the last column. Efficiency measures at the bottom of the table take the present value of lifetime gains for transitional generations as well as those in the steady state.

b. Present value of EV for all generations as percent of: present value of all lifetime income, or present value of revenue from this tax.

Finally, the table shows that the present-value efficiency gain is 3.1 percent of the present value of personal income tax revenue. When this ratio is later compared among tax instruments, we see that the personal income tax is relatively inefficient. This result might be surprising because the personal income tax has a very broad base and is not thought to distort the allocation of resources among assets, industries, or sectors. As captured in our model, however, the personal income tax does distort both labor-leisure decisions and savings decisions.

Incidence of Sales and Excise Taxes

Table 7-11 shows sales and excise tax burdens. Per capita EV dollar amounts in the second column are similar for the first ten lifetime income categories, suggesting that these taxes are regressive in relative terms for 90 percent of the population. The relative EV results in the last column suggest that these taxes are also regressive in a lifetime perspective. For the top two groups, the burden of sales taxes rises relative to the endowment tax because the latter tax does not apply to their large inheritances.

Regressivity across the first ten groups is due to two main factors: the lifetime poor spend larger portions of their incomes on goods that are taxed at the highest rates (for example, gasoline, alcohol, and tobacco), and the lifetime poor in our model have higher consumption-leisure ratios relative to the lifetime rich.

In annual incidence studies, sales and excise taxes are regressive because consumption makes up a decreasing fraction of the annual budgets of higher-income groups. For lifetime incidence, many recent authors (for example, James M. Poterba, 1989) have speculated that the lifetime burdens of sales and excise taxes may be close to proportional, since consumption over the lifetime must roughly equal income over the lifetime (depending on bequests). Our results differ because of the unique features of our model. In particular, we consider a variety of tax rates on goods that make up different fractions of the budgets of different lifetime income categories. We also consider the possibility that untaxed leisure constitutes a different fraction of the total budget of different lifetime income categories.

However, we do not use empirical techniques to measure this latter difference by income category. Instead, we simply specify that we want to have the same lifetime utility function for all individuals in the model, with different observed expenditure shares by income category explained by a set of minimum required amounts of consumption goods. We did not specify a minimum required amount of leisure. Because everyone must have the same share parameter for leisure, and the poor must spend a larger fraction of income on required goods, the lifetime poor necessarily have higher ratios of total consumption to leisure than do the lifetime rich.

The simulations described later in this chapter show how and why sales and excise taxes are regressive. For now, we note that only part of the regressivity is attributable to differing proportions of untaxed leisure. A large remaining part is attributable to the differences in tax rates and the mix of consumption goods in different budgets. Our model uses estimated consumption parameters to describe the amounts of different consumer goods that are minimum requirements. It turns out that many of the goods with higher tax rates (table 3-6) are the goods with higher estimated minimum required purchases (table 5-6). Thus, even without differences in total consumption relative to leisure, the lifetime poor have consumption bundles that are taxed at higher rates than are those of the rich.

This implies that sales and excise taxes can be made less regressive by reducing the high rates on alcohol, tobacco, and gasoline. The problem, of course, is that these taxes are designed to achieve other social objectives. They may be sensible for environmental and health reasons even if they *are* regressive. The progressivity of the overall tax system can be achieved through other instruments, exactly as we find in this chapter. Another implication is that sales and excise taxes may be made more progressive by taxing other commodities that make up higher fractions of high-income budgets. The problem in this case is that many different tax rates are hard to administer, and again progressivity might be better achieved elsewhere.[14]

Finally, the overall welfare cost of sales and excise taxes to the steady-state generation is 0.94 percent of income, and the present-value welfare cost to all generations is 0.28 percent of income (table 7-11). Again, the present-value number is smaller than the steady-state number. In this case, the current elderly prefer a tax on consumption to a tax on endowment, which would apply to the value of leisure taken in retirement.

Incidence of Payroll Taxes

The distribution of relative burdens presented in table 7-12 indicates that payroll taxes are lifetime regressive. Recall that we consider these taxes independently of any potential increase in social security benefits at the margin, since those government retirement benefits are part of lump-sum transfers in our model. That is, we calculate the incidence of the tax alone. All groups experience similar EV dollar amounts per capita, with only a slight tendency to rise with income. Lifetime incomes rise more steeply, however, so the percentage effects in the third column are regressive. In addition, the regressivity of this labor tax (compared with the endowment tax) is partly driven by the lower ratio of labor to total time endowment in the higher lifetime income categories. These ratios are high for poor individuals because of the minimum required purchases of consumption goods.

The steady-state generation enjoys a gain equal to 0.44 percent of lifetime income, when this labor tax is replaced by an endowment tax. Older generations have already paid the payroll tax during their working years, however.

---

14. Also, goods that are considered "luxuries" often have high price elasticities. Increasing taxes on such goods might lead to large excess burdens, suggesting a trade-off between equity goals and efficiency goals.

Table 7-12. *Incidence of Payroll Taxes under Standard Parameters for Steady-State Generations, at 1984 Levels, Compared with a Proportional Labor Endowment Tax*[a]

Lifetime income category	EV (billions of dollars)	EV in dollars per person	EV as percent of lifetime income
1	0.17	3,517	1.24
2	0.63	3,200	0.69
3	0.82	3,361	0.59
4	0.90	3,683	0.55
5	1.02	4,155	0.56
6	1.01	4,132	0.48
7	1.02	4,181	0.44
8	1.16	4,749	0.45
9	1.30	5,305	0.45
10	1.26	5,147	0.38
11	0.85	4,337	0.24
12	0.27	5,586	0.23
Total	10.41	4,256	0.44
Steady-state EV as percent of revenue	. . .	. . .	5.93
Efficiency measures[b]			
As percent of lifetime income	. . .	. . .	0.10
As percent of revenue	. . .	. . .	1.29

a. Positive gain from removal = the burden of the tax. The lifetime equivalent variation (EV) shows the gain in billions of 1984 dollars for each income group in the new steady state. We divide by the number of individuals in each group to get EV per person (in 1984 dollars.) We divide by the present value of lifetime labor endowments to get the percentage gain in the last column. Efficiency measures at the bottom of the table take the present value of lifetime gains for transitional generations as well as those in the steady state.

b. Present value of EV for all generations as percent of: present value of all lifetime income, or present value of revenue from this tax.

They would not pay as much labor tax during their retirement, so the switch to an endowment tax makes them worse off. These intergenerational gains and losses are shown graphically in figure 7-1 for three of the tax change simulations. Lifetime effects of the payroll tax on labor are represented by the bottom line. Small net losses are incurred by those economically born forty to sixty years ago (with chronological age 60 to 80). Net lifetime effects are positive and growing for those born later. The small bump for those born five years after the change is only an artifact of our five-year snapshots. Those born ten years after the change, and later, receive the steady-state gain equal to 0.44 percent of lifetime income. As shown in table 7-12, the present value of these net effects is 0.10 percent of the present value of all lifetime incomes.

The last line of the table indicates that the efficiency effect is 1.3 percent of the payroll tax revenue replaced. In fact, for all sets of parameters consid-

Figure 7-1. *Intergenerational Gains and Losses, All Income Groups, Standard Case*

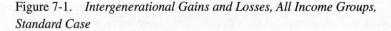

Equivalent variation as percent of lifetime income

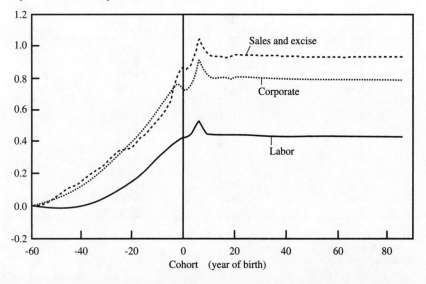

ered in the next chapter, this ratio is always lower for the payroll tax than for any other tax instrument. The payroll tax is a relatively efficient source of revenue because it has a low rate, applies to a broad base, does not discriminate among sectors, and primarily affects just the labor-leisure decision. It has few intertemporal effects, as shown in table 7-5 by the small change in the steady-state capital-labor ratio. This result highlights the policy trade-off between efficiency properties and distributional effects.

Incidence of Property Taxes

Annual incidence studies of the property tax emphasize the simultaneous consideration of the sources-side effect through the rate of return to capital and the uses-side effect through the price of housing. On the sources side, annual incidence studies typically find that capital makes up an increasing fraction of income and that the property tax reduces the net rate of return. Thus the property tax would typically be progressive on the sources-side of income. In our model, the property tax does reduce the net rate of return to capital (as seen in table 7-5, where removal raises this return 6.7 percent). But holdings of capital do not necessarily increase across lifetime income categories. In the lifetime perspective, the distributional effects of changes in the net rate of return depend on which groups save more during the life-cycle, an outcome that depends in turn on the shape of the lifetime earnings profile.

Consider the estimated wage-age profiles of chapter 4, as displayed in figure 4-2. We estimated lifetime income for each individual in our PSID sample, classified them into the twelve lifetime income groups, and then ran a separate log wage regression on each group. Middle-income groups happen to have earnings profiles that peak relatively late in their lives, compared with the lifetime poor or lifetime rich, so individuals in those middle groups in our model do not need to save as much to obtain the desired pattern of consumption over their lifetimes. High-income groups also have earnings profiles with very steep peaks and therefore save relatively more in order to smooth consumption. Table 7-3 shows that the middle-income groups indeed undertake less saving and hold less capital than the poorer and richer groups do. Thus, while the capital-labor ratio does not change uniformly across the groups, the general pattern is U-shaped. It falls to its lowest level for group 8 and rises to its highest level for group 12.

The lifetime burdens of property taxes have the same general U-shape pattern (table 7-13). The lifetime equivalent variation falls to essentially zero for group 8 and reaches its highest level for group 12. Even variations in the pattern of EVs reflect variations in the pattern of capital-labor ratios (for example, group 7 is high by both measures). Thus we obtain a very strong sources-side effect of the property tax in our model.

Effects on the uses side are also apparent, however. Burdens on the poorest two groups in table 7-13 are higher than one might expect by looking just at capital-labor ratios. The reason is that expenditures on shelter for low-income individuals are a large fraction of income. Table 7-8 shows that the property tax has a much larger effect on the price of housing than on any other commodity. Thus the uses-side explains the high relative burden on the poorest two groups.

Overall, the steady-state welfare gain is 0.3 percent of lifetime incomes. The present-value welfare cost of the property tax, over all generations, is shown to be 0.2 percent of all lifetime incomes. Surprisingly, perhaps, this tax has a relatively small excess burden. As a tax on capital, it increases the intertemporal distortion associated with all taxes on capital in this model. But table 7-2 shows that the effective tax rate in the owner-occupied housing sector is lower than in the corporate or noncorporate sector. Since the property tax applies at a higher rate to owner-occupied housing than to the corporate sector's use of capital, it helps offset the corporate income tax. It thus

Table 7-13. *Incidence of Property Taxes under Standard Parameters for Steady-State Generations, at 1984 Levels, Compared with a Proportional Labor Endowment Tax*[a]

Lifetime income category	EV (billions of dollars)	EV in dollars per person	EV as percent of lifetime income
1	0.12	2,397	0.84
2	0.57	2,938	0.63
3	0.29	1,168	0.21
4	0.47	1,921	0.29
5	0.03	104	0.01
6	0.16	659	0.08
7	1.17	4,805	0.50
8	−0.01	−57	−0.01
9	0.03	126	0.01
10	0.13	518	0.04
11	2.67	13,652	0.76
12	1.42	29,022	1.20
Total	7.04	2,880	0.30
Steady-state EV as percent of revenue	. . .	. . .	7.27
Efficiency measures[b]			
As percent of lifetime income	. . .	. . .	0.20
As percent of revenue	. . .	. . .	4.47

a. Positive gain from removal = the burden of the tax. The lifetime equivalent variation (EV) shows the gain in billions of 1984 dollars for each income group in the new steady state. We divide by the number of individuals in each group to get EV per person (in 1984 dollars.) We divide by the present value of lifetime labor endowments to get the percentage gain in the last column. Efficiency measures at the bottom of the table take the present value of lifetime gains for transitional generations as well as those in the steady state.

b. Present value of EV for all generations as percent of: present value of all lifetime income, or present value of revenue from this tax.

reduces the temporal distortion in the allocation of capital associated with disparate effective tax rates. Our model captures the net effect of these multiple distortions in a second-best economy.

Another reason that the excess burden is only 0.2 percent of income, less than other taxes we have considered, is that this tax collects less revenue. The excess burden is 4.4 percent of revenue from the property tax, somewhat higher than other instruments.

Incidence of Corporate Taxes

We arrive at an unconventional result for the tax on corporations, a tax usually assumed progressive in incidence. Although richer individuals bear a larger absolute burden from corporate taxes, the burden relative to lifetime

Table 7-14. *Incidence of Corporate Taxes under Standard Parameters for Steady-State Generations, at 1984 Levels, Compared with a Proportional Labor Endowment Tax*[a]

Lifetime income category	EV (billions of dollars)	EV in dollars per person	EV as percent of lifetime income
1	0.16	3,287	1.16
2	0.82	4,170	0.90
3	1.09	4,445	0.79
4	1.33	5,451	0.81
5	1.39	5,696	0.77
6	1.61	6,563	0.76
7	1.98	8,085	0.85
8	1.93	7,876	0.75
9	2.20	9,003	0.76
10	2.43	9,950	0.74
11	2.90	14,831	0.83
12	1.12	22,829	0.94
Total	18.95	7,749	0.80
Steady-state EV as percent of revenue	. . .	. . .	240.30
Efficiency measures[b]			
As percent of lifetime income	. . .	. . .	0.26
As percent of revenue	. . .	. . .	65.01

a. Positive gain from removal = the burden of the tax. The lifetime equivalent variation (EV) shows the gain in billions of 1984 dollars for each income group in the new steady state. We divide by the number of individuals in each group to get EV per person (in 1984 dollars.) We divide by the present value of lifetime labor endowments to get the percentage gain in the last column. Efficiency measures at the bottom of the table take the present value of lifetime gains for transitional generations as well as those in the steady state.

b. Present value of EV for all generations as percent of: present value of all lifetime income, or present value of revenue from this tax.

income is fairly flat or somewhat U-shaped (table 7-14). Since a proportional tax takes the same fraction of all groups' incomes, the initial decline of this U-shaped pattern implies that corporate taxes are lifetime regressive at the lower end of the income distribution.

Although this U-shaped pattern is similar to the property taxes pattern, it occurs for very different reasons. Property taxes reduce the rate of return to capital with sources-side effects that depend on the U-shaped pattern of capital-labor ratios. The corporate tax has no effect on relative factor returns, however, as table 7-5 shows. The pattern arises from the uses side. As it turns out, poorer individuals spend large fractions of their incomes on goods that are produced by the corporate sector. Table 7-8 showed that all effects of the corporate tax on consumer goods prices are small, but the tax does raise relative prices for goods like tobacco and gasoline that have large minimum required purchases and therefore constitute a large fraction of low-income budgets. In addition, the endowment tax replacement favors low-income individuals, who spend a smaller fraction of income on untaxed leisure in our model.

While this corporate tax replacement is regressive through the first ten lifetime income groups, it is somewhat progressive across the top two groups. The replacement of sales and excise taxes had a similar effect, for a similar reason. In both cases, the replacement tax applies to lifetime labor endowments and exempts inheritances. Because only the top two groups receive sizable inheritances, they would prefer the labor endowment tax.

Previous studies emphasize the effect of corporate taxes on the rate of return. Since capital income rises with annual income, corporate taxes are thought to be progressive. Here, however, the sources-side effects of the corporate income tax are nonexistent. Results suggest a rethinking of the incidence of the corporate tax.

These results appear to provide a specific answer to the question posed by Joseph A. Pechman and Benjamin A. Okner (1974) and others who consider alternative assumptions about the incidence of the corporate tax. They may assume the tax is borne by capital owners, "shifted back" onto labor, "shifted forward" onto consumers, or some combination of these assumptions. Our apparent answer is that the corporate tax is borne by consumers, but this interpretation has two problems.

First, the corporate tax in this model collects little revenue and therefore does not really have much burden to be shifted. It has only efficiency effects and relative price effects. It discriminates among industries that differ in the corporate share of output and in the mix of assets used in production. Thus the corporate tax is not shifted to consumers generally but instead hurts some consumers while helping others.

Second, this answer to the incidence question arises only from one model with one set of assumptions. In a model with restrictions on the free flow of capital between sectors, the tax could be borne entirely by owners of capital in the taxed sector. In models with different specifications of the corporate tax itself, or different household savings behaviors, the corporate tax could change the net rate of return and thus affect all capital owners. In fact, it is exactly this choice among alternative model assumptions that motivated the earlier literature to provide alternative incidence assumptions. Thus, without knowing the "right" model, we still do not know the "right" answer about the incidence of the corporate tax.

The assimilation of alternative models in the literature will help inform general opinions about the incidence of these taxes. We are not able here to provide alternative models. We can, however, provide alternative parameters for a given model. To the extent that alternative choices for a particular parameter lead to different conclusions about the burden of the corporate tax, our choice for that parameter is similar in nature to the earlier literature's choice of incidence assumption. Thus it would be an overstatement to say that we "calculate rather than assume" the burden of the tax. Instead, the contributions are in the rigorous model structure not available in the earlier literature and in the lifetime framework.

Finally, we note that the steady-state generation gains by 0.80 percent of their lifetime incomes when corporate taxes are removed, and the present value of gains to all generations is 0.26 percent of income. As shown in figure 7-1, older generations gain less than younger generations when this tax is replaced with an endowment tax that applies to the value of retirement leisure.

As a measure of the efficiency cost of corporate taxes, this 0.26 percent figure is considerably smaller than Harberger's (1966) finding that the welfare cost of the corporate income tax is about 0.5 percent of income. The difference is all the more surprising because our figure includes not only misallocations between sectors but also misallocations among time periods and among real assets (such as equipment, structures, inventories, land, and intangibles). One reason for the difference is that this simulation does not remove all the tax differences between the sectors. Table 7-6 shows that the removal of the corporate tax leaves effective rates in the corporate sector higher than in the noncorporate sector. We simulate the full integration of corporate and personal taxes in chapter 9.

A second reason for the difference is that the corporate tax took a bigger bite out of corporate-source income in the 1950s data used by Harberger than in our 1984 benchmark year. The tax differential between the corporate sector and the noncorporate sector was reduced by the 1962 introduction of the investment tax credit and the 1981 introduction of the Accelerated Cost Recovery System. The size of the welfare cost varies roughly with the square of this tax differential.

The main reason for the different results, however, is related to the modeling of the corporate tax itself. Harberger used the ratio of taxes paid to capital income in each sector to measure an "average effective tax rate" that was much higher in the corporate sector than in the noncorporate sector. In contrast, we use a forward-looking user cost of capital to measure a marginal effective tax rate. Table 7-2 and table 7-6 show that this rate is 0.47 in the corporate sector and 0.33 in the noncorporate sector in the benchmark case.

These rates include personal taxes and property taxes on both sectors and the extra corporate tax in the corporate sector.

When the corporate tax is removed, the effective rate in the corporate sector falls only from 0.47 to 0.42 (table 7-6). The corporate tax has little impact on this rate because the high tax on equity-financed investments is largely offset by tax credits, accelerated depreciation, and interest deductions on debt-financed investments. The rate remains higher than in the noncorporate sector because the weighted-average personal rate on dividends exceeds the personal rate on noncorporate income, and the noncorporate sector still receives investment tax credits while all corporate tax features have been removed. Thus the corporate tax removal does not have much effect on the intersectoral allocation of capital in our model. It also does not distort intertemporal allocations, for the economy-wide net rate of return is unchanged (see r/w in table 7-5). The corporate tax causes only some interasset distortions, by providing investment tax credits that reduce the effective tax rate on equipment relative to those on other assets. We investigate later whether the corporate tax becomes more distortionary under the Tax Reform Act of 1986.

Incidence of the Entire Tax System

The lifetime tax burdens of the entire U.S. tax system are presented in table 7-15. Results suggest that overall U.S. taxes are roughly proportional across middle income groups but progressive at the very bottom and at the very top of the income distribution. The negative effect on the poorest lifetime income group means that it gains slightly by having all these real-world tax instruments rather than the hypothetical tax on endowments. The variation across the middle-income groups reflects the variation in the ratios of capital income to labor income (table 7-3). The groups estimated to have late or less pronounced peaks in wage profiles tend to save less during the life cycle, have less capital income, and bear less burden from capital taxation. For the richest 2 percent lifetime income group, the more substantial overall burden primarily reflects the effects of the personal income tax.

This pattern is similar to the overall finding of Pechman and Okner (1974). Using annual incidence assumptions, they found that the ratio of total burden to income is fairly flat across almost all income groups but curls sharply up at both ends of the distribution. In fact, Joseph Pechman pointed out to us that the extreme tails of the income distribution were very different from those in other studies. He recommended that we subdivide the top and bottom deciles to show results separately for the poorest 2 percent and the richest 2

Table 7-15. *Incidence of All Taxes under Standard Parameters for Steady-State Generations, at 1984 Levels, Compared with a Proportional Labor Endowment Tax*[a]

Lifetime income category	EV (billions of dollars)	EV in dollars per person	EV as percent of lifetime income
1	−0.01	−156	−0.06
2	2.85	14,542	3.13
3	1.95	7,962	1.41
4	3.90	15,949	2.37
5	6.45	26,393	3.58
6	2.93	11,986	1.39
7	8.07	32,988	3.46
8	6.47	26,445	2.51
9	8.50	34,759	2.95
10	9.94	40,650	3.01
11	19.40	99,145	5.55
12	13.18	269,496	11.10
Total	83.62	34,195	3.52
Steady-state EV as percent of revenue	. . .	. . .	6.48
Efficiency measures[b]			
As percent of lifetime income	. . .	. . .	1.29
As percent of revenue	. . .	. . .	2.26

a. Positive gain from removal = the burden of the tax. The lifetime equivalent variation (EV) shows the gain in billions of 1984 dollars for each income group in the new steady state. We divide by the number of individuals in each group to get EV per person (in 1984 dollars.) We divide by the present value of lifetime labor endowments to get the percentage gain in the last column. Efficiency measures at the bottom of the table take the present value of lifetime gains for transitional generations as well as those in the steady state.

b. Present value of EV for all generations as percent of: present value of all lifetime income, or present value of revenue from this tax.

percent. Our measure of burden is indeed fairly flat across almost all income groups, and it also curls sharply up at the top end. Unlike that annual measure of burden, however, it curls down at the lowest income end.

The difference is attributed, at least in part, to the use of lifetime instead of annual income measures. Pechman and Okner found high relative burdens for the poorest group partly because of the annual perspective. Of course, any annual income group may contain households that would be classified differently on a lifetime basis, but the lowest annual income group is much more likely than others to contain households with temporarily low annual income. For these households, behavior and thus taxes reflect a higher lifetime income. Annual measures of sales and excise taxes are related to spending behavior and thus lifetime income. Annual measures of property tax burdens on the uses side are related to housing decisions and thus lifetime income. Therefore annual taxes appear to be a high fraction of annual income for these individuals. Because the lifetime classification eliminates this effect, taxes appear more progressive.[15]

The overall burden distribution in our model reflects the combination of lifetime-progressive income taxes (our largest source of tax revenue) and lifetime-regressive sales, excise, corporate, and payroll taxes. The property tax has a U-shaped burden, with some variations, reflecting the reduction in the net rate of return and the pattern of capital-labor ratios. In the lifetime perspective, capital is not necessarily held by the rich. It is held by those who have relatively early or more pronounced peaks in earnings, and who must therefore save to obtain smoothly increasing consumption over the life cycle.

The steady-state welfare gain from removing the tax system and replacing it with a proportional tax on endowments is 3.5 percent of lifetime incomes. This gain comes partly at the expense of older transitional generations, who are injured by the switch to a tax on endowments, so the present-value welfare gain is a smaller 1.3 percent of all incomes. This excess burden is larger than has been estimated in previous models, because our model accounts for many types of distortions in the tax system: intertemporal, intersectoral, and inter-asset distortions, as well as misallocations between consumption and leisure.

For the standard set of parameters, our simulations show that several types of taxes are regressive in the lifetime perspective. To some extent, these taxes only appear regressive compared with the hypothetical replacement tax on labor endowments. That replacement tax applies proportionately more to high-income individuals, who take proportionately more untaxed leisure.[16]

The Uniform Consumption Tax Replacement

We now consider a uniform consumption tax, or value-added tax. Because this tax does not apply to leisure of high-income groups, it is not necessarily

---

15. Pechman and Okner remove some of the lowest annual income households from their sample for this reason. If a household's measured income is near zero, for example, survival may require gifts, borrowing, or other unmeasured income. The household must still have positive consumption and thus positive sales and excise taxes paid, so the tax burden relative to measured annual income for such individuals could be arbitrarily high. We are suggesting that some of this type of effect remains even after Pechman and Okner remove the worst cases.

16. In the model we specified minimum required purchases of consumption goods but not of leisure. Therefore, when low-income groups decide how to "spend" their endowment, they must allocate relatively more to the required consumption goods. With more discretionary income, high-income groups spend relatively more on leisure. Thus the endowment tax hits them harder.

more progressive than the taxes we consider. In fact, it is exactly as progressive or regressive as a uniform sales tax. Thus the effects of replacing U.S. sales and excise taxes with this uniform consumption tax will simply tell us about the regressivity introduced by having different rates on different goods.

Each replacement tax has advantages and disadvantages. Since the endowment reflects the full value of resources used for consumption *or* leisure, the endowment tax might be considered a proportional tax on total well-being. It thus serves as a useful basis to judge the progressivity or regressivity of other taxes. It is also a lump-sum tax to judge the distortionary effects of other taxes. It is not a realistic alternative, however. The consumption tax may be a more viable policy option, and it is currently under some discussion. But it does not apply to a comprehensive measure of well-being: by exempting leisure, the tax creates its own distortions in labor-supply decisions. Finally, this alternative is not necessarily realistic in itself. To concentrate on the effects of the tax instrument being removed, we use a uniform rate of tax on all goods such as food, tobacco, and housing. More realistic alternatives might exempt food for distributional reasons and would probably not tax the consumption services of owner-occupied housing.

Results for this replacement are summarized in table 7-16. For brevity, this table shows only the equivalent variation as a percent of lifetime income for each group. The table includes a column for each U.S. tax instrument being removed, and it corresponds to figure 1-5 of chapter 1.

In the first column, personal income tax burdens range from -5 percent of income for the poorest group to $+9$ percent for the richest group. The first three negative entries do not imply that these groups receive payments through the personal income tax system, only that they gain by having a personal income tax system instead of a uniform consumption tax. In any case, the pattern is clearly progressive. The personal income tax is slightly more progressive in relation to this consumption tax than in relation to the labor endowment tax (table 7-10). As described earlier, this difference occurs simply because the labor endowment tax is more progressive than the consumption tax.

The bottom of the column indicates that this replacement would yield an overall steady-state gain equal to 2.6 percent of income (21 percent of revenue) or a present-value gain of 0.7 percent of income (5 percent of revenue). The difference is again caused by losses to transitional generations. Those who are near retirement at the time of the change would have paid low personal income taxes over the remainder of their lifetimes, but the replacement tax applies to all their remaining consumption.

Table 7-16. *Welfare Effects of a Uniform Consumption Tax Replacement under Standard Parameters*

| Lifetime income category | Lifetime equivalent variation as percent of lifetime income for steady-state generations | | | | | |
| | Removal of taxes | | | | | |
	Personal	Sales and excise	Payroll	Property	Corporate	All
1	-5.09	1.70	0.73	0.60	1.14	-2.00
2	-0.34	1.27	0.48	0.55	0.89	3.19
3	-0.70	1.22	0.54	0.21	0.78	2.48
4	0.71	1.16	0.55	0.33	0.81	3.94
5	2.53	1.19	0.64	0.09	0.78	5.66
6	0.66	1.11	0.61	0.19	0.77	3.74
7	2.22	1.04	0.53	0.59	0.85	5.64
8	2.43	1.08	0.65	0.14	0.76	5.47
9	3.01	1.06	0.67	0.17	0.77	6.09
10	3.04	0.98	0.55	0.16	0.74	5.83
11	4.19	0.72	0.16	0.73	0.83	6.81
12	9.11	0.60	0.01	1.08	0.93	11.87
All twelve in steady-state						
As percent of lifetime income	2.57	1.02	0.50	0.36	0.80	5.58
As percent of revenue	20.88	10.32	8.86	11.58	314.63	17.62
All generations[a]						
As percent of lifetime income	0.66	0.18	0.05	0.17	0.25	1.25
As percent of revenue	5.10	1.76	0.80	5.04	84.14	3.75

a. Present value of EV as percent of: present value of all lifetime income, or present value of revenue from this tax.

The 0.7 percent efficiency gain might be considered substantial, especially compared with a tax that itself distorts labor supply decisions. But progressivity makes the personal income tax more distorting. The personal marginal tax rate exceeds the total tax as a fraction of income, as is necessary to allow that average tax rate to rise with income. Distortions depend on the 0.30 marginal tax rate, whereas revenue depends on the lower average rate. Thus the personal income tax is relatively distorting per dollar of revenue. In contrast, the less progressive consumption tax needs a rate of only 0.12 to collect the same revenue.

In the second column, sales and excise taxes are clearly regressive. This appears to be similar to results under the annual approach, but sales taxes in that case are regressive because consumption is a high fraction of income for annually poor individuals. Over the lifetime, however, James M. Poterba (1989) anticipates that consumption and labor income should be close to equal. If so, lifetime consumption as a fraction of lifetime labor income should not differ much across individuals, and sales taxes would be close to proportional on a lifetime basis.

When considering the endowment tax replacement, we suggested that the lifetime regressivity of sales and excise taxes could be attributed to two factors. First, actual sales and excise taxes might be regressive because of nonuniform rates. Actual incidence depends on the pattern of tax rates and the pattern of goods consumed by the different lifetime income categories. Indeed, the point of our Stone-Geary specification is to allow for rich and poor households to purchase goods in different proportions. Table 7-16 simply replaces nonuniform sales taxes with a uniform consumption tax, so the regressivity in this table results solely from this consumption-bundle effect. Poorer households consume proportionately larger amounts of high-taxed goods such as gasoline, alcohol, and tobacco.

Second, sales and excise taxes do not apply to the "purchase" of leisure. Since leisure makes up an increasing fraction of high income purchases, we suggested that sales taxes might look regressive compared to an endowment tax that applies to the full value of time.[17]

The endowment tax replacement of table 7-11 includes both the consumption-bundle effect and the consumption-leisure effect, so a comparison of the two tables allows us to separate the two factors. For the first ten lifetime income groups, constituting 90 percent of the population, sales taxes in table 7-11 look more regressive. Therefore some of the earlier regressivity is indeed attributable to the consumption-leisure effect. For the last two groups, however, sales taxes look more progressive. The reason is that the replacement tax does not apply to inheritances.

Despite these complications, the main point is clear: U.S. sales and excise taxes are regressive on a lifetime basis for *either* replacement tax. Poterba (1989) may be right that a uniform consumption tax would be proportional to lifetime income with no bequests, but the sales and excise taxes are not uniform. The rate structure introduces regressivity.

The third column of table 7-16 considers the replacement of U.S. payroll

17. We do not estimate the fraction of endowment used for leisure in each lifetime income group, but we do point out the importance of such estimation. If endowment is the proper measure of well-being, and leisure is untaxed, the incidence of consumption taxes depends on the fraction of lifetime endowment spent on taxed goods. This fraction may differ across individuals in a lifetime perspective. In our case, we merely specify Stone-Geary utility with minimum required purchases for consumption goods but not for leisure. Because we assign the same utility function to all individuals, the lifetime poor must devote a higher fraction of their overall budget to taxable commodities.

Figure 7-2. *Intergenerational Gains and Losses, All Income Groups,*
VAT Replacement

Equivalent variation as percent of lifetime income

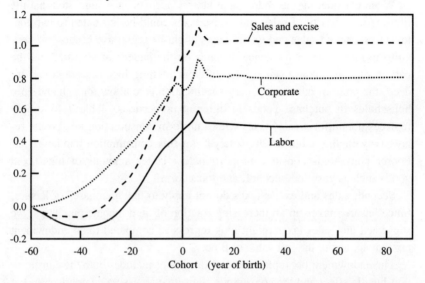

taxes with a uniform consumption tax. Again, the tax is quite regressive on
a lifetime basis. And again, this result conflicts with initial intuitions. In a
simple life-cycle model with no bequests, each individual's present value of
lifetime labor income exactly equals the present value of consumption. Therefore a uniform consumption tax is equivalent to a flat wage tax. Here the
equivalence is broken by bequests, which rise as a fraction of total endowment for higher lifetime-income groups. These high-income individuals are
required to leave the same size bequest as they receive, but they get to consume out of the extra capital income during their lifetimes. For them, the
consumption tax base exceeds the labor tax base. The simple consumption
tax is therefore more progressive than a labor income tax.

The switch from the payroll tax to consumption tax hurts the elderly and
allows gains to subsequent generations (in the steady state). These intergenerational effects are shown in figure 7-2, where again the payroll tax is represented by the bottom line. Because they are not working as much anymore,
generations economically born thirty to sixty years ago experience net lifetime losses with the switch from the payroll tax to this consumption tax.
These losses are even larger than in figure 7-1 for the switch to the endowment tax. Because the elderly are dissaving, their consumption exceeds their
endowment income.

As shown at the bottom of the column in table 7-16, the present-value gain is essentially zero. Gains to steady-state generations are almost completely offset by losses to transitional generations, so the consumption tax is no more efficient than the labor income tax. Both primarily distort only labor-supply decisions. The difference is purely distributional. The payroll tax is more regressive than the uniform consumption tax.

In the fourth column of table 7-16, the property tax has the same basic U-shaped pattern that it did with the endowment tax replacement. The property tax reduces the net rate of return and affects owners of capital on the sources side. We showed that the ratio of capital income to labor income was approximately U-shaped across the lifetime income groups. The property tax also adversely affects the cost of housing and thus low-income groups on the uses side.

The efficiency gain is only 0.17 percent of income, for two familiar reasons. First, the property tax applies primarily to use of capital in the housing sector and thus helps offset some of the misallocation due to high corporate taxes on other uses of capital. Second, the property tax is not a big tax. The last line of table 7-16 shows that the efficiency gain is 5 percent of revenue, higher than for some other tax instruments.

Finally, the distributional burden of the corporate tax in the fifth column is flat or just slightly U-shaped when compared with the uniform consumption tax. The U-shape is even less pronounced than for the endowment tax replacement (table 7-14). The new replacement tax—a general consumption tax—is not exactly like the endowment tax. Poorer individuals gain slightly less under the consumption tax replacement, because they consume relatively larger fractions of their labor endowments (rather than taking leisure). The richest individuals also have slightly less to gain under the consumption tax replacement. This replacement tax applies to consumption out of labor endowments and inheritances, whereas the endowment tax does not tax inheritances. All groups gain from replacement, however, because the corporate tax is distortionary. The efficiency gain is a very high 84 percent of revenue, since the corporate tax in this model reallocates resources without raising much revenue.

This seems to imply that the corporate tax could be entirely replaced by a small consumption tax, with gains to every income group. While this simulation does indicate such a Pareto improvement,[18] it does not suggest the best possible reform. The consumption tax replacement might be costly to intro-

---

18. A "Pareto improvement" is a change in which at least one person in society is better off, and no one is worse off.

duce, difficult to administer, and difficult to apply to all goods at a uniform rate as in this simulation. A different approach might "fix" the corporate tax in order to collect more revenue with less distortion. Such an attempt was undertaken in the Tax Reform Act of 1986. We look at that specific reform in chapter 9.

The last column of table 7-16 shows the distributional effects of replacing the entire U.S. tax system with a uniform consumption tax. The poorest lifetime income group would lose 2 percent of lifetime income and the richest group would gain 12 percent of income. Thus current U.S. taxes are progressive relative to the consumption tax. The first five columns show that most of this overall progressivity is attributable to the personal income tax. Other taxes are either regressive or proportional.

The choice of the replacement tax does not substantially affect our incidence results. The endowment tax replacement is a bit more progressive over the first ten groups, because it includes the value of leisure, which rises relative to taxable goods across the lifetime income categories. The consumption tax is a bit more progressive over the richest two groups, however, because it applies to spending out of capital income from inheritances. Most important, the pattern of results is not affected. With either replacement, we find that actual U.S. sales and excise taxes are regressive, payroll taxes are regressive, property tax burdens are U-shaped, and the corporate tax is very close to proportional in incidence. The conceptual results in this chapter suggest directions for reform that are investigated in chapter 9.

CHAPTER EIGHT

Sensitivity Analysis

MANY empirical studies of tax incidence make assumptions about how each tax instrument is shifted. Implicitly, they make assumptions about the extent to which taxpayers can avoid the taxed activity by substituting into other activities. They then vary these assumptions to perform sensitivity analysis, in which different shifting assumptions correspond implicitly to different degrees of substitutability. In our model, we make the various elasticities of substitution explicit. These elasticities directly determine the size of substitution effects and thus the ability of individuals to shift the tax burden from its statutory incidence to its ultimate economic incidence.

In our model, these changes in behavior also create inefficiency, or excess burden, in the tax system. Specifying elasticities is crucial in determining both the distributional results and the overall efficiency results. We therefore perform sensitivity analyses for every tax instrument.

In this chapter we vary some of these key assumptions of the model. Table 8-1 summarizes the standard set of parameters as well as variations in each of the alternative configurations. The first three columns serve as reminders of the notation and of parameter values in the central case. Then the bottom panel indicates the effect of those choices on certain outcomes within the model. For example, the generated capital stock in our benchmark steady state depends largely on assumptions about life-cycle behavior, estimated wage and tax profiles, the size of bequests, and the net rate of return, plus particular parameters of the utility function such as ε_1, the intertemporal elasticity of substitution, and δ, the rate of time preference. For the standard case, we use Paul L. Menchik and Martin David's (1982) data on bequests, 0.04 for the net rate of return, 0.5 for the intertemporal substitution elasticity, and 0.005 for the rate of time preference. In combination, these assumptions generate a capital stock that closely replicates a separate measure of capital derived from production data. The table shows that the generated capital is 1.05 times the other measure of capital. It also shows that the assumed bequests

Table 8-1. *Key Parameters in Each Sensitivity Case*[a]

			Variant							
	Symbol	Central	A	B	C	D	E	F	G	H
Parameters that we set										
Intertemporal substitution	ε_1	0.5	0.25							
Consumption-leisure substitution	ε_2	0.5		0.25						
Corporate-noncorporate substitution	ε_3	5.0			20.0					
Rate of time preference	δ	0.005	−0.005							
Net rate of return	r	0.04				0.03				
Endowment (hours per year)	E	4,000					5000			
Minimum required purchases (dollars)	ΣPb	8,000								
Bequests[b]		M&D[c]						0	0	
Corporate finance shares										
Retentions	c_{re}	0.33[d]								0.614[e]
New shares	c_{ns}	0.33								0.049
Debt	c_d	0.34								0.337
Outcomes, given those parameters										
Generated-capital/measure-of-capital		1.05	1.03	1.04	1.05	0.71	1.24	1.35	0.72	1.05
Bequest share		0.44	0.45	0.44	0.44	0.64	0.36	0.34	0.00	0.44
Savings elasticity		1.32	0.62	1.33	1.32	1.37	1.42	1.34	2.29	1.32
Labor-supply elasticity		0.11	0.11	0.03	0.11	0.10	0.12	0.15	0.14	0.11

a. Blank spaces indicate no change from the central case.
b. Bequests have no symbol.
c. M&D refers to bequest data from Menchik and David (1982).
d. Corporate finance shares in the central case represent the "old view."
e. Corporate finance shares in case H represent the "new view."

explain 44 percent of the total capital stock. Life-cycle saving explains the rest.

These parameters also determine the responsiveness of savings in the model. Many other studies report a value for the "savings elasticity," the percentage change in total savings for a 1 percent change in the net rate of return. Empirical work by Michael J. Boskin (1978) found an aggregate uncompensated savings elasticity of about 0.4, but E. Philip Howry and Saul H. Hymans (1978) say it is closer to zero. In a life-cycle model with no bequests, Lawrence H. Summers (1981) obtained long-run savings elasticities between 2.0 and 4.0. These figures reflect the change in steady-state savings for an exogenous change in the net interest rate. In our model, however, this savings elasticity is not well defined. With a forced change in the interest rate, the economy does not reach a new steady state. We could specify an exogenous shock that changes the equilibrium interest rate, but then the savings elasticity would depend on the nature of that shock. Basically the savings elasticity is not well defined because it is the ratio of one endogenous variable to another endogenous variable. Instead, the important parameters are the structural parameters such as the intertemporal elasticity of substitution.

Nonetheless, we wish to relate our model to previous literature by reporting a summary statistic about long-run savings responses. To calculate our "savings elasticity," we start with the assumption of a 4 percent net return and use our initialization procedures that generate baseline steady-state savings. We then raise the assumed net return slightly and use the same procedures to calculate a different baseline. All else is not held equal, but at least we can calculate the percentage change in aggregate steady-state savings for that change in the interest rate.

Table 8-1 shows that this "savings elasticity" is 1.32 in the benchmark. This figure exceeds the often cited empirical estimates of the savings elasticity mentioned above. A recognized problem, however, is that structural life-cycle models tend to imply high savings elasticities. When we choose the life-cycle framework for its analytical rigor, we subject ourselves to the problem of high savings elasticities. The problem is reduced by the inclusion of bequests, but it is hard to eliminate.[1] We could reduce this savings elasticity

---

1. In attempts to deal with this problem, Evans (1983) and Seidman (1983) introduce bequests, Starrett (1988) introduces minimum required purchases, and Engen (1992) introduces uncertainty in the future income stream. Each of these changes can help reduce the implied savings elasticity. In our model, the inclusion of bequests reduces the savings elasticity from 2.3 (in variant G, with no bequests) to 1.3 (in the central case, with bequests).

in our model by reducing the intertemporal substitution parameter, but then the generated capital stock would fall short of the measured target. We discuss alternatives below.

The structural parameters in this model also determine the responsiveness of labor supply, so we calculate an "elasticity" that measures the percentage change in aggregate labor supply for a 1 percent change in the net wage. Again, this elasticity is not well defined, because both labor supply and the net wage are endogenous in our model. Still, we can relate our model to empirical literature on uncompensated labor supply elasticities such as reviewed in Jerry A. Hausman (1985) and Gary Burtless (1987). This literature estimates a short-run response, so we use the model in a special partial equilibrium calculation. We change the net wage by 1 percent and add overall ages and income groups to calculate the percentage change in total labor supply. The last entry in table 8-1 shows that this "labor-supply elasticity" is 0.11 in the benchmark equilibrium sequence. This outcome is most affected by our choice of 0.5 for ε_2, the elasticity of substitution between consumption and leisure.

Utility Parameters

Table 8-1 summarizes eight sensitivity cases. For each case, we discuss the simulation results for each tax replacement. In this section, we vary utility parameters, including three elasticities of substitution and the rate of time preference. Later sections vary other specifications in the model, such as the net rate of return, the labor endowment, the minimum required purchase amount, the level of bequests, and corporate finance shares.

Intertemporal Elasticity

The ε_1 parameter sets the degree to which consumers will switch between present consumption and future consumption, and it therefore helps determine the responsiveness of savings to relative prices like the net rate of return to capital. Responsive savers can "avoid" a tax on capital by saving less, which ultimately decreases the marginal product of labor, decreases the wage, and "shifts" the burden onto labor.

In the central case simulations, we used 0.5 for this elasticity. This value might be considered on the high end of the estimates produced by econometric studies,[2] but it helps to generate a capital stock in our model that is close to what is actually observed in the benchmark data. If we simply reduced this elasticity from 0.50 to 0.25, the initial steady-state capital stock would fall to unreasonably low levels (about 32.5 percent of the measured capital stock). Therefore we lower this elasticity and simultaneously lower the rate of time preference. In combination, these respecifications leave us with an initial capital stock close to that of the central case simulations.

Variant A reduces the intertemporal substitution elasticity from 0.50 to 0.25, and it reduces the rate of time preference from 0.005 to −0.005. As a theoretical matter, this rate of time preference may be either positive or negative. As an empirical matter, many readers may prefer a value that is even larger than the 0.005 we use in the standard case. The only way to achieve a higher rate of time preference with the same capital stock, however, is to raise the 0.5 value for the intertemporal substitution elasticity. Our standard parameters represent our best choice among these trade-offs, and variant A represents an alternative with a lower intertemporal elasticity.

With these choices, the bequest share changes only from 44 to 45 percent of the total capital stock, but the savings elasticity shown in table 8-1 falls from 1.32 to 0.62. The labor supply elasticity is unaffected.

Results under variant A are summarized in table 8-2, for the endowment tax replacement (same results as in figure 1-6). For most taxes, it appears that incidence under this variant is very similar to that under the central case parameters. The personal income tax is just as progressive as it was before, and sales and excise taxes and payroll taxes are just as regressive. For the property tax and the corporate income tax, the U-shaped patterns are slightly more pronounced. The bottom income group and the top income group gain slightly more than they did before, whereas the middle income groups gain slightly less than they did before. For the property tax, the gains in middle income groups turn from slightly positive to slightly negative.

The more pronounced U-shaped pattern arises because these tax removals have a bigger effect on the 4 percent net rate of return to capital. The property tax removal raises the net rate of return to 0.0427 with standard parameters and to 0.0444 under variant A. The corporate tax removal now raises the rate of return to 4.04 percent. In addition, we showed that the ratio of capital income to labor income has a U-shaped pattern across the lifetime income categories (the middle income groups have later peaks in their estimated wage

2. See Hall (1988) and other studies cited in Auerbach and Kotlikoff (1987, pp. 50–51). Engen's (1992) estimates fall between 0.30 and 0.38 for this parameter.

Table 8-2. *Welfare Effects under Variant A*

Changed parameters: $\varepsilon_1 = 0.25$, $\delta = -0.005$

	Lifetime equivalent variation (EV) as percent of lifetime income for steady-state generations					
Lifetime income category	Removal of taxes					
	Personal	Sales and excise	Payroll	Property	Corporate	All
1	−4.85	2.95	1.52	0.89	1.37	−0.97
2	−0.69	1.70	0.69	0.46	0.84	2.50
3	−1.66	1.33	0.61	−0.13	0.69	0.27
4	−0.34	1.17	0.56	−0.02	0.73	1.30
5	1.14	1.06	0.59	−0.42	0.66	2.24
6	−0.76	0.87	0.50	−0.30	0.66	0.15
7	1.20	0.89	0.45	0.31	0.79	2.84
8	0.70	0.72	0.47	−0.41	0.63	1.11
9	1.27	0.65	0.47	−0.40	0.65	1.61
10	1.42	0.67	0.40	−0.35	0.63	1.71
11	3.68	0.91	0.24	0.70	0.80	5.37
12	9.12	1.04	0.22	1.31	0.95	11.47
All twelve in steady state						
As percent of lifetime income	1.39	0.92	0.45	0.01	0.72	2.57
As percent of revenue	6.64	7.15	6.14	0.29	160.69	4.69
All generations[a]						
As percent of lifetime income	0.43	0.27	0.10	0.09	0.23	0.85
As percent of revenue	1.97	1.99	1.33	2.01	42.13	1.47

a. Present value of EV as percent of: present value of all lifetime income, or present value of revenue from this tax.

profiles and therefore do not need to save as much to achieve smoothly rising consumption). Therefore the greater rise in the rate of return helps the savers at the ends of the lifetime income distribution more than the nonsavers in the middle of the distribution.

In the middle, gains are smaller because overall efficiency gains are smaller. The bottom section of table 8-2 shows that the efficiency gains from removal of the property tax are half the size they were before. Thus all groups are gaining less, on average. An explanation is that the effect of the property tax on the rate of return is more distorting when the intertemporal substitution elasticity is 0.50 than when it is only 0.25. With the lower elasticity in variant A, savers are less responsive. The capital stock grows by less, so the rate of return rises by more. Intertemporal distortions are lower in the benchmark sequence with $\varepsilon_1 = 0.25$, so tax removal provides less gain.

The entire tax system is still shown to be progressive in table 8-2, as it was with standard parameters. For most groups, the gains from the labor

Table 8-3. *Welfare Effects of Uniform Consumption Tax Replacement under Variant A*

Changed parameters: $\varepsilon_1 = 0.25$, $\delta = -0.005$

Lifetime income category	EV as percent of lifetime income for steady-state generations					
	Removal of taxes					
	Personal	Sales and excise	Payroll	Property	Corporate	All
1	−5.58	2.01	1.05	0.64	1.34	−2.85
2	−0.79	1.29	0.50	0.37	0.83	2.56
3	−1.38	1.27	0.61	−0.11	0.69	1.49
4	0.09	1.21	0.61	0.03	0.73	3.03
5	1.76	1.26	0.72	−0.31	0.66	4.53
6	−0.06	1.17	0.69	−0.17	0.67	2.71
7	1.80	1.06	0.56	0.41	0.80	5.07
8	1.62	1.14	0.73	−0.24	0.65	4.31
9	2.24	1.13	0.75	−0.21	0.67	4.99
10	2.28	1.04	0.63	−0.20	0.64	4.71
11	3.91	0.72	0.17	0.65	0.79	6.36
12	9.11	0.57	−0.02	1.16	0.93	11.82
All twelve in steady state						
As percent of lifetime income	1.96	1.06	0.55	0.09	0.72	4.71
As percent of revenue	15.83	10.84	9.94	2.74	214.22	14.75
All generations[a]						
As percent of lifetime income	0.42	0.18	0.06	0.07	0.22	0.86
As percent of revenue	3.22	1.78	1.02	1.97	54.84	2.54

a. Present value of EV as percent of: present value of all lifetime income, or present value of revenue from this tax.

endowment tax replacement are smaller than before, reflecting the smaller efficiency effects with the smaller intertemporal substitution elasticity. Gains for group 11 are not smaller, however, and gains for group 12 are larger. The tax system looks slightly more progressive because it has a bigger effect on the rate of return to capital and because the highest lifetime income individuals receive more capital inheritances.

For variant A, table 8-3 shows the effects of replacing each tax with the uniform consumption tax (results same as in figure 1-7). Results appear similar to those for the endowment tax replacement. Moreover, the differences for variant A between tables 8-3 and 8-2 are analogous to the differences for the standard parameters between the uniform consumption tax replacement and the labor endowment tax replacement. For this reason, we will not present consumption tax replacements for all of the variants B through H below. We present results just for the endowment tax replacements in cases B through H in the tables of this chapter.

Consumption-Leisure Elasticity

The ε_2 parameter sets the degree to which individuals can substitute between leisure and other (taxed) consumption goods, and it therefore determines the responsiveness of labor supply to the net-of-tax wage rate. A higher elasticity allows workers to avoid a tax on labor by working less, thus decreasing the marginal product of capital and shifting some of the burden onto capital.

In the central case parameterization, we used 0.5 for ε_2. The resulting labor supply elasticity was 0.11 (as shown in table 8-1). For sensitivity analysis in variant B, we use 0.25 for the substitution elasticity.[3] The implied labor-supply elasticity is then reduced to 0.03. Effects of replacing each tax instrument with a hypothetical tax on labor endowments are presented in table 8-4.

Personal taxes are just as progressive as in the central case and both sales and excise taxes and payroll taxes are just as regressive. In all cases, however, equivalent variations are smaller than before. These tax replacements provide smaller gains because the existing U.S. tax system is less distorting with the lower substitution elasticity. For the property tax replacement, gains are similarly lower for most groups. The top two groups gain a bit more, however, because the net rate of return to capital rises a bit more in this simulation. The effects of corporate taxes are virtually unchanged by this alternative specification.

The entire tax system is as progressive as before, but all twelve equivalent variations are lower because efficiency gains are lower. Excess burden is 0.92 percent of income instead of 1.3 percent of income. The difference is attributable to taxes that affect labor-supply decisions, such as personal taxes, sales and excise taxes, and payroll taxes. Efficiency is unchanged for property taxes and corporate income taxes.

The overall welfare cost of the tax system is larger in the central case, because a larger elasticity of substitution between consumption and leisure implies a larger distortion caused by a system that does not tax leisure. Also, in the central case, the effect on the net wage is smaller. When the consumption-leisure substitution elasticity is higher, labor is better able to avoid the tax by changing behavior.

3. If we were to use 0.8 for this substitution parameter, as in Auerbach and Kotlikoff (1987, p. 51), the uncompensated labor supply elasticity would be about 0.3 in our model. If we used their alternative value of 1.5, labor supply would be even more elastic. For our model, we felt that 0.5 for ε_2 provides a labor-supply elasticity more in line with empirical literature. For a review of labor-supply elasticity estimates, see Hausman (1985) or Burtless (1987).

Table 8-4. *Welfare Effects under Variant B*

Changed parameters: $\varepsilon_2 = 0.25$

Lifetime income category	EV as percent of lifetime income for steady-state generations					
	Removal of taxes					
	Personal	Sales and excise	Payroll	Property	Corporate	All
1	−5.21	2.04	0.76	0.74	1.13	−2.16
2	−1.09	1.21	0.31	0.57	0.89	1.51
3	−1.77	0.94	0.26	0.16	0.78	−0.08
4	−0.48	0.81	0.24	0.25	0.81	1.02
5	1.22	0.72	0.25	−0.02	0.77	2.31
6	−0.79	0.58	0.20	0.06	0.77	0.15
7	0.83	0.58	0.17	0.49	0.86	2.30
8	0.82	0.45	0.18	−0.02	0.76	1.37
9	1.36	0.39	0.19	0.00	0.77	1.86
10	1.51	0.45	0.14	0.04	0.75	2.04
11	3.21	0.72	0.06	0.78	0.85	4.88
12	8.41	0.83	0.04	1.21	0.97	10.70
All twelve in steady state						
As percent of lifetime income	1.25	0.64	0.17	0.28	0.81	2.44
As percent of revenue	5.81	4.58	2.22	7.01	265.49	4.39
All generations[a]						
As percent of lifetime income	0.44	0.20	0.03	0.18	0.26	0.92
As percent of revenue	1.93	1.37	0.38	4.06	65.69	1.58

a. Present value of EV as percent of: present value of all lifetime income, or present value of revenue from this tax.

Corporate-Noncorporate Elasticity

The ε_3 parameter sets the degree to which consumers can substitute between the output of the corporate sector and that of the noncorporate sector within an industry. It therefore determines the ability of consumers to avoid the uses-side burden associated with higher prices of corporate outputs.

In the central case, we used 5.0 for this elasticity. This parameter has never been estimated, because we just introduced the possibility that consumers can undertake such substitution between similar outputs within an industry.[4] It is therefore an obvious candidate for sensitivity analysis. This elasticity may be very high, for example, if corporate and noncorporate outputs are considered very similar and thus highly substitutable. In variant C we therefore raise ε_3 to 20.0. Whereas an elasticity of 5.0 is high, an elasticity of 20.0 means the goods are effectively perfect substitutes. Table 8-1 shows that this respecifi-

4. We developed this model of corporate and noncorporate outputs in the same industry at about the same time that Gravelle and Kotlikoff (1988) were developing a similar model. In sensitivity analysis, they also considered values as high as 20.0 for this elasticity.

Table 8-5. *Welfare Effects under Variant C*

Changed parameters: $\varepsilon_3 = 20.00$

	EV as percent of lifetime income for steady-state generations					
	Removal of taxes					
Lifetime income category	Personal	Sales and excise	Payroll	Property	Corporate	All
1	−4.28	2.69	1.24	0.79	1.20	0.02
2	−0.17	1.70	0.69	0.58	0.95	3.22
3	−0.87	1.35	0.60	0.14	0.83	1.49
4	0.39	1.19	0.55	0.22	0.86	2.45
5	2.03	1.09	0.57	−0.05	0.82	3.65
6	0.07	0.89	0.48	0.01	0.81	1.46
7	1.71	0.89	0.44	0.44	0.90	3.55
8	1.63	0.74	0.45	−0.07	0.80	2.58
9	2.17	0.68	0.45	−0.06	0.81	3.02
10	2.30	0.69	0.38	−0.03	0.79	3.08
11	3.99	0.90	0.24	0.71	0.88	5.65
12	9.11	1.02	0.23	1.15	0.99	11.21
All twelve in steady state						
As percent of lifetime income	2.07	0.93	0.44	0.23	0.85	3.60
As percent of revenue	9.98	7.25	5.96	5.56	305.86	6.62
All generations[a]						
As percent of lifetime income	0.70	0.28	0.10	0.18	0.27	1.33
As percent of revenue	3.21	2.10	1.30	3.92	80.15	2.32

a. Present value of EV as percent of: present value of all lifetime income, or present value of revenue from this tax.

cation has no effect on the capital stock, savings elasticity, or labor supply elasticity.

Table 8-5 summarizes simulation results. In comparing these results to those of the central case, it is apparent that this elasticity does not affect the incidence results to any appreciable extent. All numbers in table 8-5 are virtually the same as corresponding values in tables 7-10 to 7-15. Distributional effects do not arise because our model does not specify any differences in the corporate-noncorporate consumption mix of the lifetime rich compared with the lifetime poor. Any such effect would have to be tenuous, requiring both a different mix of goods consumed by rich and poor as well as a different sectoral mix for those goods.

Comparing table 8-5 to earlier tables also shows that this substitution parameter has little effect on efficiency measures. The respecification has only a slight effect on the level of gains in the last two columns. With the higher substitution parameter, corporate taxes (and therefore overall taxes) are slightly more distorting. In this case the explanation is that we specify a fixed coefficient input-output matrix in which each corporate or noncorporate good is produced, using intermediate inputs of both corporate and noncorporate outputs. Thus substitution can take place only in consumption. But the price of any corporate or noncorporate output is always a composite of corporate and noncorporate input prices. As a result, ultimate output prices do not change as much as would be implied by changes in the relative tax treatment of the two sectors. In addition, we use 1984 marginal effective tax rates that simply do not differ much between the corporate and noncorporate sectors (see table 7-2). Because tax-induced distortions between corporate and noncorporate goods prices are small, the elasticity of substitution between corporate and noncorporate outputs does not much matter.[5]

Other Specifications

The remaining cases, D through H, allow us to test the effects of alternatives for other assumptions in the model. We also eliminate some of the new features of our model, such as minimum required purchases and bequests, in order to relate our results to earlier literature.

The Net Rate of Return

Somewhat arbitrarily, the standard set of parameters assumes that the real net rate of return is 4 percent in the benchmark steady state. Here, for variant D, we change this return to 3 percent and generate a new baseline. Simulation results are then shown in table 8-6. Perhaps surprisingly, these results are remarkably similar to those for the standard parameters, at least for the first four tax replacements. The distributional patterns are almost identical. The only major difference is that the 3 percent return generates less capital income and therefore less tax revenue. Equivalent variations are the same fractions of incomes as before, but they are all higher fractions of revenue. These taxes seem less efficient, because their welfare costs comprise higher fractions of the amounts transferred to government.

For the corporate income tax, in variant D, the distributional effect is still

5. Interestingly, Gravelle and Kotlikoff (1988) get very high efficiency effects in a similar model in which corporate and noncorporate outputs coexist in the same industry because of imperfect substitutability on the part of consumers. They have no input-output matrix, and they use Harberger's 1957 average effective tax rates that were much higher in the corporate sector. In that case, large tax differences combine with large substitution elasticities to create large misallocations.

Table 8-6. *Welfare Effects under Variant D*

Changed parameters: $r = 0.03$

| | EV as percent of lifetime income for steady-state generations | | | | | |
| | Removal of taxes | | | | | |
Lifetime income category	Personal	Sales and excise	Payroll	Property	Corporate	All
1	−4.09	2.70	1.10	0.93	0.63	0.26
2	−0.70	1.74	0.58	0.75	0.39	2.51
3	−1.40	1.41	0.47	0.30	0.36	0.84
4	−0.07	1.25	0.42	0.40	0.37	1.91
5	1.40	1.18	0.42	0.08	0.36	2.93
6	−0.51	0.98	0.34	0.13	0.35	0.79
7	1.09	0.94	0.31	0.55	0.37	2.72
8	1.31	0.85	0.31	0.01	0.34	2.13
9	1.72	0.79	0.31	0.02	0.36	2.45
10	1.92	0.77	0.25	0.04	0.34	2.58
11	3.64	0.85	0.16	0.74	0.36	4.92
12	8.60	0.92	0.16	1.15	0.40	10.33
All twelve in steady state						
As percent of lifetime income	1.61	0.98	0.31	0.32	0.36	2.95
As percent of revenue	10.55	9.44	5.01	14.56	−1,906.28	7.21
All generations[a]						
As percent of lifetime income	0.81	0.37	0.12	0.23	0.16	1.40
As percent of revenue	5.12	3.41	1.85	10.03	−1,194.72	3.31

a. Present value of EV as percent of: present value of all lifetime income, or present value of revenue from this tax.

slightly regressive or U-shaped. Equivalent variations are smaller fractions of incomes, for all groups and in total. With less capital income, capital taxes are less distorting. This tax generated little revenue under the standard parameters, however, and it generates negative revenue with the lower net rate of return. Thus the bottom of the column for corporate taxes shows a large negative number for this welfare effect as a fraction of revenue. For all taxes together, variant D shows the same pattern as the case with standard parameters.

The Labor Endowment

We used data to derive estimates of wage rates and hours worked, but we had to choose an arbitrary figure for the maximum number of hours available for either work or leisure. Faced with a similar problem, Alan J. Auerbach and Laurence J. Kotlikoff (1987) chose 5,000 hours a year. That choice implies that an individual could work almost 100 hours a week. For our central case, we chose 4,000 hours a year, or about 77 hours a week. Now we test

Table 8-7. *Welfare Effects under Variant E*

Endowment = 5,000 hours a year

Lifetime income category	EV as percent of lifetime income for steady-state generations					
	Removal of taxes					
	Personal	Sales and excise	Payroll	Property	Corporate	All
1	−3.22	2.17	0.93	0.64	1.04	0.22
2	0.45	1.43	055	0.64	0.89	3.37
3	−0.21	1.15	0.49	0.23	0.79	1.79
4	0.81	1.03	0.46	0.29	0.81	2.59
5	2.05	0.94	0.47	0.03	0.77	3.43
6	0.50	0.80	0.41	0.09	0.76	1.72
7	1.91	0.81	0.38	0.50	0.85	3.62
8	1.72	0.67	0.39	−0.00	0.75	2.57
9	2.12	0.62	0.40	0.00	0.76	2.90
10	2.18	0.64	0.35	−0.00	0.73	2.87
11	3.52	0.82	0.25	0.60	0.81	4.99
12	7.60	0.92	0.25	0.98	0.90	9.48
All twelve in steady state						
As percent of lifetime income	2.08	0.83	0.39	0.26	0.79	3.42
As percent of revenue	11.99	7.09	6.30	6.54	252.43	7.17
All generations[a]						
As percent of lifetime income	0.79	0.27	0.09	0.19	0.25	1.29
As percent of revenue	4.29	2.20	1.34	4.61	68.30	2.53

a. Present value of EV as percent of: present value of all lifetime income, or present value of revenue from this tax.

the importance of that assumption by using Auerbach and Kotlikoff's choice of 5,000 hours in variant E.

Table 8-1 indicates the pros and cons of that respecification. On the one hand, the benchmark sequence generates more capital stock (which might have allowed us some reduction in the central case intertemporal elasticity of substitution, or some increase in the assumed rate of time preference). The bigger endowment means more savings for retirement. On the other hand, the savings elasticity is slightly higher than in the central case. Choices in the central case tried to keep this outcome low.

As shown in the simulation results of table 8-7, the personal income tax looks less progressive than before. With the larger endowment, the nontaxation of leisure is worth more to the high-wage groups. The total steady-state gain is about 25 percent larger than in the central case, but the value of the lifetime endowment is also 25 percent larger. Thus the steady-state gain is still 2 percent of lifetime income, as it was before. As shown farther down the column, the removal of personal taxes has a bigger efficiency effect than in the central case. The welfare cost is now more than 4 percent of revenue in present value.

For all the tax instruments in table 8-7, the top income group gains less than in the central case, because the replacement tax on labor endowments hits them harder. Thus the personal tax looks less progressive, sales taxes look more regressive, and property taxes look less U-shaped. In general, the additional endowment dampens the percentage effects of taxes, because taxes apply to a smaller percentage of this broader definition of income. For the entire tax system in the last column, results are less progressive. Efficiency effects are 25 percent larger in absolute size, but division by the larger figure for income yields percentage gains about the same as in the central case.

Lessons from this section are twofold. First, since progressivity is defined as an increasing ratio of tax to income, calculating progressivity depends not only on the tax in the numerator but also on the definition of income in the denominator. Second, despite the common presentations of excess burden as a percent of income or revenue, efficiency effects of taxes also matter in absolute magnitudes.

Minimum Required Purchases

Previous life-cycle models used simpler functional forms, but our central case employs a multigood Stone-Geary sub-utility function with econometric estimates for the marginal expenditure shares (β) and minimum required purchases (b). To address the effect of this specification on results, in variant F we simply set the b parameters to zero.[6] Table 8-1 indicates that benchmark steady-state behavior generates a larger capital stock, a lower bequest share, and slightly higher savings and labor-supply elasticities.[7]

Table 8-8 shows simulation results from the removal of each tax instrument. The personal income tax, in the first column, is not obviously more or less progressive than in the central case. All losses are smaller or gains are

---

6. A different procedure might reestimate the β parameters under the constraint that the b are zero, but then the sensitivity case would involve changes to both sets of parameters. Instead, variant F isolates the effect of b, holding β constant.

7. As pointed out by Starrett (1988), the introduction of minimum required purchases should serve to reduce the savings elasticity. To investigate this issue, we calculate a separate elasticity for each lifetime income group. For poor groups, the introduction of minimum required purchases does indeed reduce the savings elasticity. For the richer lifetime income groups, however, the minimum required purchases represent an insignificant fraction of incomes and expenditures. Because these groups are responsible for most of total savings, their behavior drives the aggregate elasticity.

Table 8-8. *Welfare Effects under Variant F, with No Minimum Required Purchases*

Lifetime income category	EV as percent of lifetime income for steady-state generations					
	Removal of taxes					
	Personal	Sales and excise	Payroll	Property	Corporate	All
1	−3.00	1.14	0.48	1.30	1.26	−1.11
2	0.95	1.09	0.50	0.95	1.16	3.46
3	0.15	0.94	0.52	0.44	1.05	1.92
4	1.37	0.97	0.57	0.47	1.09	3.14
5	2.99	0.93	0.64	0.16	1.06	4.44
6	0.97	0.87	0.61	0.18	1.05	2.37
7	2.60	0.99	0.61	0.61	1.15	4.68
8	2.51	0.86	0.66	0.06	1.05	3.67
9	3.02	0.86	0.69	0.05	1.08	4.21
10	3.11	0.94	0.65	0.07	1.05	4.30
11	4.72	1.32	0.55	0.80	1.14	7.07
12	9.81	1.59	0.61	1.22	1.27	12.87
All twelve in steady state						
As percent of lifetime income	2.95	1.02	0.61	0.39	1.10	4.65
As percent of revenue	13.85	8.50	8.72	7.52	426.99	8.31
All generations[a]						
As percent of lifetime income	1.05	0.37	0.14	0.26	0.35	1.74
As percent of revenue	4.66	2.97	1.89	4.70	102.71	2.95

a. Present value of EV as percent of: present value of all lifetime income, or present value of revenue from this tax.

larger, so everyone is better off than in the central case. Thus we turn first to explaining the efficiency effect at the bottom of the column. This efficiency gain is almost 50 percent larger than in the central case, and all groups seem to share in it.

Although substitution parameters are unchanged, the removal of the minimum required purchases gives consumers much more flexibility in their choices about what and when to consume. They do not have to buy *b* of consumption goods, so the tax induces more of a switch into leisure. Thus labor taxes are more distorting. They do not have to buy *b* every period, so they have more choice about saving for the future. Thus capital taxes are more distorting. Because the personal income tax applies both to labor income and to capital income, its removal provides larger gains in this case.

Every other tax in table 8-8 affects either the consumption-leisure choice or the savings choice, so all the efficiency effects across the bottom of the table are larger than in the central case. For the removal of sales and excise taxes, the present-value gain is almost 3 percent of revenue. In this case, however, not all groups share in it. Since low-income groups are affected less than before, this tax instrument looks less regressive. In the central case, remember, the regressivity of sales and excise taxes case was originally attributed to the minimum required purchases. Low-income groups bought proportionally more highly taxed goods like alcohol, tobacco, and gasoline. Without that specification, sales and excise taxes in variant F actually look fairly proportional.[8]

In addition, the regressivity of the payroll tax in the central case was partly attributed to the minimum required purchases, because low-income groups consumed more taxed goods while high-income groups consumed relatively more untaxed leisure. Without that effect, in variant F, the payroll tax is also fairly proportional. Finally, the property tax burden is approximately U-shaped as before, and the corporate tax burden is fairly proportional as before.

The entire tax system in variant F is more progressive than in the central case, as shown in the last column of table 8-8. This net effect reflects the less regressive sales and excise taxes, and less regressive payroll taxes. We conclude that the innovation of minimum required purchases has important effects on both efficiency and progressivity. It leads to different purchases by the different income groups, and it leads to less flexibility in consumption choices. The former affects progressivity, and the latter affects efficiency.

Bequests

Simple life-cycle models also often ignore bequests. More complex models may include bequests, but they ignore differences across lifetime income categories. Since this is the first general equilibrium model with different lifetime income groups, it is also the first such model with bequests that differ by lifetime income group. The next variant is designed to determine the effect of these innovations on our distributional results. In variant G, we set to zero both the bequests and the minimum required purchases. As shown in table 8-1, the generated capital stock falls to 72 percent of the target measure. The bequest share, of course, is zero.

We change both bequests and minimum required purchases for three reasons. First, we can still isolate the effect of bequests by comparing this case to the previous variant F, which changed only the minimum requirements. Second, if we just set bequests to zero without changing any of the other

8. The top income group gains more than other groups from the removal of sales and excise taxes, because the replacement tax applies to labor endowment and not to their relatively high capital inheritances.

Table 8-9. *Welfare Effects under Variant G, with No Bequests or Minimum Required Purchases*

| Lifetime income category | EV as percent of lifetime income for steady-state generations | | | | | |
| | Removal of taxes | | | | | |
	Personal	Sales and excise	Payroll	Property	Corporate	All
1	−4.45	0.91	0.51	0.87	0.82	−3.38
2	−0.15	1.02	0.47	0.70	0.66	1.78
3	−0.67	0.91	0.50	0.37	0.59	0.78
4	0.64	0.97	0.54	0.43	0.62	2.18
5	2.49	0.96	0.61	0.24	0.61	3.83
6	0.43	0.92	0.56	0.29	0.60	1..78
7	1.91	1.05	0.55	0.60	0.66	3.78
8	2.17	0.95	0.60	0.24	0.60	3.42
9	2.71	0.97	0.63	0.26	0.62	4.02
10	2.68	0.93	0.64	0.13	0.59	3.76
11	3.73	1.02	0.64	0.34	0.64	5.08
12	9.00	1.19	0.74	0.53	0.72	10.72
All twelve in steady state						
As percent of lifetime income	2.30	0.98	0.60	0.34	0.62	3.70
As percent of revenue	11.88	7.96	7.77	12.43	398.84	7.13
All generations[a]						
As percent of lifetime income	0.80	0.37	0.14	0.23	0.21	1.44
As percent of revenue	3.95	2.83	1.70	7.93	116.68	2.64

a. Present value of EV as percent of: present value of all lifetime income, or present value of revenue from this tax.

parameters, the generated capital stock would fall to unreasonably low levels. The previous case shows that the elimination of minimum required purchases substantially raises the generated capital stock, so this change helps offset the fall in the capital stock from dropping bequests. Third, variant G provides an interesting comparison with earlier models with neither bequests nor minimum required purchases. The pathbreaking article by Lawrence H. Summers (1981), for example, shows that multiperiod life-cycle models can generate extraordinarily high savings elasticities, and table 8-1 confirms that the savings elasticity rises from 1.3 to 2.3 in this case.

Results in table 8-9 suggest that personal taxes and the overall tax system are still progressive. As in variant F, however, both sales and excise taxes and payroll taxes switch from regressive to proportional. The similarity to variant F indicates that this result is driven primarily by the elimination of minimum required purchases. Members of the highest-income group do not gain as much, however, because they no longer have high inheritances (which were exempted from the replacement tax on labor endowments).

Property taxes are much less dramatically U-shaped than in the central case, for two reasons. First, without minimum required purchases of housing, the uses-side effect on housing prices no longer hits low-income families. Second, without inheritances, the replacement tax on labor endowments no longer favors the highest-income group. We attribute the remaining U-shaped pattern solely to differences in savings behavior, because middle-income groups have later peaks in their wage profiles, they save less than other groups, and they are less affected by the sources-side change in the rate of return.

The corporate tax still has no pronounced distributional pattern. Since it does not change the rate of return or stock of capital, it only distorts the allocation of capital. In variant F, efficiency effects were larger than in the central case because the capital stock was larger. In variant G, efficiency effects are smaller because the capital stock is smaller.

Finally, consider the overall picture from variant G. Efficiency effects are all larger than in the central case because the lack of minimum requirements makes consumption-leisure choices and savings choices more flexible. Distributional effects are smaller than in the central case for all but personal taxes. The progressivity of the personal income tax depends directly on the estimated lifetime tax profiles for each group, and the progressivity of the entire tax system depends directly on the personal income tax. All other taxes in table 8-9 are roughly proportional. These results confirm the intuition from earlier-generation models, that consumption taxes and labor taxes are proportional in a lifetime context. Conversely, these results confirm the importance of including these two features in our new model. Minimum required purchases introduce differences in the consumption patterns of different income groups and thus introduce interesting effects on the uses side. Bequests introduce differences in the capital endowments of different income groups and thus introduce interesting effects on the sources side.

The "New View"

Alternative theories hypothesize about why firms pay dividends. In the "old view," used above, dividends have some intrinsic value such that dividend tax reductions provide more incentive to invest.[9] When this intrinsic value is modeled as a reduction in the required rate of return, James A. Poterba and Lawrence H. Summers (1985) show that the cost of capital involves a traditional weighted average of the dividend rate and the capital gains rate.

---

9. See McLure (1979).

In contrast, the "new view" assumes that firms face a constraint in their re-purchase of shares at the margin, so the dividend tax must eventually be paid. It is therefore capitalized into the value of shares, and firms always rely on retained earnings (dividend reductions) as the marginal source of finance. In this case, the cost of capital depends on the capital gains rate and not on the dividend rate.[10]

The new view has more theoretical appeal, perhaps, but it conflicts with simple observations of firms that both pay dividends and issue new shares. In addition, the constraints on share repurchases do not seem to bind, because many firms are increasing this activity.[11] In empirical tests, Poterba and Summers (1983) find evidence against the new view, and Alan J. Auerbach (1984) finds evidence against the old view.

The reason for dividends and the effect of taxes on financial behavior do not concern us here. We model only the effects of taxes on real investment. The important distinction for our purposes is just the implication for whether dividend taxes affect investment. Formally, in our model, dividend taxes affect incentives only for new-share issues. In the central case we assume that marginal corporate equity is evenly divided between retentions and new shares. Because dividend taxes are important, we call this the old view. Observed financing is irrelevant here because retained earnings may be exhausted: even if retentions are used to finance most observed invest-ment, they may be unavailable to finance a firm's additional investment. In variant H we assume that new corporate investment is financed in the same proportions as past investment, with only 5 percent by new-share issues. Because the resulting weight for dividend taxes is so low, we call this the new view.

One interpretation is that we are concerned with the number of firms at each margin, and another interpretation is that we distinguish between the old view and the new view. The two interpretations are indistinguishable in this model because they have the same implications for whether dividend taxes affect the cost of capital. Table 8-1 shows that this alternative has no effect on the capital stock, bequest share, or elasticities.

Table 8-10 shows results for variant H, the new view of dividend taxation. Personal taxes are just as progressive as before, but losses are bigger and gains are smaller than in the central case. Thus all groups feel the reduced efficiency effect at the bottom of the column. Personal taxes are not as dis-

10. See Auerbach (1979), Bradford (1981), and King (1977).
11. See Shoven (1987).

Table 8-10. *Welfare Effects under Variant H (New View)*

Lifetime income category	EV as percent of lifetime income for steady-state generations					
	Removal of taxes					
	Personal	Sales and excise	Payroll	Property	Corporate	All
1	−4.97	2.65	1.24	0.77	0.82	−0.77
2	−1.10	1.66	0.69	0.55	0.53	2.17
3	−1.55	1.30	0.58	0.10	0.51	0.70
4	−0.32	1.14	0.54	0.18	0.52	1.64
5	1.44	1.03	0.55	−0.11	0.53	2.95
6	−0.52	0.84	0.46	−0.04	0.52	0.76
7	0.85	0.84	0.43	0.41	0.51	2.57
8	1.13	0.68	0.43	−0.13	0.52	1.94
9	1.63	0.62	0.43	−0.12	0.53	2.36
10	1.79	0.64	0.36	−0.08	0.51	2.45
11	3.11	0.86	0.24	0.69	0.48	4.63
12	7.95	0.98	0.24	1.15	0.49	9.93
All twelve in steady state						
As percent of lifetime income	1.39	0.88	0.43	0.19	0.51	2.79
As percent of revenue	7.56	6.78	5.72	4.37	−298.13	5.35
All generations[a]						
As percent of lifetime income	0.46	0.27	0.10	0.18	0.15	0.96
As percent of revenue	2.41	1.98	1.26	3.82	−88.27	1.75

a. Present value of EV as percent of: present value of all lifetime income, or present value of revenue from this tax.

torting as in the central case, because the personal tax on dividends no longer represents a disincentive to investment in the corporate sector. Both the intersectoral and intertemporal distortions are smaller.

The choice between the old view and the new view primarily affects investment incentives, not labor supply. For sales and excise taxes as well as payroll taxes, therefore, all distributional and efficiency effects are almost identical to those of the central case. The property tax has a reduced effect on efficiency, however, as shown in the fourth column of table 8-10. In this second-best world, the welfare cost of taxation depends on the combination of multiple tax instruments. In simple models it depends on the square of the combined tax rate. When the new view reduces the effective tax on capital through the personal taxation of dividends, it reduces the importance of remaining taxes on capital such as the property tax. For all groups, welfare gains from property tax removal are smaller.

For the corporate tax, essentially the same story applies. The new view reduces the effective tax rate in the corporate sector and thus reduces intersectoral distortions. Removal of the corporate tax yields smaller welfare gains for all income groups in the model. The present-value efficiency effect is 0.15

percent of income, compared with 0.26 percent in the central case. This efficiency effect is rather small in absolute size, but it was 65 percent of revenue in the central case, in which the corporate tax raised very little revenue. Under the new view, with 1984 provisions, it loses revenue. The positive tax on corporate equity is more than offset by the combination of interest deductions, investment tax credits, and accelerated depreciation allowances. Thus the bottom of the fourth column of table 8-10 shows negative figures for the welfare cost of the tax as a percent of revenues.

Finally, the entire tax system, in the last column, has similar distributional effects but smaller efficiency effects, compared with the central case. We conclude that the new view significantly affects the measure of tax distortions but not the measure of progressivity.

What We Learn from Sensitivity Calculations

The theoretical literature provides alternative models of economic behavior, with different predictions about the incidence of taxation. The empirical literature provides tests of these predictions, but these tests are often inconclusive. As a consequence, no single model can yield the "right" answer for who bears the lifetime tax burden. For our basic framework, we have chosen a set of assumptions that include life-cycle behavior, nested CES utility functions, and certain future incomes. We cannot vary the basic framework, but we can vary the model by changing assumptions about the Stone-Geary subutility function, the importance of bequests, the size of labor endowments, and the values of certain parameters. Our framework thus encompasses a family of different models.

Each such "model" employs a particular assumption about each behavior and a point estimate for each parameter. It uses one set of input numbers to calculate one set of output numbers. Thus the results are not statistical concepts with probability distributions. In this context, sensitivity analysis is just a crude substitute for calculating confidence intervals. Since the parameter may lie in a range of possible estimates, the simulation results may lie in a range of possible outcomes. Sensitivity analysis provides definitive results about the numerical importance of alternative parameters, and it aids our understanding about the economic impact of alternative theories.

In the first few alternatives, we vary only parameters of the utility function. We find that a lower intertemporal elasticity of substitution raises the impact of capital taxation on the net rate of return. Since the top two groups have more capital income, from their greater inheritances, capital taxation looks somewhat more progressive. Virtually no effects on progressivity were found from changes in the elasticities of substitution between consumption and leisure or between corporate and noncorporate outputs. Qualitative conclusions about the lifetime incidence effects of U.S. taxes are thus quite robust to changes in these elasticities. All three elasticities affected efficiency, however, because more substitution implies taxes are distorting.

Next, a change in the assumed labor endowment affects the measure of income and therefore the measure of progressivity (the tax as a fraction of income). It also affects efficiency because it determines the amount of leisure compared with labor in the benchmark. A change in the size of minimum required purchases affects distributional results because it affects differences in consumption patterns among income groups. It also affects efficiency because it determines the extent to which consumers can switch from taxed goods into untaxed leisure, and from one period to another.

Bequests are found to affect distributional results, for the simple reason that they are not equally distributed among groups. High-income groups, which have larger capital endowments, are more greatly affected by capital taxes. Results are also sensitive to the replacement tax, which may or may not apply to inheritances. Finally, capital taxation is sensitive to assumptions about the disincentive effects of personal taxes on dividends.

Certain qualitative results are robust to these changes, however. The personal income tax is always progressive on a lifetime basis, since it remains progressive in each annual tax calculation. The corporate income tax has only a small effect on the net rate of return in all of these calculations, because it remains small in terms of revenue. The overall tax system is always progressive on a lifetime basis. Even large variations in the incidence of other tax instruments cannot reverse the large impact of progressive personal income taxes on the overall progressivity of the entire tax system.

CHAPTER NINE

Evaluation of Policy Reforms

IN THE PREVIOUS chapter we used our life-cycle, general equilibrium tax model to evaluate lifetime tax incidence. We can also use our model to investigate the efficiency and distributional effects of various real-world policies or proposed reforms.

In this chapter we discuss results from three types of policy simulations: the Tax Reform Act of 1986, a major revision of tax law that took place after the base year for our model (1984); corporate tax integration, a potential reform that has for years been a popular subject of discussion; and a value-added tax, often suggested as an alternative to the current confusing hybrid of income tax features and consumption tax features.[1] We measure the changes in excess burdens and the incidence associated with each of these policies, using lifetime equivalent variations (EVs) for each of the twelve lifetime income groups. Results from the Tax Reform Act and integration simulations is presented in this chapter. Our discussion of the VAT simulations is based on results previously shown in chapters 7 and 8.

The Tax Reform Act of 1986

This major revision of tax law made impressive changes to the structure of U.S. personal and corporate income taxation. It was designed to improve the equity and efficiency of the tax system, primarily by broadening the tax base, reducing both personal and corporate marginal tax rates, and reducing the differences in effective tax rates among different assets and forms of income. It was intended to reduce distortions in labor supply decisions by re-

1. Since our benchmark data set is from 1984, it reflects rules prior to the Tax Reform Act of 1986. Thus, our model simulates the possible efficiency and redistributive effects of the act but is not based on actual post-act data.

ducing personal marginal tax rates. It was also intended to reduce distortions in capital asset allocations, or "level the playing field," by lengthening depreciation periods and repealing the investment tax credit.

Although the 1986 act was designed to improve overall tax efficiency, it did not reduce all types of tax distortions. The reform was expected to reduce labor supply and interasset distortions, but it also increased corporate taxes and might therefore be expected to worsen misallocations between the corporate and noncorporate sectors. In addition, if the reform raised effective tax rates on income from capital, it would exacerbate existing distortions in decisions about when to save and when to consume. Since our model encompasses all of these producer and consumer choices in a second-best world, it can weigh the relative sizes of these distortions and calculate the net gain or loss.

The reform had distributional goals as well. The act removed many poor households from the tax rolls by increasing personal exemptions and the standard deduction, and increasing the earned income credit. More subtly, the reform was expected to redistribute tax burdens from the poor to the rich by increasing corporate tax collections and the overall tax rate on income from capital. In many annual incidence calculations, the act was found to burden those with high annual incomes. Individuals with high annual earnings also have high savings and high capital income.

Joseph A. Pechman (1987) finds the act to be "distinctly progressive."[2] His study shows that the lowest income decile enjoys a 44 percent reduction in tax liabilities, and the highest decile incurs a 3 percent increase in tax liabilities. Percentage increases in liabilities increase monotonically with income.

Pechman's analysis differs from ours in several important ways. First, Pechman classifies households according to annual incomes, while our analysis is based on the distribution of lifetime labor endowments. Second, Pechman assumes the corporate tax is a tax on capital in general, while our findings suggest that the corporate tax has more significant effects on the prices of particular consumption goods. Third, Pechman's analysis is able to incorporate more of the detailed changes in the treatment of personal taxes than our analysis allows. We do, however, capture the reduction in personal tax rates made possible by the increase in corporate tax collections. Finally,

---

2. He classifies households according to annual, comprehensive income, and uses the Brookings MERGE file to account for the effects of the act on all individuals and corporate income tax liabilities.

of course, Pechman's model concentrates on the distribution of taxes paid, while we use a more comprehensive welfare measure that includes efficiency.

In our simulation of the Tax Reform Act, we do not examine the effects of all of the personal income tax base–broadening provisions. Instead, we focus primarily on the aspects of the reform that affect the costs of capital. To capture the important changes in the structure of the corporation income tax, we use some of the specific tax parameters in our model. As indicated in tables 3-17 and 3-18, our benchmark data set specifies 0.495 for u, the statutory corporate tax rate, a figure that includes the 0.46 federal rate plus an average of state rates. The effective annual depreciation allowances are 0.340 and 0.135 for equipment and structures, respectively, and the investment tax credit is 0.10 for equipment.

One way the act affects the values of these parameters is through a reduction in the statutory federal corporate tax rate from 46 percent to 34 percent. The reform also altered depreciation allowances and eliminated the investment tax credit for both corporate and noncorporate investors. We simulate the act by reducing u from 0.495 to 0.383, a figure that reflects the reduced federal rate of 34 percent plus the average state rate. The reform changed depreciation allowances on equipment and structures in a complicated way, but the changes can be summarized by using the present-value-equivalent, exponential rate of depreciation for tax purposes. Don Fullerton and Andrew B. Lyon (1988) calculate that this rate changed from 34 percent to 38 percent for equipment, and from 13.5 percent to 7.6 percent for structures.[3] Finally, since the 1986 act repealed the investment tax credit, we change this parameter from 10 percent to zero.

As mentioned, the act was designed to increase corporate income tax revenues and decrease individual income tax rates.[4] Our model omits the second-earner deduction, specific itemized deductions, and other details associated with personal income taxes. Although our simulation does not capture every detailed feature of the act, it does capture the spirit of that reform. The corporate tax changes described above do indeed raise revenue in our model, and

3. The change in the rate for equipment reflects offsetting effects. Although many types of equipment were assigned longer depreciation lifetimes, all types changed from 150 percent declining balance to double declining balance. In addition, the basis for depreciation was formerly reduced by half the investment tax credit. Our figures account for the increase in basis associated with the repeal of the ITC.

4. The Treasury Department and the Joint Committee on Taxation of Congress projected that the corporate tax changes associated with the 1986 act would raise over $20 billion a year. Poterba (1992) finds that actual increases in federal corporate tax receipts have fallen far short of projections.

Table 9-1. *Effective Marginal Tax Rates on Capital Assets*

Sector	Base case	Remove corporate taxes	Tax Reform Act of 1986	Integration of corporate and personal tax systems
Corporate				
Equipment	0.200	0.413	0.471	−0.141
Structures	0.511	0.442	0.525	0.321
Inventories	0.571	0.413	0.523	0.343
Land	0.587	0.442	0.543	0.378
Intangibles	0.074	0.338	0.144	−0.055
Overall	0.466	0.421	0.498	0.238
Noncorporate				
Equipment	−0.138	−0.138	0.298	−0.129
Structures	0.324	0.324	0.362	0.318
Inventories	0.333	0.333	0.334	0.330
Land	0.371	0.371	0.373	0.366
Intangibles	−0.012	−0.012	−0.012	−0.012
Overall	0.328	0.328	0.355	0.324

our simulation calculates the degree of personal rate reduction that would make the package revenue-neutral. In our model, average personal tax rates are reduced through a proportionate decrease in the marginal tax rate and in the intercept of each individual's tax function.[5]

Before the act, equipment and intangibles were heavily favored relative to other capital assets. Table 9-1 shows effective marginal tax rates on each asset, including corporate taxes, personal taxes, and property taxes. These rates reflect the net effects of depreciation allowances, investment tax credits, and expensing of investment in new intangibles. In the base year, 1984, the effective marginal tax rate in the corporate sector was 20 percent for equipment, 51 percent for structures, 57 percent for inventories, and 59 percent for land. The rate for intangibles was only 7 percent, because of expensing. These tax preferences pertain to the noncorporate sector as well. The different effective tax rates reflect differences in user costs of capital, suggesting significant interasset distortions and possibly large excess burdens. Table 9-1 also shows an intersectoral distortion associated with the tax system. In the base case the 47 percent overall effective rate on corporate capital is considerably higher than the 33 percent rate on noncorporate capital.

As a basis for comparison, the second column of table 9-1 repeats effective

5. Recall that our model specifies a linear income tax function facing each group. These schedules use the same marginal tax rate for all income categories, but average tax rates vary because of differences in the intercepts.

tax rates from chapter 7, where we removed the corporate tax system. In this earlier simulation, we simply set the corporate rate and the investment tax credit (ITC) to zero, and replaced the revenue with a proportional tax on lifetime labor endowments. As we can see in table 9-1, this simulation does nothing to affect tax rates on noncorporate capital. Removing corporate taxes does reduce the overall effective rate of taxation on corporate capital and nearly eliminates the interasset distortions in that sector. Because the overall corporate tax rate is reduced toward the overall noncorporate rate, the intersectoral distortion is reduced slightly as well.

The next column shows the Tax Reform Act of 1986. By eliminating the investment tax credit and modifying depreciation schedules, the act also works toward leveling the playing field across the different types of capital assets. Compared with prior law, the 47 percent effective tax rate on equipment in the corporate sector is now much closer to the rates on structures, inventories, and land. As indicated in the table, the effects of the 1986 act are somewhat similar to the effects of corporate tax removal in that both simulations reduce interasset distortions. The removal of corporate taxes does more to level the corporate playing field, by removing advantages to equipment and intangibles, but it has no effect on the noncorporate sector. It also reduces intersectoral distortions. In contrast, the 1986 act repeals the ITC and levels the playing field in both sectors, but it does little to change the intersectoral distortion.[6]

Table 9-2 shows the effects of the act on the welfare levels of the twelve different lifetime income categories. The overall pattern reflects a combination of effects from the sources side and the uses side, because the act affects both relative factor returns and the relative prices of consumer goods.

The poorest category enjoys a relatively larger welfare gain from the act than other groups do, primarily because of an effect on the uses side. This reform raises taxes on equipment, so equipment-intensive industries are hurt and other industries are helped in relative terms. Tables 3-19 and 3-20 (in chapter 3) show that the most equipment-intensive industry is "services," and table 3-11 shows that this producer good is the major input to the consumer good called "personal care services." The increased relative price of services hurts the lifetime rich, because these services comprise a larger fraction of

6. The base-case effective tax rates on corporate and noncorporate capital are 0.466 and 0.328, respectively. With removal of corporate taxes, the gap narrows to 0.421 and 0.328. In contrast, the 1986 act raises both the corporate and noncorporate effective tax rates, to 0.498 and 0.355, respectively. The gap between these rates is slightly smaller in percentage terms but larger in absolute terms.

Table 9-2. *Welfare Effects of the Tax Reform Act of 1986, Standard Parameters, for Steady-State Generations, at 1984 Levels, with Multiplicative Scaling of Personal Tax Rates*[a]

Lifetime income category	Lifetime EV (billions of dollars)	EV in dollars per person	EV as percent of lifetime income
1	0.08	1,626	0.57
2	0.20	1,007	0.22
3	0.41	1,675	0.30
4	0.46	1,875	0.28
5	0.65	2,653	0.36
6	0.69	2,818	0.33
7	0.48	1,979	0.21
8	0.87	3,560	0.34
9	1.01	4,127	0.35
10	1.07	4,357	0.32
11	0.43	2,206	0.12
12	0.04	774	0.03
Total	6.38	2,610	0.27
Efficiency measure[b]	. . .	. . .	0.06

a. The lifetime equivalent variation (EV) shows the gain in billions of 1984 dollars for each income group in the new steady state. We divide by the number of individuals in each group to get EV per person (in 1984 dollars). We divide by the present value of lifetime labor endowments to get the percentage gain in the last column. Efficiency measures at the bottom of the table take the present value of lifetime gains for transition generations as well as those in the steady state.

b. Present value of EV for all generations as percent of the present value of all lifetime income.

their consumption bundles. Tables 5-6 and 5-7 (in chapter 5) show that minimum required purchases of services are small relative to discretionary purchases.

On the other hand, goods that make up relatively larger fractions of poorer households' budgets are produced with relatively little equipment. These consumer goods include food, alcohol, tobacco, housing, and gasoline. Table 3-11 shows that these consumer goods are produced mainly with the outputs of industries 1 (agriculture, forestry, and fisheries), 5 (food and tobacco), 8 (petroleum refining), 15 (trade), and 17 (real estate). Finally, tables 3-19 and 3-20 indicate that these industries are less equipment intensive than other industries. The repeal of the investment tax credit reduces relative costs of capital for these industries, and it thus reduces their competitive output prices. On the uses side, poorer groups gain from a reform that reduces the relative prices of their consumer goods.[7]

The incidence of the 1986 act across the lifetime income categories also

7. Since our model has only one type of housing, however, it does not capture the effects on lower-income groups of the increased cost of rental housing relative to owner-occupied housing.

reflects the sources-side effect of a slightly lower net rate of return to capital. The steady-state net rate of return is reduced from 0.040 to 0.039 as a result of the increased effective tax on capital income. Because of the reduced return to capital, the lifetime income categories with relatively high capital-labor ratios show relatively smaller welfare gains. The reader may recall, from table 7-3, that capital-labor ratios have a U-shaped pattern across the twelve lifetime income categories.

In sum, we find that the lifetime distributional effects of the 1986 Tax Reform Act are fairly consistent with the annual results from Pechman (1987). The act is, overall, a lifetime-progressive reform. The poorest households enjoy larger relative gains, 0.57 percent of lifetime income, because of the reduced prices of their consumption bundles. The richest households gain only 0.03 percent, because of a slightly reduced return to capital. On average, in the steady state, all lifetime income groups together gain by 0.27 percent of lifetime incomes.

Next we examine the effect of the Tax Reform Act on all generations, in present value, as a measure of the overall effect of the reform on economic efficiency. The bottom number in table 9-2 indicates the present value of welfare gains across all generations. This value is rather small, a mere 0.06 percent of lifetime income. This efficiency measure is smaller than the steady-state gain because the most elderly cohorts at the time of the reform experience net losses, or gains that are smaller than the steady-state gain in welfare.[8] Although the 1986 act reduces labor-supply distortions and interasset distortions, it does not affect intersectoral distortions. It exacerbates the intertemporal distortion because of an overall increase in the effective tax rate on capital. The net positive efficiency gain, however, shows that the reductions in labor-supply and interasset distortions are large relative to the increase in the intertemporal distortion.

We also perform sensitivity analysis on this reform for each of the eight variants used for the lifetime incidence simulations in chapter 8. Table 9-3 repeats the distributional pattern of welfare gains under the central-case parameters and adds results for each of the sensitivity cases.

The distributional effects in these sensitivity cases are very similar to those in the central case, except for variants F and G. In both these variants we remove the minimum required purchases that give rise to differences across income categories in their bundles of consumption goods. As a consequence,

---

8. Older generations are either hurt or have much less to gain by the 1986 act because of the increase in capital tax rates relative to labor tax rates.

Table 9-3. *Sensitivity Analysis for Welfare Effects of the Tax Reform Act of 1986, with Multiplicative Scaling of Personal Tax Rates*

Lifetime income category	Central case	Variant A, $\varepsilon_1 = 0.25$ $\delta = -0.005$	Variant B, $\varepsilon_2 = 0.25$	Variant C, $\varepsilon_3 = 20.0$	Variant D, $r = 0.03$	Variant E, $E = 5{,}000$	Variant F, $b = 0$	Variant G, no bequests, and $b = 0$	Variant H, new view
			Lifetime equivalent variation (EV) as percent of lifetime income for steady-state generations						
1	0.57	0.93	0.51	0.58	0.25	0.46	0.34	0.26	0.55
2	0.22	0.28	0.16	0.22	-0.02	0.19	0.23	0.05	0.18
3	0.30	0.41	0.25	0.30	0.08	0.27	0.34	0.12	0.29
4	0.28	0.38	0.23	0.28	0.06	0.26	0.36	0.12	0.27
5	0.36	0.50	0.32	0.36	0.15	0.33	0.45	0.18	0.37
6	0.33	0.45	0.29	0.33	0.13	0.31	0.44	0.16	0.33
7	0.21	0.27	0.17	0.21	0.01	0.20	0.34	0.08	0.17
8	0.34	0.47	0.30	0.34	0.16	0.32	0.47	0.17	0.35
9	0.35	0.49	0.31	0.35	0.17	0.33	0.50	0.19	0.36
10	0.32	0.45	0.29	0.32	0.15	0.32	0.48	0.21	0.33
11	0.12	0.15	0.09	0.13	-0.05	0.16	0.30	0.17	0.07
12	0.03	0.01	-0.00	0.04	-0.15	0.08	0.24	0.15	-0.06
Total	0.27	0.37	0.23	0.27	0.08	0.26	0.40	0.16	0.26
Efficiency measure[a]	0.06	0.09	0.05	0.06	0.01	0.05	0.09	0.01	0.04

a. Present value of EV for all generations as percent of the present value of all lifetime income.

the poorest and richest income categories have welfare gains more similar to that of the middle-income categories. In variant G we also eliminate bequests and inheritances, which eliminates much of the capital held by the higher income categories. As a result, the rise in capital taxation under the Tax Reform Act does not offset the net gain to those higher-income categories.

Table 9-3 also shows how parameters affect the relative size of the different distortions. Efficiency gains are relatively smaller when the labor supply elasticity is low, as in variant B, because the improvement in the labor supply distortion is smaller. Efficiency gains are relatively larger when the intertemporal elasticity is low, as in variant A, because the gain from improvements in the labor supply and interasset distortions are offset to a lesser extent by the worsening of the intertemporal distortion. Efficiency gains are smaller when the initial assumed rate of return is low, as in variant D, because a given absolute change in capital taxation translates into a bigger relative change in effective tax rates and intertemporal distortions.

Corporate Tax Integration

The corporate income tax is a popular target of criticism among economists and policy analysts. Some criticize its mere existence, arguing that the burdens associated with the tax are passed on to different types of people in mysterious ways. "Corporations" cannot bear the ultimate burden of the tax; only people can bear burdens, whether they be stockholders, employees, or customers of the corporations. Because this idea often goes unrecognized by the general public, cynics claim that the corporate income tax is a politician's dream: they can assert that "everyone" will be better off under a tax policy that shifts the burden away from households and onto corporations.

Others criticize the structure of the corporate tax because it generates distortions. It raises costs for some assets more than others, and it affects some industries more than others. Our model captures these distortions in the allocation of real capital, but it does not capture other additional distortions in financial decisions. In particular, the corporate tax base includes all income from equity but excludes interest payments on debt. It therefore distorts debt-equity choices of firms. In addition, personal taxes apply to interest and dividends but not fully to the retained earnings of the firm.[9] Thus the current

9. Retained earnings may raise stock prices and thus provide capital gains to the individual stockholders, but these accrued capital gains are not taxed until the stocks are actually sold. Thus

system also distorts the dividend payout decisions of firms. Because our model treats these financial decisions as exogenous, we understate the possible gains from a reform that reduces these distortions.

To deal with these multiple real and financial distortions caused by the corporate tax, some advocate the "integration" of the corporate and individual income tax systems. The general idea behind integration is to tax corporate-source income only once, at the stockholder's personal rate. Many methods of partial integration have been used in other countries, and other, more complete methods of integration have been suggested.[10] In this chapter we simulate only one full-integration plan. Following what is often labeled the partnership method, we attribute all corporate-source income to individual investors as if they were partners. As a practical matter, the corporation could still pay a withholding tax on this income. It would then issue statements to stockholders, so that individuals would get a rebate if that withholding exceeded the amount of their personal taxes. Our model ignores these administrative pros and cons.

To capture the real effects of integration in our model, we replace the corporate marginal tax rate u in the cost-of-capital formula with the individual investor's tax rate. For this purpose we use 0.292, the personal tax rate on dividend income. The corporate "partnership" still receives the investment tax credit, as would a noncorporate partnership. Since this personal tax on all corporate-source income takes the place of separate personal taxes on just dividends or capital gains, we set the model's personal tax rates on dividend income and capital gains to zero. As a consequence, tax collections will fall. We replace the lost revenue with a uniform consumption tax such as a flat-rate value-added tax.[11]

For this integration plan, the effective tax rates on capital are shown in table 9-1. Compared with the base case, integration sharply reduces the cost of capital to the corporate sector. Although interasset distortions remain, intersectoral distortions disappear. The overall effective tax rate in the corporate sector is now less than the overall effective tax rate in the noncorporate sector, but the reason is that the corporate sector uses more tax-favored assets such

---

retained earnings have a deferral advantage over dividends. In addition, the effective tax on capital gains was reduced by the exclusion and by the step-up of basis at death.

10. McLure (1979) and the U.S. Department of Treasury (1992) discuss several of the different methods.

11. This replacement tax is the same type as one used for some of the simulations in chapters 7 and 8.

as equipment and intangibles, whereas the noncorporate sector uses more heavily taxed assets such as land and structures. For any given asset in table 9-1, the effective tax rates in the two sectors are similar. Because the severities of the interasset and intersectoral distortions are basically unchanged, the efficiency gains due to changes in these types of distortions are basically zero.

Integration does improve efficiency by reducing financial distortions and intertemporal distortions. As mentioned, our model does not capture gains from reducing distortions in debt-equity and dividend payout decisions of firms. By reducing effective tax rates on capital, however, integration reduces intertemporal distortions in our model. We find that the net rate of return to capital rises from 0.040 to 0.042, in the steady state, because of this integration plan.[12]

The welfare effects of integration are shown in table 9-4. As with previous results, distributional effects reflect a combination of factors on the uses side and the sources side. On the uses side, integration changes the relative prices of consumer goods in a way similar to the removal of corporate taxes. The reader may recall from chapter 7 that corporate taxes raise the relative prices of goods consumed by poorer individuals more than the prices of goods consumed by the rich. The removal of corporate taxes therefore benefits the lifetime poor more than the other categories, in terms of consumer prices. Table 9-4 shows that integration similarly produces this benefit to the lifetime poorest.

On the sources side, integration increases the net rate of return to capital and benefits those income categories with a relatively high capital share of income. Table 9-4 shows relatively high welfare gains to precisely the categories with the highest shares of capital income in table 7-3. We can note that this pattern of sources-side welfare gains is opposite to that of the Tax Reform Act in table 9-2; integration raises the net rate of return to capital while the 1986 act reduces it. Overall, as a result of both the sources-side and uses-side effects, the benefits of integration have a roughly U-shaped distribution across the lifetime income categories. Table 9-4 shows that all the categories enjoy welfare gains in the steady state, by 1.07 percent of lifetime income overall.

Table 9-4 also indicates the efficiency effect of the integration plan. The present value of welfare gains over all generations is 0.38 percent of the present value of all lifetime incomes. This gain is high relative to that of the Tax Reform Act. Integration reduces the intertemporal distortion in this

12. Contributing to this intertemporal efficiency gain is the choice of a consumption tax as our replacement tax, since consumption-based taxes do not distort the choice between present and future consumption.

Table 9-4. *Welfare Effects of Corporate Tax Integration, Standard Parameters, for Steady-State Generations, at 1984 Levels, with Revenue Replaced by a Uniform Consumption Tax*[a]

Lifetime income category	Lifetime EV (billions of dollars)	EV in dollars per person	EV as percent of lifetime income
1	0.20	4,075	1.44
2	1.26	6,443	1.39
3	1.35	5,505	0.97
4	1.77	7,255	1.08
5	1.50	6,121	0.83
6	1.89	7,738	0.90
7	3.15	12,862	1.35
8	2.19	8,946	0.85
9	2.53	10,348	0.88
10	2.74	11,220	0.83
11	4.83	24,700	1.38
12	2.13	43,626	1.80
Total	25.54	10,445	1.07
Efficiency measure[b]	. . .	. . .	0.38

a. The lifetime equivalent variation (EV) shows the gain in billions of 1984 dollars for each income group in the new steady state. We divide by the number of individuals in each group to get EV per person (in 1984 dollars). We divide by the present value of lifetime labor endowments to get the percentage gain in the last column. Efficiency measures at the bottom of the table take the present value of lifetime gains for transition generations as well as those in the steady state.

b. Present value of EV for all generations as percent of the present value of all lifetime income.

model, but the replacement tax on consumption increases somewhat the labor supply distortion. In contrast, the act reduced interasset distortions and labor-supply distortions but increased the intertemporal distortion. The 0.38 percent present-value gain from integration is smaller than the 1.07 percent steady-state gain, because the older, transitional generations are harmed by the switch from income to consumption taxes.

We test the sensitivity of these results, using our eight alternative cases. The results of integration under each of the different variants are shown in table 9-5. For all cases, the pattern of distributional effects is little changed from the central case. The pattern of gains is basically U-shaped, even for variant F, which removes the differences in consumption bundles across income categories by setting minimum required purchases at zero. By removing the uses-side effects discussed above, variant F might be expected to reduce the relative gains to the poorest group. On the other hand, the removal of

Table 9-5. *Sensitivity Analysis for Welfare Effects of Corporate Tax Integration, with Uniform Consumption Tax Replacement*

Lifetime EV as percent of lifetime income for steady-state generations

Lifetime income category	Central case	Variant A, $\varepsilon_1 = 0.25$ $\delta = -.005$	Variant B, $\varepsilon_2 = 0.25$	Variant C, $\varepsilon_3 = 20.0$	Variant D, $r = .03$	Variant E, $E = 5{,}000$	Variant F, $b = 0$	Variant G, no bequests, and $b = 0$	Variant H, new view
1	1.44	1.43	1.52	1.49	1.03	1.34	2.23	1.42	0.79
2	1.39	1.18	1.48	1.45	0.90	1.46	2.07	1.28	0.58
3	0.97	0.59	1.06	1.03	0.52	1.06	1.61	0.97	0.41
4	1.08	0.74	1.17	1.14	0.62	1.15	1.68	1.04	0.45
5	0.83	0.35	0.92	0.88	0.35	0.91	1.42	0.87	0.35
6	0.90	0.48	0.99	0.95	0.40	0.96	1.45	0.90	0.38
7	1.35	1.15	1.45	1.41	0.78	1.39	1.88	1.20	0.55
8	0.85	0.40	0.94	0.90	0.31	0.90	1.38	0.87	0.35
9	0.88	0.43	0.97	0.93	0.32	0.92	1.40	0.89	0.37
10	0.83	0.40	0.93	0.88	0.32	0.85	1.32	0.78	0.35
11	1.38	1.30	1.50	1.45	0.85	1.29	1.79	0.97	0.57
12	1.80	1.90	1.93	1.87	1.20	1.64	2.17	1.20	0.74
Total	1.07	0.76	1.18	1.13	0.55	1.09	1.60	0.96	0.45
Efficiency measure[a]	0.38	0.26	0.40	0.40	0.31	0.38	0.51	0.37	0.16

a. Present value of EV for all generations as percent of the present value of all lifetime income.

minimum required purchases affects the replacement tax as well as the removed tax.[13]

The distributional pattern of gains is slightly changed in variant G, which removes both bequests and minimum required purchases. Without bequests in the model, the capital shares of the lifetime richest groups are reduced significantly. Therefore groups 11 and 12 show smaller relative gains than in the central case. This result confirms that the major distributional effect of integration in our model is the sources-side effect of the higher net rate of return to capital.

As mentioned, the simulated integration plan improves efficiency by reducing the intertemporal distortion caused by capital income taxation. This efficiency effect is confirmed in all the sensitivity cases of table 9-5. The efficiency measure is significantly lower in variant A than in the central case, 0.26 percent compared with 0.38 percent, because the intertemporal elasticity of substitution is lower. The efficiency measure is significantly higher in variant F than in the central case, at 0.51 percent, because the capital stock is higher.[14] The efficiency gain is much smaller in variant H than in the central case, at 0.16 percent, because the "new view" places a smaller weight on dividend payouts of the corporation. Therefore, under the new view, the double taxation of dividends does not raise the effective tax rate on corporate capital as much as it does under the old view. As a consequence, the intertemporal and intersectoral distortions are smaller in the benchmark equilibrium, and integration provides less efficiency gain.

Value-Added Taxation

Another proposal that is receiving much attention is the value-added tax. This tax would apply to value added at each stage of production, measured by sales revenue minus the cost of all intermediate inputs. If full deductions are allowed for the cost of capital goods, the VAT is a consumption-based

13. With minimum required purchases of consumption goods, the lifetime poor have more expensive bundles of goods under the corporate tax. They also have relatively high consumption relative to leisure, however, which increases their burden from the replacement tax on consumption. When we remove the minimum purchases, we reduce the gains to the poor from the repeal of corporate taxes, but we also reduce the burden to the poor of the replacement tax. Thus, under variant F, the relative gain to the lifetime poor from integration with a VAT replacement is actually very similar to that of the central case.

14. Table 8-1 shows the generated capital stock in the model relative to a separate estimate of U.S. capital. This percentage is 105 in the central case and 135 in variant F.

tax. On each final product, the total revenue collected from a VAT is equal to the sum of amounts paid at each stage. Since the value of the final product is just the sum of value added at each stage, this consumption-based tax is equivalent to a retail sales tax.

A specific VAT proposal may exempt certain goods and place different rates of tax on different industries. We do not consider these many variants. However, if the VAT applies at the same rate in all industries, it is equivalent to a uniform consumption tax. Thus, though the VAT and sales tax would be administered differently, they would have the same economic effects. In this model, the VAT is simply an alternate way of collecting a sales tax. For this reason we use the terms "VAT" and "uniform consumption tax" interchangeably.

The relative merits of consumption-based and income-based taxes continue to be debated among policymakers and economists. Proponents of consumption taxes stress that these taxes are intertemporally efficient. In contrast, income taxes affect the rate of return to capital and therefore the relative prices of present and future consumption.[15] Opponents of consumption taxes point out that these taxes are regressive, in the annual perspective, because consumption as a fraction of annual income is higher for those with low annual income than for those with high annual income. Thus, from an annual perspective, income-based taxes are more easily designed to be progressive.

From a lifetime perspective, however, consumption-based taxes might not be so regressive. Several authors, including James M. Poterba (1989), stress that lifetime consumption should be roughly equal to lifetime income. If that is the case for all income categories, the lifetime incidence of a consumption tax should be close to proportional. Thus a reform that replaces a lifetime regressive tax with a uniform consumption tax should benefit the poor more than the rich.

In chapters 7 and 8 we presented some results for the replacement of each tax in our current tax system with a uniform consumption tax. These simulations served mainly as part of our sensitivity analysis—to test the robustness of our lifetime incidence results to the choice of the replacement tax. For the purposes of this chapter, we can simply change the interpretation. Each of those replacements can be viewed as a viable policy option. Here we evaluate the potential efficiency gains as well as the lifetime distributional effects as-

---

15. Consumption-based taxes are not perfectly efficient, however, since they still fail to tax leisure. A switch from income taxation to consumption taxation will decrease the intertemporal distortion but may increase the labor supply distortion.

sociated with the replacement of some or all of our current tax instruments with the proposed consumption tax or VAT.

Table 7-16 shows the welfare effects associated with a switch to a VAT under our standard parameters. In this standard case, the intertemporal elasticity of substitution is 0.50, and the rate of time preference is 0.005. Table 8-3 shows results from sensitivity variant A, which uses a lower intertemporal elasticity of substitution (0.25) and a lower rate of time preference (− 0.005).

We first examine the efficiency gains from replacement of the various tax instruments with the uniform VAT. The last two rows in tables 7-16 and 8-3 show the present values of welfare gains. Since values in all columns are positive, efficiency increases with any such replacement. The uniform consumption tax still involves a labor-supply distortion, however, so the efficiency gains from using this replacement reflect the net effects from reductions in other types of distortions.[16]

Both tables indicate that the efficiency gain as a percent of lifetime income is largest for the replacement of personal taxes. This gain is 0.66 percent under standard parameters, because the personal tax base includes wages, which distort labor-supply decisions, and interest income, which distorts savings decisions. As a percent of revenue, however, the replacement of corporate taxes produces the largest efficiency gain. The present value of welfare gains is 84 percent of the present value of revenue under standard parameters. This huge welfare gain reflects the corporate tax distortions among commodities, between sectors, and among assets, as well as the fact that the corporate income tax does not collect much revenue.

The sales tax also might be used to replace state and local property taxes. Efficiency gains are fairly large from this replacement, at 5.04 percent of revenue, because property taxes reduce the net rate of return to capital and thus generate significant intertemporal distortions. In the second column of tables 7-6 and 8-3, actual U.S. sales and excise taxes are replaced by the uniform consumption tax. The smaller efficiency gains for this replacement reflect the elimination of distortions across commodities, because actual sales and excise taxes are not uniform across all goods.

The efficiency gain is close to zero for the replacement of payroll taxes, basically because neither these labor taxes nor consumption taxes distort sav-

---

16. More specifically, the uniform consumption tax does not distort allocations across time periods, across goods, between sectors, or among assets. Each efficiency gain therefore reflects the degree of each such distortion inherent in the replaced tax instrument.

ings decisions.[17] Overall, under the standard parameters, replacing the entire U.S. tax system with a national VAT would generate an efficiency gain equal to 1.25 percent of lifetime incomes, or 3.75 percent of tax revenues.

Comparing the present values in table 8-3 with those in table 7-16, we see that these efficiency gains are larger under the standard parameters. In variant A, replacing the entire tax system with a VAT provides an efficiency gain of only 0.86 percent of lifetime incomes or 2.54 percent of tax revenues. This difference arises because the standard case uses a higher intertemporal elasticity than variant A does. Thus, in the standard case, the savings distortions under current taxes are larger, and the efficiency gains from removing those distortions are higher. The contrast between values in tables 7-16 and 8-3 is especially clear for taxes on personal income and on property, taxes that generate the largest intertemporal distortions.

The simulated efficiency gains discussed above support the case for consumption-based taxes. But what about distributional effects? Tables 7-16 and 8-3 also show percentage welfare gains, by lifetime income category, for a generation alive in the new steady state. Both tables make clear that the replacement of personal income taxes with a VAT would be a regressive change in taxes. Under standard parameters, the poorest lifetime income category is made worse off by 5.09 percent of lifetime income, while the richest category is made better off by 9.11 percent. The use of the VAT to replace sales and excise taxes or corporate taxes, on the other hand, would benefit the lifetime poor relatively more than the lifetime rich. The reason is that a switch to a uniform consumption tax would remove the regressive uses-side effects of either the actual U.S. sales and excise taxes or of corporate taxes. Recall from chapters 7 and 8 that the uses-side effects of these taxes served to increase the prices of goods purchased by the poor more than the prices of goods purchased by the rich.

Replacing payroll taxes with a consumption tax also benefits the poor relatively more than the rich, because the consumption tax base effectively includes spending out of the income from inheritances, whereas the payroll tax base does not. Finally, the replacement of the entire tax system with a uniform consumption tax, or VAT, would be a regressive reform. This result reflects the dominance of the progressive personal income tax being removed. In the standard case, the lifetime poorest would be worse off by 2 percent of lifetime

17. Payroll taxes and consumption taxes are not identical, however, even in present-value terms, because of intergenerational transfers. The VAT applies to consumption out of either labor income or inheritances, whereas the payroll tax applies only to labor income.

income, while the richest would be better off by 12 percent of lifetime income.

Our simulation results highlight the trade-offs between efficiency and equity in the debate about the choice between income-based and consumption-based taxes. For example, intertemporal efficiency is greatly improved by replacing the personal income tax with a consumption tax, but such a switch is lifetime regressive. A switch from either sales and excise taxes or payroll taxes to a uniform consumption tax is a progressive reform but generates a much smaller efficiency gain. Our results suggest that the most promising reform, in terms of efficiency and equity goals, might be the replacement of corporate taxes with a consumption-based tax. Here our results are somewhat surprising. This corporate tax replacement would be slightly progressive in nature, at least at the lower half of the lifetime income distribution, and it would generate relatively large efficiency gains as a percent of revenue.

References

Ando, Albert, and Franco Modigliani. 1963. "The 'Life Cycle' Hypothesis of Saving: Aggregate Implications and Tests." *American Economic Review* 53 (March): 55–84.

Armington, Paul S. 1969. "A Theory of Demand for Products Distinguished by Place of Production." International Monetary Fund, *Staff Papers* 16: 159–76.

Atkinson, Anthony B., and Joseph E. Stiglitz. 1980. *Lectures on Public Economics.* McGraw-Hill.

Auerbach, Alan J. 1979. "Wealth Maximization and the Cost of Capital." *Quarterly Journal of Economics* 93 (August): 433–46.

———. 1984. "Taxes, Firm Financial Policy, and the Cost of Capital: An Empirical Analysis." *Journal of Public Economics* 23 (February–March): 27–57.

———. 1985. "The Theory of Excess Burden and Optimal Taxation." In *Handbook of Public Economics,* vol. 1, edited by Alan J. Auerbach and Martin Feldstein, 61–127. Amsterdam: North Holland.

———. 1989. "The Deadweight Loss from 'Nonneutral' Capital Income Taxation." *Journal of Public Economics* 40 (October): 1–36.

Auerbach, Alan J., and Laurence J. Kotlikoff. 1987. *Dynamic Fiscal Policy.* Cambridge University Press.

Auerbach, Alan J., Laurence J. Kotlikoff, and Jonathan Skinner. 1983. "The Efficiency Gains from Dynamic Tax Reform." *International Economic Review* 24 (February): 81–100.

Bacharach, Michael. 1971. *Biproportional Matrices and Input-Output Change.* Cambridge University Press.

Ballard, Charles L. 1983. "Evaluation of the Consumption Tax with Dynamic General Equilibrium Models." Ph.D. dissertation, Stanford University.

———. 1987. "Tax Policy and Consumer Foresight: A General Equilibrium Simulation Study." *Economic Inquiry* 25 (April): 267–84.

Ballard, Charles L., and Steven G. Medema. 1991. "The Marginal Efficiency Effects of Taxes and Subsidies in the Presence of Externalities: A Computational General Equilibrium Approach." Working Paper, Michigan State University.

Ballard, Charles L., Don Fullerton, John B. Shoven, and John Whalley. 1985. *A General Equilibrium Model for Tax Policy Evaluation.* University of Chicago Press for National Bureau of Economic Research.

Berkovec, James, and Don Fullerton. 1992. "A General Equilibrium Model of Housing, Taxes, and Portfolio Choice." *Journal of Political Economy* 100 (April): 390–429.

Bernheim, B. Douglas. 1991. "How Strong Are Bequest Motives? Evidence Based on Estimates of the Demand for Life Insurance and Annuities." *Journal of Political Economy* 99 (October): 899–927.

Bernheim, B. Douglas, John Karl Scholz, and John B. Shoven. 1991. "Consumption Taxation in a General Equilibrium Model: How Reliable Are Simulation Results?" In *National Saving and Economic Performance*, edited by B. Douglas Bernheim and John B. Shoven, 131–62. University of Chicago Press for National Bureau of Economic Research.

Blomquist, N. S. 1981. "A Comparison of Distributions of Annual and Lifetime Income: Sweden Around 1970." *Review of Income and Wealth* 27 (September): 243–64.

Boskin, Michael J. 1978. "Taxation, Saving, and the Rate of Interest." *Journal of Political Economy* 86 (April): S3–S27.

Bovenberg, A. Lans. 1989. "Tax Policy and National Saving in the United States: A Survey." *National Tax Journal* 42 (June): 123–38.

Bradford, David F. 1981. "The Incidence and Allocation Effects of a Tax on Corporate Distributions." *Journal of Public Economics* 15 (February): 1–22.

———. 1986. *Untangling the Income Tax*. Harvard University Press.

Browning, Edgar K. 1986. "Pechman's Tax Incidence Study: A Note on the Data." *American Economic Review* 76 (December): 1214–18.

Browning, Edgar K., and William R. Johnson. 1979. *The Distribution of the Tax Burden*. Washington: American Enterprise Institute.

Burman, Leonard E., Thomas S. Neubig, and D. Gordon Wilson. 1987. "The Use and Abuse of Rental Project Models." In *Compendium of Tax Research 1987*. U.S. Department of the Treasury, Office of Tax Analysis.

Burtless, Gary. 1987. "The Work Response to a Guaranteed Income: A Survey of Experimental Evidence." In *Lessons from the Income Maintenance Experiments*, edited by Alicia H. Munnell, 22–52. Federal Reserve Bank of Boston Conference Series 30.

Caddy, Vern. 1976. "Empirical Estimation of the Elasticity of Substitution: A Review." Preliminary Working Paper OP-09, IMPACT Project, Industrial Assistance Commission, Melbourne, Australia.

Creedy, John. 1985. *Dynamics of Income Distribution*. Oxford: Basil Blackwell.

Davies, David G. 1986. *United States Taxes and Tax Policy*. Cambridge University Press.

Davies, James B., France St-Hilaire, and John Whalley. 1984. "Some Calculations of Lifetime Tax Incidence." *American Economic Review* 74 (September): 633–49.

Davies, James B., and John Whalley. 1991. "Taxes and Capital Formation: How Important is Human Capital?" In *National Saving and Economic Performance*, edited by B. Douglas Bernheim and John B. Shoven, 163–200. University of Chicago Press.

Deaton, Angus, and John Muellbauer. 1980. *Economics and Consumer Behavior*. Cambridge University Press.

Economic Report of the President, February 1985.

Economic Report of the President, January 1987.

Engen, Eric M. 1992. "Precautionary Saving, Consumption, and Taxation in a Life-Cycle Model with Stochastic Earnings and Mortality Risk." Ph.D. dissertation, University of Virginia.

Evans, Owen J. 1983. "Tax Policy, the Interest Elasticity of Saving, and Capital Accumulation: Numerical Analysis of Theoretical Models." *American Economic Review* 73 (June): 398–410.

Fitzgerald, John, and Tim Maloney. 1990. "The Impact of Federal Income Taxes and Cash Transfers on the Distribution of Lifetime Household Income, 1969–1981." *Public Finance Quarterly* 18 (April): 182–97.

Friedman, Milton. 1957. *A Theory of the Consumption Function*. Princeton University Press.

Friesen, Peter H., and Danny Miller. 1983. "Annual Inequality and Lifetime Inequality." *Quarterly Journal of Economics* 98 (February): 139–55.

Fullerton, Don. 1987. "The Indexation of Interest, Depreciation, and Capital Gains and Tax Reform in the United States." *Journal of Public Economics* 32 (February): 25–51.

Fullerton, Don, and Roger H. Gordon. 1983. "A Reexamination of Tax Distortions in General Equilibrium Models." In *Behavioral Simulation Methods in Tax Policy Analysis*, edited by Martin Feldstein, 369–426. University of Chicago Press.

Fullerton, Don, and Yolanda Kodrzycki Henderson. 1989. "A Disaggregate Equilibrium Model of the Tax Distortions among Assets, Sectors, and Industries." *International Economic Review* 30 (May): 391–413.

Fullerton, Don, and Andrew B. Lyon. 1988. "Tax Neutrality and Intangible Capital." In *Tax Policy and the Economy*, vol. 2, edited by Lawrence Summers, 63–88. MIT Press.

Fullerton, Don, John B. Shoven, and John Whalley. 1978. "General Equilibrium Analysis of U.S. Taxation Policy." In *1978 Compendium of Tax Research*. U.S. Treasury Department, Office of Tax Analysis.

———. 1983. "Replacing the U.S. Income Tax with a Progressive Consumption Tax: A Sequenced General Equilibrium Approach." *Journal of Public Economics* 20 (February): 3–23.

Galper, Harvey, Robert Lucke, and Eric Toder. 1988. "A General Equilibrium Analysis of Tax Reform." In *Uneasy Compromise: Problems of a Hybrid Income-Consumption Tax*, edited by Henry J. Aaron, Harvey Galper, and Joseph A. Pechman, 59–114. Brookings.

Gieseman, Raymond. 1987. "The Consumer Expenditure Survey: Quality Control by Comparative Analysis." *Monthly Labor Review* 110 (March): 8–14.

Goulder, Lawrence H., and Barry Eichengreen. 1989. "Savings Promotion, Investment Promotion, and International Competitiveness." In *Trade Policies for International Competitiveness*, edited by Robert C. Feenstra, 5–12. University of Chicago Press.

Goulder, Lawrence H., John B. Shoven, and John Whalley. 1983. "Domestic Tax Policy and the Foreign Sector: The Importance of Alternative Foreign Sector Formulations to Results from a General Equilibrium Tax Analysis Model." In *Behavioral Simulation Methods in Tax Policy Analysis*, edited by Martin Feldstein, 333–67. University of Chicago Press.

Goulder, Lawrence H., and Lawrence H. Summers. 1989. "Tax Policy, Asset Prices and Growth: A General Equilibrium Analysis." *Journal of Public Economics* 38 (April): 265–96.

Gravelle, Jane G. 1991. "Income, Consumption and Wage Taxation in a Life-Cycle

Model: Separating Efficiency from Redistribution." *American Economic Review* 81 (September): 985–95.

Gravelle, Jane G., and Laurence J. Kotlikoff. 1988. "Does the Harberger Model Greatly Understate the Excess Burden of the Corporate Tax? — Another Model Says Yes." Working Paper 2742. Cambridge, Mass: National Bureau of Economic Research (October).

———. 1989. "The Incidence and Efficiency Costs of Corporate Taxation When Corporate and Noncorporate Firms Produce the Same Good." *Journal of Political Economy* 97 (August): 749–80.

Hall, Robert E. 1988. "Intertemporal Substitution in Consumption." *Journal of Political Economy* 96 (April): 339–57.

Hall, Robert E., and Dale W. Jorgenson. 1967. "Tax Policy and Investment Behavior," *American Economic Review* 57 (June): 391–414.

Harberger, Arnold C. 1962. "The Incidence of the Corporation Income Tax." *Journal of Political Economy* 70 (June): 215–40.

———. 1966. "Efficiency Effects of Taxes on Income from Capital." In *Effects of Corporation Income Tax: Papers Presented at the Symposium on Business Taxation,* edited by Marian Krzyzaniak, 107–117. Wayne State University Press.

Harris, Richard. 1984. "Applied General Equilibrium Analysis of Small Open Economies with Scale Economies and Imperfect Competition." *American Economic Review* 74 (December): 1016–32.

Hausman, Jerry A. 1985. "Taxes and Labor Supply." In *Handbook of Public Economics,* vol. 1, edited by Alan J. Auerbach and Martin Feldstein, 213–63. Amsterdam: North Holland.

Haveman, Robert H. 1988. "Facts vs. Fiction in Social Policy." *Challenge* 31 (March–April), 23–28.

Heckman, James J. 1979. "Sample Selection Bias as a Specification Error." *Econometrica* 47 (January): 153–61.

Houthakker, Hendrik S., and Lester D. Taylor. 1970. *Consumer Demand in the United States, 1929–70, Analysis and Projections.* Harvard University Press.

Howry, E. Philip, and Saul H. Hymans. 1978. "The Measurement and Determination of Loanable Funds Saving." *Brookings Papers on Economic Activity* 3: 655–85.

Hulten, Charles R., and Frank C. Wykoff. 1981. "The Measurement of Economic Depreciation." In *Depreciation, Inflation, and the Taxation of Income from Capital,* edited by Charles R. Hulten, 81–125. Washington: Urban Institute Press.

Irvine, Ian. 1980. "The Distribution of Income and Wealth in Canada in a Lifecycle Framework." *Canadian Journal of Economics* 13 (August): 455–74.

Jorgenson, Dale W., and Martin A. Sullivan. 1981. "Inflation and Corporate Capital Recovery." In *Depreciation, Inflation, and Taxation of Income from Capital,* edited by Charles R. Hulten, 171–237. Washington: Urban Institute Press.

Kasten, Richard. 1987. *The Changing Distribution of Federal Taxes: 1975–1990.* U.S. Congressional Budget Office.

Kimbell, Larry J., and Glenn W. Harrison. 1986. "On the Solution of General Equilibrium Models." *Economic Modelling* 3 (July): 197–212.

King, A. Thomas. 1979. "Estimation of a Linear Expenditure System for the United States in 1973." *Journal of Economics and Business* 31 (Spring): 190–95.

King, Mervyn A. 1977. *Public Policy and the Corporation*. Wiley.

King, Mervyn, and Don Fullerton, eds. 1984. *The Taxation of Income from Capital: A Comparative Study of the United States, the U.K., Sweden, and West Germany*. University of Chicago Press.

Kmenta, Jan. 1971. *Elements of Econometrics*. Macmillan.

Kotlikoff, Laurence J. 1988. "Intergenerational Transfers and Savings." *Journal of Economic Perspectives* 2 (Spring): 41–58.

Kotlikoff, Laurence J., and Lawrence H. Summers. 1981. "The Role of Intergenerational Transfers in Aggregate Capital Accumulation." *Journal of Political Economy* 89 (August): 706–32.

———. 1987. "Tax Incidence." In *Handbook of Public Economics*, vol. 2, chap. 16. Amsterdam: Elsevier Science Publishers.

Lillard, Lee A. 1977a. "The Distribution of Earnings and Human Wealth in a Life-Cycle Context." In *The Distribution of Economic Well-Being: Studies in Income and Wealth*, vol. 41, edited by F. Thomas Juster, 557–618. Ballinger for National Bureau of Economic Research.

———. 1977b. "Inequality: Earnings vs. Human Wealth." *American Economic Review* 67 (March): 42–53.

Lyon, Andrew B., and Robert Schwab. 1990. "Consumption Taxes in a Life-Cycle Framework: Are Sin Taxes Regressive?" University of Maryland, Department of Economics.

McLure, Charles E., Jr. 1975. "General Equilibrium Incidence Analysis: The Harberger Model after Ten Years." *Journal of Public Economics* 4 (February): 125–61.

———. 1979. *Must Corporate Income Be Taxed Twice?* Brookings.

Maddala, G. S. 1983. *Limited-Dependent and Qualitative Variables in Econometrics*. Cambridge University Press.

Menchik, Paul L., and Martin David. 1982. "The Incidence of a Lifetime Consumption Tax." *National Tax Journal* 35 (June): 189–203.

Merrill, O. H. 1972. "Applications and Extensions of an Algorithm That Computes Fixed Points to Certain Upper Semi-Continuous Point-to-Set Mappings." Ph.D. dissertation, University of Michigan.

Modigliani, Franco, and Richard Brumberg. 1954. "Utility Analysis and the Consumption Function: An Interpretation of Cross-Section Data." In *Post-Keynesian Economics*, edited by Kenneth K. Kurihara, 388–436. Rutgers University Press.

Moss, Milton. 1978. "Income Distribution Issues Viewed in a Lifetime Perspective." *Review of Income and Wealth* 24 (June): 119–36.

Musgrave, Richard A. 1959. *The Theory of Public Finance: A Study in Political Economy*. McGraw-Hill.

Musgrave, Richard A., Karl E. Case, and Herman Leonard. 1974. "The Distribution of Fiscal Burdens and Benefits," *Public Finance Quarterly* 2 (July): 259–311.

Pechman, Joseph A. 1985. *Who Paid the Taxes, 1966–1985*. Brookings.

———. 1987a. "Pechman's Tax Incidence Study: A Response." *American Economic Review* 77 (March): 232–34.

———. 1987b. "Tax Reform: Theory and Practice." *Journal of Economic Perspectives* 1 (Summer): 11–28.

————. 1990. "The Future of the Income Tax." *American Economic Review* 80 (March): 1–20.

Pechman, Joseph A., and Benjamin A. Okner. 1974. *Who Bears the Tax Burden?* Brookings.

Poterba, James M. 1989. "Lifetime Incidence and the Distributional Burden of Excise Taxes." *American Economic Review* 79 (May): 325–30.

————. 1992. "Why Didn't the Tax Reform Act of 1986 Raise Corporate Taxes?" In *Tax Policy and the Economy,* vol. 6, edited by James M. Poterba, 43–58. MIT Press.

Poterba, James M., and Lawrence H. Summers. 1983. "Dividend Taxes, Corporate Investment, and 'Q'." *Journal of Public Economics* 22 (November): 135–67.

————. 1985. "The Economic Effects of Dividend Taxation." In *Recent Advances in Corporate Finance,* edited by Edward Altman and Marti G. Subrahmanyam, 227–84. Homewood, Ill.: Irwin.

Seidman, Laurence S. 1983. "Taxes in a Life Cycle Growth Model with Bequests and Inheritances." *American Economic Review* 73 (June): 437–41.

Shoven, John B. 1987. "The Tax Consequences of Share Repurchases and Other Non-Dividend Cash Payments to Equity Owners." In *Tax Policy and the Economy,* vol. 1, edited by Lawrence H. Summers, 29–54. MIT Press.

Shoven, John B., and John Whalley. 1972. "A General Equilibrium Calculation of the Effects of Differential Taxation of Income from Capital in the U.S." *Journal of Public Economics* 1 (April): 281–321.

————. 1973. "General Equilibrium with Taxes: A Computational Procedure and an Existence Proof." *Review of Economic Studies* 40 (October): 475–90.

————. 1984. "Applied General Equilibrium Models of Taxation and International Trade: An Introduction and Survey." *Journal of Economic Literature* 22 (September): 1007–51.

Slemrod, Joel. 1983. "A General Equilibrium Model of Taxation with Endogenous Financial Behavior." In *Behavioral Simulation Methods in Tax Policy Analysis,* edited by Martin Feldstein, 427–59. University of Chicago Press.

Slesnick, Daniel T. 1986. "Welfare Distributional Change and the Measurement of Social Mobility." *Review of Economics and Statistics* 68 (November): 586–93.

Starrett, David A. 1988. "Effects of Taxes on Saving." In *Uneasy Compromise: Problems of a Hybrid Income-Consumption Tax,* edited by Henry J. Aaron, Harvey Galper, and Joseph A. Pechman, 237–68. Brookings.

Stern, Robert M., Jonathan Francis, and Bruce Schumacher. 1976. *Price Elasticities in International Trade: An Annotated Bibliography.* London: Macmillan for the Trade Policy Research Centre.

Summers, Lawrence H. 1981. "Capital Taxation and Accumulation in a Life Cycle Growth Model." *American Economic Review* 71 (September): 533–44.

Tobin, James. 1958. "Estimation of Relationships for Limited Dependent Variables." *Econometrica* 26: 24–36.

University of Michigan, Institute for Social Research. Various Years. *A Panel Study of Income Dynamics.*

U.S. Congressional Budget Office. 1987. *The Changing Distribution of Federal Taxes: 1975–1990.* Washington.

———. 1992. *Effects of Adopting a Value-Added Tax.*

U.S. Treasury Department. 1987. *Compendium of Tax Research 1987.* Office of Tax Analysis.

———. 1992. *Report of the Department of Treasury on Integration of the Individual and Corporate Tax Systems* (January).

U.S. Department of Commerce. Various years. *Survey of Current Business.*

U.S. Department of Labor, Bureau of Labor Statistics. 1984–85. *Consumer Expenditure Survey.*

Zeldes, Stephen P. 1989. "Consumption and Liquidity Constraints: An Empirical Investigation." *Journal of Political Economy* 97 (April): 305–46.

Index

241